ENGLISH COTTAGE GARDENING

ENGLISH COTTAGE GARDENING

FOR AMERICAN GARDENERS

TEXT AND PHOTOGRAPHS BY MARGARET HENSEL

FOREWORD BY TASHA TUDOR

Including a Cultural Chart compiled with the help of Gary Koller,
Assistant Director of Horticulture at The Arnold Arboretum

With Garden Plans by Gordon Morrison

W.W. NORTON & COMPANY
NEW YORK · LONDON

Dedication

*This book is dedicated to all of the gardeners whose gardens
and love of gardening made it possible.*

The text of this book is composed in Galliard,
with the display set in Galliard.
Composition by the Maple-Vail Book Manufacturing Group.
Manufactured by Dai Nippon Printing Co., Ltd., Hong Kong
Book design by Marilyn Fowles Appleby.

Library of Congress Cataloging-in-Publication Data

Hensel, Margaret.
English cottage gardening for American gardeners / by Margaret Hensel.
p.   cm.
Includes index.
1. Cottage gardens, English.   2. Cottage gardens, English—United
States.   3. Cottage gardens, English—Pictorial works.   I. Title.
SB405.H498   1992
712′.6—dc20   90–28433
ISBN 0-393-04789-X

W.W. Norton & Company, Inc., 500 Fifth Avenue, New York, N.Y. 10110
W.W. Norton & Company, Ltd., 10 Coptic Street, London WC1A 1PU

2 3 4 5 6 7 8 9 0

CONTENTS

FOREWORD

IT WAS AT the Berkshire Botanical Garden in Stockbridge, Massachusetts, that I first met Margaret Hensel. She stood out in the usual garden group like some exotic flower. She had the looks of a fourteenth-century painting and a delightful exuberance for things horticultural. Needless to say, I was impressed.

Over a number of years, she has frequently photographed my garden, so I have come to know her. It was both an honor and a surprise to be asked to write a foreword to *English Cottage Gardening for American Gardeners.*

I thoroughly enjoy Margaret's delight in exuberant gardens, gardens overflowing with the old favorites—hollyhocks, foxgloves, poppies, forget-me-nots, sweet-scented shrub roses, and even vegetables. She lets the reader see, through her words, the pleasing disorder of masses of lady's mantle, pinks, violas, and fragrant sweet alyssum—all spilling over warm brick paths in happy profusion.

This book encourages that most rewarding of complaints, Garden Fever. As I read the book this fall, it made me wish to rush out and plant dozens of blue and white campanulas among my shrub roses, along with more dozens of my favorite mignonettes. In my eagerness to put some of the book's ideas into practice in my own garden, I for once regretted the coming of winter's peace. Now, it is a special book that makes a lover of winter long for spring in the autumn!

And, kind reader, do you not agree with Margaret Hensel that it is time for Americans to turn more often to lovely flowers in their yards and along their walks, turning away from the dull shrub plantings that one all too often sees? How boring those shrub plantings are! How unimaginative! "Yes," you may say, "but shrubs require no care." Well, nothing truly worthwhile is ever easy. But you will be surprised by joy if you choose to follow the spirit of this book and create a small Eden of your own.

Tasha Tudor
Corgi Cottage 1990

(Opposite) The entrance to a cottage garden is framed by a brick archway covered with pink climbing roses and borders featuring globe thistle (Echinops ritro), *yellow fernleaf yarrow* (Achillea filipendulina), *shasta daisies, pale pink shrub roses and an edging of dianthus.*

ACKNOWLEDGMENTS

FIRST, THANKS to Ellen Steese, my former editor at *The Christian Science Moniter,* for her love of travel and gardens and for my first trip to England; to my former editors at *The American Horticulturist*—Judy Powell, who suggested I write a column about garden design, and Barbara Ellis, who continued to provide encouragement and a forum for my ideas on design and plants; and to my editors (past and present) at *Horticulture,* John Barstow, Tom Cooper, Anne Eldridge, Leonie Foy, Tina Schwinder, and Roger Swain.

Thanks to Naomi Alson and Will Ketchum for their silver-sided barn on the banks of the Housatonic River, where I planted some of my first cottage garden combinations; to Margarite Bradley and Pat Bruno at Positive Images, who helped edit the selection of photographs; to Gary Koller of the Arnold Arboretum for his help on the cultural chart; to Dan Coleman of *Horticulture* for his nomenclature editing; to Suzy Verrier for reading over the sections on roses and offering her suggestions; to Gordon Morrison for all his hours of advice and his fine garden plans; to Marilyn Appleby for the beauty and clarity of her design work and her willingness to listen; and to Gordon Hayward, who helped me over my absolute horror of computers and pointed the way to several of the gardens in this book.

Thanks to the many people in England who gave encouragement, advice, and directions to obscure country gardens and provided delightful meals and warm welcomes after long days of driving and photographing. I am particularly grateful to Jean and Paul Cragg of Wapsbourne Farm, Ann Dee of Old Farm, Ralph Harrisson of Knowle Rock, Rosemary Verey of Barnsley House, Timmy Beddow, and my dear friend Sarah Munster.

Special thanks to Erik Anderson, a long-time friend and photographer, who encouraged me to "see" and to continue photographing gardens; to my clients Lori and Terence Hill, Mags and Art Voorhees, and Patty and Tom Morse for their continued patronage and friendship; and to Starling Lawrence, my editor at W. W. Norton, who waited patiently for this book through the years of its creation.

Thanks also to my aunt Mary Dilks for her exuberant love of life and gardens; to Louise Olsen and her late husband, Ralph, who designed and planted the garden of my childhood with its shrub and climbing roses, lilacs, and lily-of-the-valley, a place where I learned so much about what comfort, solace, and quiet joy a garden can give; a very deeply felt thanks to my parents for sharing with me their love of nature and for our many days at "the meadow" searching for lady slippers in the spring and gathering apples and wild asters on sunny autumn afternoons; and to Paul Smyth, who, with his glorious imagination, helped me back and forth over Windsor Mountain into the garden of my dreams.

Notes on Equipment:

The photographs in *English Cottage Gardening for American Gardeners* were all shot using Nikon equipment. The cameras I used were Nikkormat, Nikon F, and Nikon F3 HP. The lenses used were 24 mm 2.8, Micro 55 mm 3.5, 50 mm 1.8, 105 mm 2.5, and 135 mm 2.8. The film was all Kodak, primarily Kodachrome 64.

(Opposite) A bank in Tasha Tudor's Vermont garden is thickly planted with salmon-pink Papaver orientale *'Helen Elizabeth' and* P. orientale *'Water-melon', self-seeded white foxgloves (*Digitalis *hybrids), and wild field daisies.*

(Top) A wooden bench surrounded by wild field daisies and old-fashioned shrub roses is a focal point at the entrance to Tasha Tudor's vegetable garden.

*(Left) In June, pink and purple foxgloves (*Digitalis *hybrids) are a highlight in Tasha's peony garden.*

CHAPTER 1

COTTAGE GARDENING

(Opposite) Thatchers, a cottage garden in Kent with red and yellow climbing roses, and borders spilling over with Alstroemeria ligtu *hybrids, lavender-pink fleabane* (Erigeron × *hybridus*)*, and huge clumps of globe thistle* (Echinops ritro) *and primrose-yellow giant scabies* (Cephalaria gigantea)*. To the right, drifts of magenta-rose campion* (Lychnis coronaria)*, a short-lived, long-blooming perennial, frame the path.*

(Right) The ancient wooden door at Thatchers is accented by the climbing rose 'Sparkling Scarlet', its canes trained against the house and tied to wires.

THIS BOOK BEGAN by a happy accident: one sunny June morning, on the way to photograph the gardens at Sissinghurst Castle, I happened to drive through the small village of Benover, in Kent. On the lefthand side of the road I spotted the most wonderful thatched cottage with hollyhocks and cascades of red and yellow roses surrounding the windows and the wild, picturesque tangle of old-fashioned perennials to either side of the path leading to the front door.

I stopped the car and asked the white-haired man trimming roses for permission to take some photographs. He cheerfully gave his consent. I then spent the rest of the afternoon walking up and down the path taking photographs, studying the selection and placement of flowers, and—to my surprise—identifying a good many that were hardy from USDA Zone 4 to Zones 8 and 9 in the United States.

Later that afternoon, the couple who owned the cottage invited me to tea. Seated beneath an old apple tree, they talked about their garden. Each plant had a story. Some were gifts from friends or neighbors, others had been purchased at tiny roadside stands or grown from seed. Over the years, the couple had tried many different plants, some successes, others utter failures. But it was apparent that every experience had become part of the richness of their life together.

That evening, on the way back to the farmhouse where I was staying, I thought about that cottage garden—comparing it in my heart and mind to the large, well-known English gardens I had been photographing. Unlike those estates, with their mile-long valleys of rhododendrons, or Gertrude

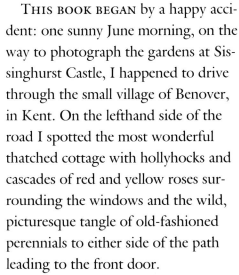

(Right) A dooryard garden in Suffolk with borders featuring oriental poppies (Papaver orientale), *and bearded irises, with clumps of hardy geraniums, dianthus, and fleshy-leaved bergenias softening the edges of the brick walk.*

(Below) A whitewashed cottage at the edge of a field, its tiny yard of lupines glowing in the late afternoon light. In summer, the garden will be full of annuals, including nasturtiums and masses of self-seeded, delicate blue love-in-a-mist (Nigella damascena).

Jekyll—inspired perennial borders embellished with balustrades and fountains, this simple garden was deeply personal and something that American gardeners, such as myself, with small gardens and equally modest amounts of spare time and cash, could create.

Here, I thought, was something charming and quintessentially English, but on an intimate scale that could easily be translated into the small gardens and front yards of urban and suburban America. (See Chapter 2, "Doors and Dooryards.")

That evening, sitting before the fire, my imagination began to run wild. Certainly there had to be more gardens with the romantic, old-fashioned qualities of this one. I envisioned a whole book on picturesque thatched cottages surrounded by small gardens overflowing with plants: red hollyhocks and yellow hollyhocks, delphiniums, daisies, and climbing roses draped in great fragrant cascades over everything from toolsheds to doorways. Full of color photographs, the book would also contain garden plans and hundreds of ideas for small owner-designed and owner-maintained gardens that could realistically be translated or adapted by American gardeners.

An ancient wisteria vine frames the windows and doorway of a village cottage near Cranleigh Surrey.

The next morning, I set aside my carefully planned itinerary and went off in search of picturesque country lanes and villages. During the months (and years) that followed, I visited such out-of-the-way places as Great Tew and Little Tew in Oxfordshire, Winterborne Whitchurch in Dorset, and Monk Eleigh in Suffolk. In these and other villages, I found thirteenth- and fourteenth-century timber-framed and whitewashed or thatched cottages covered with wisteria and ivy, dooryards full of lupines, and garden gates arched with roses.

But more often it was word-of-mouth or the advice of a friend that led me down some quiet country road to a garden full of roses and lavender and homemade topiary. Occasionally, a bit of country humor in topiary form turned a dooryard into a barnyard with lumpy yew or boxwood ducks and chickens nesting precariously on lopsided balls and squares.

Often it was a simple gesture, such as a doorway surrounded with honeysuckle or clematis, or roses cascading over a picket fence, that made a cottage memorable. Sometimes it was the pure exuberance of the gardens that I found so wonderful—where one or two window boxes or hanging baskets would have been enough, there were dozens, filled with every conceivable color of geranium, petunia, and lobelia.

Beginning in early spring, many cottage gardens featured the most delightful and often extravagant combinations of spring bulbs. In some, seemingly wild sweeps of self-sown snowdrops and scillas were followed by species tulips and daffodils in all shapes and sizes. While in others, brick paths were lined with a carnival of red, pink, yellow, and orange tulips.

In most cottage gardens, seemingly spontaneous mixes of old-fashioned perennials were the highlights from late spring through the summer—everything from peonies and poppies, to daisies and delphiniums, to phloxes and Michaelmas daisies. Cottage pinks, bellflowers, and lady's mantle, self-seeded and sprawling along the edges of paths and between the stones, created delicate, impromptu combinations of flowers and foliage.

The horticultural skill of the cottage gardeners I talked with ranged from knowledgeable plantsmen and plantswomen to rank amateurs. Some gardened full time, their gardens beautiful and demanding obsessions; others gardened as a leisurely weekend and evening hobby.

The more cottage gardens I visited and photographed, the more apparent it became that this was not going to be merely a cute book on rose-covered thatched cottages. Although there

In Great Tew in Oxfordshire, a thatched cottage is embraced by the voluminous, friendly forms of clipped yew hedges. Borders of bright red roses edge the path to the front door framed by clematis and hardy, rose-purple sweet peas (Lathyrus latifolius).

were plenty of these cottages around, cottage gardening is not just growing old-fashioned flowers. Gardeners with modern houses, large houses, small houses, narrow city back yards, small village lots, and seemingly impossible hillsides were all cottage gardening.

I found cottage gardeners transforming flat landscapes surrounding modern bungalows into wild and romantic places, mixing old-fashioned roses, primulas, and pinks with everything from hostas to hybrid tea roses, while others were creating exuberant flower borders within the once formal framework of clipped hedges and lawns, or carpeting a make-believe woodland of shrub roses with sprawling mounds of blue-flowered catmint *(Nepeta mussinii),* lady's mantle *(Alchemilla mollis),* and oriental poppies *(Papaver orientale).* Many of the same plants were used again and again, but each gardener had his or her own way of mixing them, so every garden was different.

Occasionally I found a cottage garden that covered an acre or more, but most were small, many of them only dooryards or flower-lined paths to the

(Top right) Surrounded by cement sidewalks, the tiny patch of ground in front of a row house features bright orange and scarlet oriental poppies (Papaver orientale), *orange wallflowers* (Cheiranthus cheiri), *and the silver variegated foliage of spotted dead nettle* (Lamium maculatum).

(Top left) A white picket fence painted the same color as the window frames ties together the house and garden. A pink spirea creates a striking focal point.

(Above) A dirt path leads through a garden of dahlias, white sneezewort (Achillea ptarmica), *pink yarrow* (Achillea millefolium), *and pink and white summer phlox* (Phlox paniculata) *to the front door of a cottage framed by hollyhocks* (Althaea rosea).

(Left) Village gardens with hanging baskets of petunias and fuchsias with annuals and early flowering rock plants spilling over the narrow borders into the road.

front door. Often enclosed by fences, walls, or hedges, these intimate spaces were closely connected to the house by flowering shrubs and perennials, or vines trained around windows and doorways.

There are numerous kinds of cottage gardens, but certain design elements characterize this garden style, most of which can easily be utilized by American gardeners. It is how these design elements are used that gives each garden its unique character.

Paths, for example, are crucial to a cottage garden, for practical as well as aesthetic reasons. Thoughtfully placed brick, stone, or grass paths can help organize and divide space and establish very different frameworks for exuberant displays of perennials, flowering shrubs, and roses. Gates, fences, arbors, and benches (of various materials, styles, and colors) are also key elements in creating the romantic look and feel of a cottage garden.

Much careful thought and planning (rarely on paper) may go into designing cottage gardens, but they tend not to look designed. And that is definitely part of their appeal. They are romantic places, and however tiny or well planned, there always seems to be enough space to squeeze in a few additional fragrant herbs or perhaps a

Borders thick with oriental poppies (Papaver orientale) *and Shirley poppies* (Papaver rhoeas) *line a gravel path to a farm house in Somerset. To the right, red valerian* (Centranthus ruber) *spills over the edge of the path.*

decorative row of leeks or parsley. Cottage gardens are the most wonderful excuses for combining everything from peonies and chives to apple trees and roses. With their easy, idiosyncratic mix of this and that, some of the best cottage gardens give the pleasant illusion that they just happened.

Full of old-fashioned charm and occasional whimsy, cottage gardens are not only do-able but wonderfully enjoyable. These gardens are lived in and loved by their owners, enthusiastic gardeners (both experienced and inexperienced) who are always shifting plants around and trying new combinations, planting yet another rosebush into an already crowded border or simply letting plants self-seed.

Many of these cottage gardeners work with modest or even severely limited gardening budgets, but they never let the lack of money stifle their imaginations or limit their dreams. If trees have to be chopped down or bricks and stone laid, they do it themselves or with the help of friends. If they need plants, they often propagate them from cuttings or divisions, or grow them from seed.

In the years I spent researching this book, I learned a great deal about horticulture and design but even more about how these gardeners make the most of what they have, whether it is a large garden or a tiny dooryard.

The story of cottage gardening is the story of transformations—of weedy hillsides and junk-filled vacant lots turned into beautiful gardens. But, more important, it is about the spirit of gardening, about the delights, enthusiasms, and triumphs of the imagination.

A timber-framed house, its doorway framed with red and white roses, is separated from the road by a low yew hedge that also provides a background for pink annual tobacco (Nicotiana *hybrids*).

(Left) A tiny dooryard garden in Kent is planted with hydrangeas and roses and enclosed by a white picket fence.

(Above) In Somerset, a dooryard garden at the edge of a gravel driveway creates an inviting entrance to a doorway framed by honeysuckle and variegated ivy. The white daisies, windows, door, bench, and roses (to the left) unite this little scene.

CHAPTER 2

DOORS AND DOORYARDS

(Right) A window box of lobelia and pelargoniums.

(Opposite) A brick path edged with borders of Siberian iris (Iris sibirica), orange-scarlet oriental poppies (Papaver orientale), and daisies leads to the honeysuckle-covered doorway of a thatched cottage in Suffolk. To the left (where the path curves), a Rosa rugosa will begin blooming later in June and continue through the summer.

I DISCOVERED some of the loveliest cottage gardens in the most unexpected ways and places. Because there were no books or maps showing the locations of these small, old-fashioned gardens, my search became like a treasure hunt, full of clues, hand-drawn maps from village storekeepers and farmers, and, of course, the most delightful surprises.

Like the garden in Benover, with its hollyhocks and roses, a good many of these cottage gardens were only small dooryards. Located along the roadsides, or in out-of-the-way villages, they ranged in size from 20 feet to 12 inches wide, mere slivers of soil between a cottage and the road. Sometimes there was no soil at all, and flowers flourished in everything from plastic buckets and coffee cans to old car tires turned inside out. The best of these creations were a marvelous mix of texture, color, and fragrance, with flowers for bouquets and herbs for cooking.

In contrast to some of the larger, more elaborate cottage gardens featured in this book, many of these dooryard gardens achieved a memorable charm through small details: variously styled fences, gates, paths, or trellises and easily created plant combinations. These simple effects could easily be adapted to American gardens to transform even the smallest front yards into delightful and delightfully personal spaces.

Although these gardens varied in size, their layouts often shared the same basic structure—a path to the front door through a square or rectangular yard. Brick, stone, gravel, or concrete, the paths were edged with plantings as individualistic as the gar-

At Thatchers in Kent, the entrance gate (framed by a weathered picket fence) opens into borders full of old-fashioned perennials, featuring huge clumps of yellow yarrow (Achillea filipendulina) *and blue globe thistle* (Echinops ritro). *Love-in-a-mist* (Nigella damascena), *mountain bluets* (Centaurea montana), *and columbine* (Aquilegia *hybrids*) *line the edge of the brick path, while climbing roses 'Sparkling Scarlet' and 'Golden Showers' frame the door and windows.*

deners who created them. Some were simple yet elegant seasonal pictures: a double line of apple trees to the front door underplanted with tulips and clouds of blue forget-me-nots, or a hedge of lavender either side of the path. Sometimes paths were lined with shrub roses underplanted with perennials. A good many were edged with perennial borders.

One of my favorites was at Thatchers, the cottage garden in Benover, Kent. Begun over twenty years ago by Dorothy and John Foy, the borders on either side of the walk to the front door had evolved into wonderful jumbles of old-fashioned cottage plants, in bloom from spring right into fall. As with most perennial borders, creating this succession of bloom involved much trial and error. In some years, primulas lined the walks; in others, cornflowers, honesty, and love-in-a-mist self-seeded so heavily that the borders were solid waves of blue. Various lilies were tried: one year spectacular and the next year nothing.

Spring bulbs, on the other hand, proved an unqualified success. Originally planted in small groups between the perennials, dark blue scilla, chionodoxa, species crocus, muscari, and narcissus multiplied into broad sweeps. Now each April and May the borders are so thick with these spring blooms you can scarcely see the ground.

Along the edges of the borders, basket-of-gold *(Aurinia saxatilis,* or *Alyssum saxatile),* cushion spurge *(Euphorbia epithymoides,* or *E. polychroma),* and purple rock cress *(Aubrieta deltoidea)* provide bright spots of early spring color. In May and early June, mountain bluets *(Centaurea montana)* and yellow and lavender columbines *(Aquilegia* hybrids) are features along the edges and toward the middle of the borders. Brilliant orange-scarlet oriental poppies *(Papaver orientale)* and blue and yellow bearded irises are focal points in mid-border.

Later in June, Peruvian lilies *(Alstroemeria ligtu* hybrids) in scarlet, orange, yellow, and pink and huge clumps of yellow fernleaf yarrow *(Achillea filipendulina)* and blue globe thistle *(Echinops ritro)* are features. Pink and blue fleabane *(Erigeron × hybridus),* biennial honesty *(Lunaria annua),* masses of self-sown rose campion *(Lychnis coronaria)* and annual love-in-a-mist *(Nigella damascena)* serve as fillers. (See Plan for Thatchers.)

But it is the climbing roses along the front of the cottage that are the real highlight in June. And, oddly enough, they are one of the few things that were really planned. To get just the right combination, John tried a dozen different shades of red and yellow roses before he came up with the present combination of 'Sparkling Scarlet' and 'Golden Showers', both perpetually blooming climbers that, after a heavy flush in June, continue to flower right through September.

In August, the borders feature soft pink summer phlox *(Phlox paniculata)* and a mixture of mauve, pink, and lavender Michaelmas daisies *(Aster novae-angliae* hybrids and *A. novibelgii* hybrids). Planted years before, their cultivar names are anybody's guess.

The placement and generous proportions of these feature perennials is part of the key to this garden's success. Years ago the poppies, yarrows, globe thistles, and Michaelmas daisies were planted as seasonal features. Repeated on both sides of the walk, they have given the borders a symmetry and a strong backbone as they continue to evolve through the many changes of perennials and sweeps of self-seeding annuals.

Both the yarrows and globe thistle are now huge, with crowns 3–4 feet across. No one quite remembers when they were planted or whether they were ever divided. They simply grew bigger and bigger year after year, no

At Thatchers in Kent, the climbing rose 'Golden Showers' frames leaded windows with flowers from June into September.

doubt crowding out less vigorous perennials in the process. But each June they produce hundreds of flowers, so Dorothy and John figure, "Why fool with a good thing?"

Thatchers, like many of the dooryard gardens I saw, is separated from the road by a hedge. This 4-foot hedge gives some privacy from passing cars, and its mix of hawthorn, hazel, holly, blackberry bushes, and

(Right) The doorway of a seaside cottage in Suffolk is surrounded with self-seeded pink and red hollyhocks (Althaea rosea).

(Below) In the village of Great Tew in Oxfordshire, a rolling, billowing yew hedge encloses a cottage garden.

The doorway of a farm house in Somerset is bright with wire baskets and pots full of fuchsias, pelargoniums, and petunias. Mounds of yellow-flowered Corydalis lutea (surrounding the posts) bloom from May through August.

wild roses also provides flowers in spring, berries in autumn, and the wonderful tapestry of leaf textures so characteristic of English hedgerows. Combined with the rustic picket fence and wrought iron gate, the hedge frames the borders and creates a most inviting entrance to the garden.

Throughout England I saw dooryard gardens surrounded by the most imaginative combinations of fences, walls, and picturesque gates. Driving through English villages and country lanes was like leafing through a living catalog of garden ideas. Here were scores of different gates and fences that could easily be built and adapted to a variety of homes here in America—everything from New England Colonial-style houses to Midwestern, stucco bungalows and California tract houses. I wondered why anyone in his or her right mind would ever put up a chain link fence.

Depending upon the style of the cottage or the effect the owner was after, fence styles ranged from elegant cast iron filigree to unpainted wooden pickets covered with lichen and held together with baling wire. Picket fences were painted red, blue, green, yellow, and white, with individual pickets shaped like arrows, hearts, and diamonds. Sometimes pickets were used as a gate set into a stone wall.

In a small dooryard garden such as Thatchers, situated right next to the road, a gate becomes a powerful poetic symbol, the division between trucks and traffic and a quieter, private world. In larger cottage gardens, a gate often becomes a transition between one area and the next—between a lawn and a small orchard, or a rose garden and a kitchen garden.

(Above) Enclosed by a rustic wooden fence, a dooryard garden features hybrid tea, shrub, and climbing roses. To the left, roses and honeysuckle create a thick mass of fragrant flowers along the side of the garage.

(Top) Separated from the road by a weathered picket fence, a tiny dooryard in Kent features yellow and pink hollyhocks, red climbing roses, and window boxes full of pink, white, and red pelargoniums. To the left, the gate to the front door is framed by a shrubby potentilla, its bright yellow flowers poking through the pickets.

(Right) A simple yet elegant metal fence is painted blue to match the door and doorway of a tiny brick cottage.

(Lower right) A white metal gate set in a stone wall covered with moss and old-fashioned roses marks the entrance to a cottage garden.

(Below) The simple elegance of a metal gate contrasts with the rustic simplicity of a split rail fence at the entrance to a kitchen courtyard in Kent.

In Gloucestershire the look of a cement garden path is softened by an edging of grass and the lavender 'Hidcote'. Climbing roses, including 'American Pillar' (to the far right), cascade over a low stone wall. Alstroemeria ligtu hybrids provide a spot of brilliant, contrasting color.

Sprawling clumps of red valerian (Cen-tranthus ruber) and the variegated, silver foliage of spotted dead nettle (Lamium maculatum) accent a gate.

The garden features roses and masses of chartreuse lady's mantle (Alchemilla mollis) spilling over stone walls and the edges of the path.

The styles of these garden gates are as varied as the fences. A gate often helps to establish a garden's character. Made of rough, natural wood, a gate may introduce a wild sprawl of perennials. An elaborate filigree iron gate may emphasize the formality of a garden path lined with standard roses and underplanted with lavender and squares of blue and white annual lobelia.

White is the predominant gate color, but they come in dozens of other hues, including apple green, blue, yellow, and some shocking shades of pink. Sometimes a cottage's front door or window frames are painted the same color as the gate to strengthen the link between house and garden.

One of my favorite garden gates is in a tiny village discovered one rainy Sunday afternoon. With thatched cottages, a mill pond, and white ducks paddling about in the roadside puddles, the scene was like a Helen Allingham painting, and in the center of the village stood a small stone cottage with a brilliant yellow gate. That single splash of yellow was so appealing that I stopped the car, put on my rain gear, and went over for a closer look. Striking as it was from a distance, the real import of that yellow gate became clear only when I looked into the garden. The whole yard, a mere 10 feet by 10 feet, was the most wonderful froth of yellow, white, and silver: clouds of perennial and annual baby's breath and half a dozen different kinds of yellow and white daisies. Exuberant clumps of *Artemisia schmidtiana* 'Silver Mound' lined the walk, and bold spikes of blue delphiniums on either side of a deep blue front door provided the perfect foil.

Since that rainy Sunday I have thought of that garden many times. As a simple design exercise I imagined that yellow gate painted red, blue, green, or white. With each color, the entire garden changed, but never for the better. Red created too sharp a contrast, and white too little. A green

gate was boring. A blue gate provided an interesting contrast but sacrificed the garden's cohesion and quiet harmony.

Dooryard gardens are also enclosed by combinations of fences, walls, and hedges. Hemlock, box, holly, beech, or combinations of these and other shrubs become hedges that assume all sorts of forms—everything from rolling waves to great, bulging masses of box that look more like undulating green dragons than plants.

Occasionally, topiary becomes part of a hedge, a stretch of box ending in a big obelisk or a shape as fanciful as a

(Above) Over 150 years old, this clipped yew arch has framed this doorway for generations. Lavender and clipped balls of box (Buxus sempervirens) *either side of the walk complete this simple but wonderfully idiosyncratic garden.*

(Right) Topiary and perennial sweet peas (Lathyrus latifolius) *frame a doorway.*

wineglass or bowling pin. In one Oxfordshire village, a mammoth pair of hemlock balls enhances a driveway entrance. Next door, a pair of 8-foot-tall clipped yew ducks perched on top of wobbly box boxes provides whimsy to an otherwise bare and humorless lawn.

Many cottages and houses with dooryard gardens have thatched or tiled roofs and whitewashed or honey-colored Cotswold stone walls and are picturesque examples of vernacular architecture. But just as many are plain, if not downright ugly, houses. Simple architectural details—the shape and color of a door or window, or an arbor or trellis over a door—give even the most ordinary cottage an air of individuality. Sometimes these architectural details are combined with simple, low-maintenance plantings. A yellow door with pink and red roses planted to either side, or a blue door with masses of yellow daisies, gives a front yard color and vitality.

Although some dooryard gardens rely on such simple effects as topiary, vines, or roses, a good many dooryard gardeners combine many different plants in wonderful and sometimes unlikely color combinations that transform even the most unpromising sites into visually exciting spaces. One

A pink shrub rose and perennials create a colorful and exuberant foundation planting against a stone cottage.

of my favorite examples of this style of dooryard planting is in a tiny Gloucestershire village. Built on a steep, narrow slope, right beside the road, the garden is a pleasant hodgepodge of bright and pastel flowers. Created by a woman well into her seventies, it provides another excellent example of how little it takes to give an ordinary house charm and individuality.

The resourcefulness and imagination of this gardener are impressive. Confronted with such an awkward site, many homeowners would have planted juniper 'Blue Rug' or some other low-maintenance nonentity. But this woman was determined to grow flowers and create something beautiful for herself and the village.

In a seaside garden in Suffolk, roses and lavender frame the charming entrance to a small brick cottage.

(Top) Gaillardia, chrysanthemums, and red valerian (Centranthus ruber) *spill over the path to a country doorway framed by yellow roses.*

(Above) *This tiny, terraced dooryard features long-blooming miniature roses. Primulas, dianthus, hardy geraniums, and various campanulas, including* Campanula persicifolia, C. carpatica, *and* C. rotundifolia, *are tucked in between the stones. Lavender and lady's mantle* (Alchemilla mollis) *spill over the narrow borders and soften the edges of the concrete steps.*

To increase the growing space, she terraced the hillside into three levels, each about 1½ –2 feet wide. She then built the retaining walls, using small stones gathered from the back yard and the neighborhood. The soil was then enriched with homemade compost. Except for the miniature roses and spring bulbs, the plants all were gifts from neighbors or were grown from cuttings or seed.

Despite its small size, this garden has a lengthy succession of bloom, beginning in early spring with white and pink arabis and pink aubrietas, blue forget-me-nots, and primulas. Groups of smaller-flowered spring bulbs, including muscari and miniature narcissus, are interplanted between these and other perennials.

Pink and red miniature roses begin flowering in June and remain an important feature into September. Around the roses, several different campanulas, heucheras, hardy geraniums, and clumps of pink and white dianthus make pretty fillers. Yellow daisies, lavender, and various hybrid lilies flower in July. Such annuals as dusty miller, nigella, nasturtiums, and pink and white petunias also play their part, providing continuous color from late May right to frost.

Over the years, this tiny garden has become a small but important part of village life. Each week of the growing season something new is in bloom, and everyone from children on their way to school to women headed to market stops and takes a look or talks to its owner as she weeds. Often the conversations are about gardens, and just as often a plant or a few seeds are given away, to brighten another dooryard garden down the road.

The most challenging sites for dooryard gardens are those without any soil at all. Paved in concrete or stone, these gardens are still overflowing with flowers—masses of annuals and tender perennials planted in

everything from discarded kitchen sinks and tires to wooden beer kegs. Painted any one of a dozen colors, these tubs and tires are festive and, often, surprisingly elegant.

Occasionally, the display of hanging flowers is restrained, perhaps nothing more than a geranium on either side of the door, but just as often there are dozens of pots, the front of a cottage practically covered with hanging baskets of annuals. Sometimes the containers are filled with a single type of plant, perhaps petunias, nasturtiums, or ivy geraniums. Simple color combinations are

created by combining either pink geraniums and white alyssum or blue lobelia and orange nasturtiums. But the best, and certainly the most colorful, containers are those overflowing with half a dozen different annuals.

The secret to these exuberant displays is simple. In early spring, each container is planted solidly with small plants, as many as 12 plants per 12-

Painted tubs and clay pots planted with marigolds, pelargoniums, and calendulas transform a cement dooryard into a garden. Along the front of the house, a narrow raised border is planted with clematis and climbing roses.

Located along a busy highway, this modest dooryard garden features standard roses. Discarded car tires turned inside out are planted with red and white pelargoniums and petunias.

The concrete dooryard of an old post office in Wiltshire is transformed into an elegant and inviting entryway with a line of pots and wire baskets planted with lobelias, pelargoniums, and petunias.

The door and windows of a thatched cottage in the Cotswolds are festooned with pale pink climbing roses. A narrow border against the cottage is thickly planted with roses, campanulas, and lupines (gone to seed) and edged with lavender.

inch container. This assures a very full pot, but any available soil in the pot is quickly used up—a condition that results in stiff competition for nutrients and water throughout the growing season. The trick to keeping these containers so lush and overflowing is regular feeding and thorough watering. It is critical to water daily, sometimes twice a day, especially if the weather is sunny, hot, and windy. Removing faded flowers, particularly from plants such as petunias, will also keep container plants lush for longer periods of time.

As I drove past all these dooryard gardens, I invariably found myself comparing these charming spaces to the sterile settings of most modest American homes. Unlike the anonymous concrete paths and boring lawns in front of so many suburban American homes, these roadside dooryards were lovely, intimate, and welcoming spaces.

Now, whenever gardening friends complain about how cramped their front or back yards are and how little space they have to grow flowers, I tell them how I have seen coffee cans and old tires turned into gardens. The magic is not in having the biggest garden on the block but in making whatever space you do have as beautiful as it possibly can be.

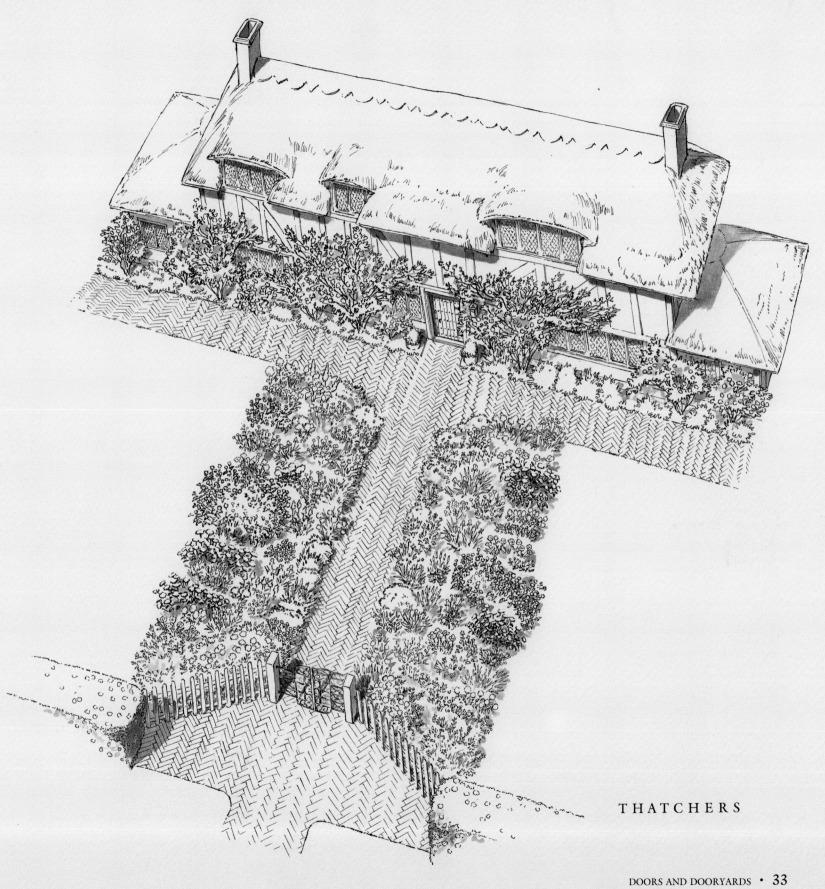

THATCHERS

CHAPTER 3

COTTAGE PLANTS

(Right) Magenta Geranium sanguineum *and* G. sanguineum *var.* striatum *mingle to form a dense mound along the edge of a terrace.*

(Opposite) In Tasha Tudor's Vermont garden, a border is a delightful sprawl of shrub roses and old-fashioned perennials, including foxgloves (Digitalis purpurea), *lupines* (Lupinus *hybrids*), *and hybrid delphiniums with daisies and mounds of hardy geraniums spilling over the grass path.*

"WHAT EXACTLY is a cottage plant?" I asked English cottage gardeners. Not surprisingly, each gardener had his or her own list of favorites. For some, cottage plants were those historically associated with cottage gardens: delphiniums, roses, hollyhocks, old-fashioned pinks, and oriental poppies. For others, cottage plants were those they remembered from the cottages and small country gardens of their childhoods: French lilacs surrounding a white wooden arbor, or masses of madonna lilies beside the front door of a grandmother's cottage.

My own list grew to include over a hundred different plants, a good number of which I never expected to find in cottage gardens. By themselves, hybrid tea roses lack the informality and charm so characteristic of cottage gardening. A collection of hybrid tea roses mulched with wood chips will never be called cottage plants. However, even the stiffest hybrid teas lose their formality when combined with shrub roses and underplanted with sprawls of blue and pink lavender and hardy geraniums.

I often found that the same herbaceous plants were used again and

again. Some plants, such as hardy geraniums (*Geranium* species and hybrids), lady's mantle (*Alchemilla mollis*), and catmint (*Nepeta mussinii*), were vital in creating the overflowing look so characteristic of cottage gardening. Throughout the book, I have focused on these and other key plants, suggesting different ways they can be used. To help American gardeners, plants featured in the text also appear in the cultural chart at the end of the book.

Many people in the United States and England imagine a cottage garden as a kind of eclectic farmyard where

The owner of this Sussex garden devised a most ingenious way to frame a doorway devoid of soil: a rose planted in a raised bed then trained over a homemade arbor.

everything from herbs and fruit trees to cabbages and campanulas are jumbled together. At first glance many of the cottage gardens I photographed did seem a mad scramble, but once I took a closer look there was usually some method to the placement of various plants.

Most of these cottage gardens use what I call feature plants. These act as focal points and give structure to a border, highlight an arbor, gate, or path, or draw attention to some architectural element of a house.

FEATURE PLANTS

Roses, probably more than any other plant, make a cottage garden. In June and early July roses cover arbors, walls, doorways, and windows. Roses are also key features in borders or planted at the base of small trees, their canes trained up the trunks. Occasionally a tree and its climbing rose is the garden, the only feature in a tiny dooryard.

Climbing roses don't really climb, they need support. A most efficient and economical way to grow a lot of climbing roses in a small space is to train them up wooden posts. Fence posts 4 inches in diameter, with metal screw eyes placed at strategic points, make excellent supports. Strong twine or plastic-coated wire can then be used to attach the rose canes. A border 4 feet wide and 20 feet long can easily accommodate 5 rose posts and still have room for perennials and spring bulbs.

Shrub roses also play an important part in creating the lush bloom of cottage-style gardens. *Rosa rugosa* hybrids like the white 'Blanc Double de Coubert' and the amber-yellow 'Agnes' can give structure to a garden and substance to June displays when used in borders or as part of the foundation plantings surrounding a house.

Many shrub roses bloom just once, whereas others, including hybrid perpetuals such as the white 'Frau Karl Druschki' and the clear rose-pink 'Baroness Rothschild', flower repeatedly. The *Rosa rugosa* hybrid 'Roseraie de l'Hay' is one of the best. A dense, bushy shrub with dark green leaves, 'Roseraie de l'Hay' has large, semi-double, dark pink blooms that are deliciously scented and continue right through the summer. In autumn its foliage turns a rich golden yellow.

Even some of the best shrub roses are frequently bare and gawky about the ankles and knees. Devoid of foliage and flowers, a rose's "legs" are often so unattractive they can destroy the effect of a plant in full bloom. If shrub roses are a feature, cottage gar-

An unknown climbing rose frames a doorway.

deners often rely on masses of hardy perennials to hide the bottom third of the shrub. These same perennials, with attractive, long-lasting foliage, also help keep borders interesting through the summer.

At East End Farm in Somerset, Margaret Wray grows over a hundred different roses in a lovely, rustic setting of ancient stone barns and walls. Her shrub roses are underplanted with imaginative combinations of perennials, including almost a dozen different hardy geraniums and masses

of deep blue Italian bugloss (*Anchusa azurea*) as high as the roses. Margaret's paths are edged with catmint (*Nepeta mussinii*) and lamb's ears (*Stachys byzantina,* or *S. lanata*) and mixtures of fleshy-leaved bergenias (*Bergenia cordifolia*), forget-me-nots (*Myosotis alpestris*), and lavish clumps of horned violets (*Viola cornuta*). (See Chapter 6, "Roses Cottage Style.")

With or without roses, hardy perennials play an important role in a cottage garden's distinctive style. Some of the larger, showier specimens

A climbing rose is trained over a metal arbor framing the entrance to a courtyard in Sussex. To the left are the silvered leaves of spotted dead nettle (Lamium maculatum).

also become features. Peonies, oriental poppies, lupines, and bearded irises are popular seasonal highlights during May and June, followed by various delphiniums and yarrows, as well as hollyhocks *(Alcea rosea,* or *Althaea rosea),* blanket flowers *(Gaillardia × grandiflora),* and globe thistles *(Echin- ops ritro).* In August, *G. × grandiflora* and *E. ritro* continue blooming while monkshood *(Aconitum napellus)* and summer phlox *(Phlox paniculata)* assume feature status, followed by Michaelmas daisies, *(Aster novae- angliae* hybrids and *A. novi-belgii* hybrids) in August and through Sep- tember.

Delphinium hybrids are often fea- tured in cottage-style borders in June and again in August or September, if the plants are cut back to the crown to induce a second flowering. Like many cottage perennials, delphiniums can be used to create very different effects. Planted in regularly spaced groupings along the length of rectangular peren- nial borders, as at Charleston Manor in Sussex, delphiniums can reinforce the symmetry of a garden's layout. Delphiniums can also be planted in irregular-sized groupings and under- planted with sprawling mounds of hardy geraniums and dianthus or combined with various lilies for a very informal look.

The brilliant combination of scarlet Maltese cross (Lychnis chalcedonica) *and yellow circle flower* (Lysimachia punctata) *become a feature in this scramble of old-fashioned perennials. To the left are white peach-leaved bellflowers* (Campanula persicifolia) *and lady's mantle* (Alchemilla mollis), *with delphinium and yellow fernleaf yarrow* (Achillea filipendulina) *in the background.*

In combination with variously col- ored perennials, delphiniums can help create distinctly different moods. Pale blue *Delphinium* 'Summer Skies', for example, when combined with masses of clear-yellow daylilies *(Hemerocallis* hybrids), pink shrub roses, and white *Potentilla* 'Abbotswood', create a soft, romantic picture. Deep violet *Delphin- ium* 'King Arthur' or darker violet *D.* 'Black Knight' (two other Pacific Coast hybrids), on the other hand, can create a richly dramatic effect when combined with dark red lilies, shrub roses, *Anchusa azurea* 'Loddon Royalist', and *Achillea millefolium* 'Red Beauty'.

Cottage gardeners also use color combinations to create features of plants that would never be features all by themselves. I remember one gar- den in particular: on two different lev- els it had perhaps three dozen different plants in bloom, but the combination of scarlet Maltese cross *(Lychnis chalcedonica)* and yellow circle

flower *(Lysimachia punctata)* were what really caught my eye. Used alone in a border (in similarly small quantities), neither would necessarily make a feature. In this garden, however, they created an unexpected combination of sharp, bright colors that unified the whole scene.

I also discovered that even the most unassuming plants can become features if planted in sufficient numbers. Lavender is a wonderful, old-fashioned cottage plant, with fragrant

(Left) In May and June, lupine (Lupinus *hybrids) in a wide variety of colors including yellow, shades of pink and red, violet-purple, and white are a frequent feature in cottage gardens. Here a clump of yellow lupine brightens a partially shady garden in Kent.*

(Above) Roses, yellow annual pot marigolds (Calendula officinalis), *and red valerian* (Centranthus ruber) *spill out onto the sidewalk and create a colorful little garden in front of an old cottage in Oxford. Later in July, red and yellow hollyhocks will join the riot of colors.*

spikes of blue, pink, or white flowers; it is not a show-stopper if mixed in a border, but it becomes a star when massed beneath hybrid teas roses or as a hedge along a walk or terrace, as at Crabb Cottage in Somerset. (See Conclusion.)

A plant can also assume feature status depending on where it is placed in the garden or border and what plants surround it. A clump of bearded irises or red valerian (*Centranthus ruber,* or *Valeriana rubra)* surrounded by low-growing hardy geraniums and dianthus becomes a significant feature simply because the two plants are taller and bolder than their companions. Those same clumps of irises or red valerian planted at the edge of a narrow border or path will also command attention. (See Chapter 8, "Yew Tree Cottage.")

Siberian iris *(Iris sibirica)* is featured in a good many cottage gardens. Although best in full sun, this iris will also tolerate partial shade and is an excellent choice for gardens and dooryards on the north or shady side of a house. Available in a range of colors, including lavender, pink, rose, and white, as well as dozens of shades of blue, *I. sibirica* is combined with everything from daisies and delphiniums to shrub roses. From 24 to 40 inches tall with slender, upright

(Top) Clumps of catmint (Nepeta mussinii) *help hide the bare canes of shrub roses and encircle a sundial surrounded by* Geranium endressii.

(Right) Lavender-pink and dark purple hybrid delphiniums combined with dark pink sweet Williams (Dianthus barbatus) *create a dramatic feature in a July cottage garden. To the right, a mound of potentilla provides a contrast of form and foliage texture.*

(Above) A silver-leaved artemesia provides a subtle complement to the brilliant magenta flowers of Geranium psilostemon (G. armenum).

foliage that remains attractive all season, *I. sibirica* is planted as an accent along the edges of borders or as a feature in mid-border.

In bloom from late May to early July (depending upon variety), *I. sibirica* is undemanding and will grow in a wide range of cultural conditions, from a somewhat poor, dry soil to average border conditions in full sun or partial shade. At Cobblers, in East Sussex, they are even grown in the damp soil of a pond edge and form an important part of the garden's framework.

Ponds are not standard cottage garden features, but the pond at Cobblers has all the charm of an informal dooryard, with plenty of color and cottage-style details, including a winding brick path and white painted benches. It also offers a great lesson in planting a narrow border. This pondside border is too narrow for all the different layers of plants that usually make up a perennial border. Therefore each perennial selected as a seasonal feature also has to have foliage that remains attractive throughout the growing season.

Large clumps of blue and white *Iris sibirica*, for example, combined with golden-orange globeflowers (*Trollius* species and hybrids) and *Primula japonica*, are major spring focal points.

The *I. sibirica*, in combination with various astilbes, *Hosta sieboldiana*, and ornamental grasses, including Bowles' golden sedge (*Carex elata* 'Bowles Golden'), then provide an interesting green framework for a succession of July and August perennials, including pink cultivars of purple loosestrife (*Lythrum salicaria*), prairie mallow (*Sidalcea malviflora*), cardinal flower (*Lobelia cardinalis*), and the orange-yellow flowers of bigleaf goldenray (*Ligularia dentata*).

Maintenance for this cottage-style pond border is surprisingly low. Many of the plants are still in their original positions, but others, including *Iris sibirica* and *Lythrum salicaria*, are periodically divided when the clumps get too large. To save time and minimize the disturbance of the pond's edge, Cobblers' owner doesn't lift the whole plant when it is time to divide. Instead, he takes a sharp spade and cuts down around the outside edge of the plant, then through the center, and pries up a section like a piece of cake. The hole is then filled with enriched soil, and fillers such as primroses (*Primula* species) and lady's mantle (*Alchemilla mollis*) are planted to cover the bare ground.

Along the edge of the pond at Cobblers in Sussex, white and dark blue Siberian irises (Iris sibirica) *are interplanted with dark pink and orange-pink* Primula japonica *and astilbes. In the background, orange-yellow globe flowers* (Trollius *hybrids*) *create spots of bright color.*

(Opposite) *A cottage garden in Wiltshire with purple-flowered chives* (Allium schoen-oprasum), *blue-flowered catmint* (Nepeta mussinii), *and lady's mantle* (Alchemilla mollis) *planted along the edge of the raised beds. In the foreground are large plants of sage* (Salvia officinalis), *and in the background, bright red peonies and oriental poppies provide highlights.*

(Top) *At the edge of a border,* Geranium 'Johnson's Blue' *mingles with dianthus and daisies.*

(Above) *An intimate garden corner is highlighted by a weathered garden bench surrounded by hardy geraniums, pink* Geranium endressii *and blue-purple* G. ibericum *or* G. platypetalum *and the chartreuse flowers of self-seeded lady's mantle* (Alchemilla mollis) *winding up through the seat.*

FILLERS

Some of the loveliest cottage gardens are so thickly planted that everything, including paths, steps, and benches, is surrounded by flowering plants. Feature plants can give a garden structure, but to create the effusive planting style so characteristic of cottage gardens, plants such as Siberian irises, roses, and peonies need to be set off by fillers: sprawling mounds of forget-me-nots, clouds of dame's rocket, or masses of columbines, love-in-a-mist, and daisies.

Some of my favorite fillers for the June border are the hardy geraniums. Beneath roses or planted between peonies and lupines, pink-flowered *Geranium endressii, G. endressii* 'Wargrave Pink', *G.* 'Johnson's Blue', and *G. sanguineum* var. *striatum (G. sanguineum lancastriense)* create a rich, full look. These hardy geraniums grow from 10 to about 36 inches. They have interesting and, for the most part, long-lasting foliage with growth habits that vary from the dense masses of *G. sanguineum* var. *striatum* to the open sprawling habit of *G. sanguineum* 'Album'. *G. psilostemon (G. armenum)*, with its magenta flowers and black centers, can grow up to 3 or 4 feet tall. Planted amid other tall plants in a border it is a

A lichen-covered statue surrounded by mountain bluets (Centaurea montana), *with shaggy blue flowers from late May into early July, lady's mantle* (Alchemilla mollis), *and a variegated euonymus, is a picturesque focal point in a country garden.*

Circle flower (Lysimachia punctata), *with spikes of bright yellow flowers in June and July, has spread and formed a dense cover in the raised bed behind a bench.*

striking accent, whereas a well-established grouping can resemble a small shrub and become a significant feature in June and July. (See Chapter 10, "Spontaneity, Combinations, and Magic in My Garden.")

Another plant often used as a filler is circle flower *(Lysimachia punctata)*. Mentioned earlier in this chapter as a feature plant in combination with *Lychnis chalcedonica, L. punctata* is easy to grow in sun with moist soil or in partial shade. Given the conditions it prefers, it also spreads with unrestrained enthusiasm, so I must admit I had a certain prejudice against it. Weedy as it is, I found it in so many different cottage gardens, combined with everything from roses to lupines and lady's mantle, that it obviously has its value.

A better-mannered plant is the horned violet *(Viola cornuta),* with apricot, white, yellow, and blue flowers reminiscent of pansies. Their lank stems, up to 2 feet long, will wind through the bottom of shrub roses and bloom profusely from May to October and sometimes as late as November in Zone 5. Although I have not found them reliably hardy in that zone, they will often winter over in a reasonably protected spot, particularly if snow cover is early and constant.

Poppies are also a good compliment for roses—not the big flashy orientals, but the fragile, translucent blooms of annual Shirley poppies *(Papaver rhoeas)* and perennial Iceland poppies *(P. nudicaule)*. As bright as they are, with colors ranging from bright pink, yellow, scarlet, and orange, the paperlike petals of these poppies are so delicate they blend with any number of different colored roses. Under a pink rose such as 'Kazanlik', for example, small groupings of pink and apricot-orange poppies can look particularly lovely combined with *Geranium sanguineum* 'Album' and dark blue Italian bugloss *(Anchusa azurea)*. Iceland poppies, although perennial, may flower the first year from seeds sown the previous fall. If plants self-sow too thickly in subsequent years, their roots are noninvasive, and unwanted seedlings can easily be weeded out. (See Chapter 6, "Roses Cottage Style.")

Mountain bluet *(Centaurea montana)* is another easy-to-grow filler, with cornflower blue flowers from late May into early July. From 2 to 3 feet tall, *C. montana* looks good with everything from hostas to delphiniums and daisies, as well as masses of lady's mantle *(Alchemilla mollis)*. In the areas of rich, well-drained soil of my own garden, I find that *C. mon-*

At East End Farm in Somerset, the shrub rose 'Moonlight', with clusters of scented, creamy-white blooms from June through August, is underplanted with translucent, dark pink Shirley poppies (Papaver rhoeas), *lavender-blue catmint* (Nepeta mussinii), *and peach-leaved bellflowers* (Campanula persicifolia).

tana benefits from division every third or fourth year to keep the plants from spreading and flopping. If it is deadheaded it will continue to flower. If not, it readily self-sows. This can be a problem or an asset, depending upon how you look at it and where the plants are placed. Because *C. montana* is so easy to grow and divide, cottage gardeners often use it as cheap, quick-growing filler to keep weeds from getting established in new beds.

Many cottage gardeners I talked with often let some of their plants go to seed each year. This assures a steady crop of short-lived perennials such as hollyhocks *(Alcea rosea,* or *Althaea rosea)*, rose campion *(Lychnis coronaria)*, with small, crimson-magenta flowers, and dame's rocket

(Above) A border at Eyhorne Manor features lupine (Lupinus *hybrids*) *surrounded by self-sown honesty* (Lunaria annua) *and dame's rocket* (Hesperis matronalis). *Lady's mantle* (Alchemilla mollis) *spills over the edge of the borders onto the grass path.*

(Below) The woolly, silver-gray leaves of rose campion provide a striking complement to its bright, crimson-magenta flowers. In bloom from June into July, this short-lived perennial often behaves like a biennial but will self-sow. In the background yellow fern-leaf yarrow (Achillea filipendulina) *and the purple spikes of loosestrife provide contrast.*

weeding, I noticed some of the "weeds" had developed their second and third set of leaves and looked exactly like tiny digitalis, hardy geraniums, forget-me-nots, and violas. From then on it was easy to tell garden plants from dandelions and pigweed.

EDGING PLANTS

Edgings are another important group of plants for creating a cottage garden. Although hundreds of different plants can be used a edgings, a few are used frequently. Catmint (*Nepeta mussinii*) is a favorite for the edges of walks, walls, steps, and banks. Planted along paths, its loose panicles of blue flowers make a striking contrast with lamb's ears (*Stachys byzantina,* or *S. lanata*), snow-in-summer (*Cerastium tomentosum*), and clumps of cushion spurge (*Euphorbia epithymoides,* or *E. polychroma*).

Nepeta mussinii grows from 15 to 18 inches high with neat, small-leaved foliage and flowers in late spring and early summer. If cut back after the first flowering, it will often bloom a second time. Although it prefers a well-drained, drier soil, it will thrive in the average border in full sun or partial shade. A sterile hybrid with gray-green leaves, *N.* × *faassenii* grows

(*Hesperis matronalis*), with fragrant white or purple flowers reminiscent of *Phlox paniculata,* as well as biennials such as foxgloves (*Digitalis purpurea*) and honesty (*Lunaria annua*). It also helps create the spontaneous, overflowing look so characteristic of cottage gardens.

The initial trick with self-sowing fillers—annual, biennial, and perennial—is telling them apart from the weeds. I pulled countless digitalis, campanula, and hardy geranium seedlings before I learned. One day, while about 18 inches high and is often confused with and sold as *N. mussinii*. The most dramatic is *N.* 'Six Hills Giant', which grows about 3 feet tall. (See Chapter 10, "Spontaneity, Combinations, and Magic in My Garden.")

Catmint is particularly attractive planted in continuous lines as an edging for rose gardens, herbaceous borders, terraces, and paths. As an underplanting for shrub and climbing roses, *N. mussinii* or *N.* 'Six Hills Giant' complements a wide range of colors, from deep scarlet and pink to salmon and gold. Their various shades of blue flowers combine well with almost every color of perennial and look particularly well with *Geranium endressii* 'Wargrave Pink'. They also make an elegant edging for squares of mint, cabbages, and potatoes in an herb or vegetable garden.

Lady's mantle *(Alchemilla mollis)* is another useful plant for softening edges. Frequently planted in perennial borders, its panicles of chartreuse flowers blend surprisingly well with everything from roses to delphiniums and hollyhocks. The most common use for *A. mollis* is as an edging along paths and terraces. I have also seen it planted around the edges of ponds, combined with hostas or various ornamental grasses, such as Bowles' golden sedge.

(Top) A dense circle of Geranium endressii *'Wargrave Pink' surrounds a sundial placed as a focal point at the end of a path.*

(Above) Along the edge of a partially shaded path, Nepeta *'Six Hills Giant' billows over with spikes of purple-blue flowers.*

The rounded, gray-green leaves of *A. mollis* have a velvety surface, where dew and rain settle in pearly drops. Even when not in bloom, its foliage makes it an attractive accent from early May until late October. In England, where rainfall is usually more abundant than most areas of the United States, *A. mollis* self-seeds with absolute abandon in the cracks of terraces, between stones in walls, along paths, in full sun or partial shade. If allowed their way, in a season or two a few plants can multiply into a billowing mass of foliage and flowers, softening even the most unattractive cement walks.

After *A. mollis* has finished blooming, its flower stalks can look an absolute mess, particularly after a heavy rain. Then it can be grabbed by the handful and cut back to the new leaves at the crown. If faded flower stalks are removed promptly after bloom, seeds won't have a chance to sow. But for all this plant's enthusiasm, its roots are noninvasive, so if you don't deadhead plants in time and they self-seed a bit too enthusiastically, small seedlings are easily removed.

Another edger that can self-seed with enthusiasm is red valerian (*Centranthus ruber,* or *Valeriana rubra*). In bloom in late June and July, then spo-

(Opposite) At Weeks Farm in Kent, lady's mantle (Alchemilla mollis) *has self-seeded, softening the edges of a wide stone and concrete path. To the left of the gate is a dense mass of circle flower* (Lysimachia punctata) *with bright yellow flower spikes.*

(Above) Self-seeded lady's mantle (Alchemilla mollis) *provide a picturesque setting for a garden bench in a country garden in Sussex.*

Great sprawling mounds of blue- and white-flowered lavender create an intimate, embracing entrance to a cottage in Somerset.

radically into September, it grows about 24–36 inches tall with panicles of dark rose-colored flowers. It is also available in a white form; both will thrive in poor, well-drained soil in sun. *Centranthus ruber* grows wild in Cornwall and Devon, self-seeding in the walls along the sea and the roofs of cottages. The effect is exceedingly picturesque and well worth a trip along the shore in June.

It was Crabb Cottage in Somerset, the garden of Peter Parker-Smith, that really convinced me of the value of *C. ruber*. Here it has self-seeded (with Peter's help) in the cracks of the path and dry stone wall. In bloom with roses and self-seeded yellow corydalis *(Corydalis lutea)*, it sprawls over the edges and creates a most dramatic accent. Like *A. mollis, C. ruber* seems to look well with just about everything. (See Conclusion.)

Lavender *(Lavandula angustifolia)* is another versatile edging for sunny paths or terraces. A walk or path edged with a solid line of lavender is one of the easiest ways to create a charming cottage garden entry. Blue is the most commonly planted lavender and is much more dramatic than the white or pink. Roughly half a dozen cultivars are available here in the United States, ranging in height from the 12-inch, lavender-blue 'Munstead

Dwarf' to the 22-inch, deep violet-blue 'Hidcote'.

As with most cottage plants, the spacing between lavenders will depend upon the effect you're after. Young plants of 'Hidcote' planted 8–12 inches apart will create a dense hedge and bloom from July, with some bloom continuing into September. Lavender requires little care if planted in a location with good drainage and full sun. The needlelike foliage of all lavenders will remain a feature from late spring into autumn, or year round if the climate is mild. The removal of faded flower stalks and dead wood after a hard winter is one of lavender's few maintenance requirements. Older plants tend to get a bit woody, but many gardeners like their gnarled appearance and fill in gaps with younger plants.

Features, fillers, and edgings, as I mentioned earlier, are not mutually exclusive. Fillers such as peach-leaved bellflower *(Campanula persicifolia)* and hardy geranium *(Geranium endressii)* or edgers like lady's mantle *(Alchemilla mollis)*, red valerian *(Centranthus ruber)*, and lavender *(Lavandula angustifolia)* can easily become features, depending on where they are used and how they are combined with surrounding plants.

In a small herb garden outside the kitchen window at Eyhorne Manor in Kent, Lychnis coronaria *has self-seeded alongside various mints and a huge clump of yellow-flowered tansy* (Tanacetum vulgare).

Jean Sinfield creates strong seasonal features at Yew Tree Cottage by combining blue or white *C. persicifolia* with *G. endressii*, and *A. mollis*, then repeating the groupings in several borders. Because the borders aren't designed around important feature plants, they have a light, almost airy look. The layout is rather formal, with a strong sense of symmetry, but the gardens don't look stiff. (See Chapter 8, "Yew Tree Cottage.")

A good many cottage garden plants, including *C. persicifolia*, *G. endressii*, and *A. mollis*, along with forget-me-not *(Myosotis alpestris)*, coral-

At Eyhorne Manor the kitchen garden borders are densely planted with herbs, including over a dozen different varieties of thyme. In the upper garden, self-seeded lupines create bright focal points amid a sea of green foliage.

bell *(Heuchera × brizoides)*, circle flower *(Lysimachia punctata)*, Siberian iris *(Iris sibirica)*, and horned violet *(Viola cornuta)*, will grow in full sun or partial shade and are excellent choices for a partially shady or north facing border, or along the edge of a path in the dappled shade beneath apple or pear trees.

Versatility is the key to cottage plants and their use in the garden. Although it helps to begin with a basic plant vocabulary, including a few features and fillers for each season and some edgers with long-lasting foliage, it is just as important to remember that there are few set rules. One gardener might like lady's mantle sprawling over walks and terraces, while another prefers it a bit more restrained and combined with delphiniums in a border. Some cottage gardeners like their peonies surrounded by masses of forget-me-nots; others plant peonies with daisies and lilies. Cottage gardens are highly personal and often idiosyncratic. Plants are rarely used in the same way twice, and that is the joy of cottage gardening.

A bold clump of red valerian (Centranthus ruber) *softens the edge of a stone wall. In the background, pink climbing roses frame a doorway.*

Lavender interplanted with various pinks (Dianthus *hybrids*) *creates a bright, informal edging along a grass path.*

CHAPTER 4

DURBANS: A WEEKEND COTTAGE GARDEN

(Opposite) Throughout the borders, various herbs are planted in combination with perennials. In the border to the right of the path, clumps of chives (Allium schoenoprasum) *are planted in front of lupines, and* Geranium endressii *'Wargrave Pink' is combined with lavender and mint.*

(Right) The 'Russell Strain' lupines at Durbans begin blooming in May and continue into July.

COTTAGE GARDENING is easy. Just about anyone can do it. You don't need to know the names of a hundred different perennials or how to grow prize-winning delphiniums when you begin. Many of the gardens featured in this book were created totally from scratch, some by gardeners who didn't know a peony from a potato when they started. If you don't need lots of experience to create a cottage garden, though, you do need time and a bit of patience. A garden often takes years to become fully established, with walls and fences covered with climbing roses and paths picturesquely crowded with lady's mantle and pinks.

Most of the gardens in this book are at least 12 years old, some much older. All of these established gardens are lovely and full of ideas on design and plant combinations. But they may not be the most helpful for a new gardener, so I also wanted to feature a new garden full of easy-to-grow, common plants to encourage people who have, perhaps, never before gardened. One misty morning in West Sussex, I found just the garden.

Driving down a winding country lane, I passed a shingle farmhouse, almost hidden behind a thick hedgerow. Through a picket fence I caught a quick glimpse of an old-fashioned garden overflowing with daisies and delphiniums. This merited further investigation, so I stopped the car and walked back for a closer look. Here, it seemed, was the classic cottage garden: violas and thyme spilling over a stone path, and borders thick with blue and white lupines and pink foxgloves. A gnarled old apple tree festooned with pink climbing roses completed a garden that looked like it had been cultivated for generations. As it turned out, the garden was only in its third year and had been planted by a man who had never so much as staked a tomato.

Three years earlier, when Clive and Theo McBain bought Durbans, the garden was waist high in weeds. The remnants of a once pretty country garden were scarcely discernible in a thicket of brambles. Fallen fences were covered with vines and honeysuckle gone wild, and the whole garden looked like a scene from "Sleeping Beauty." Neglected as it was, the garden also had many assets, and its framework was still intact. A background of mature trees and a thick hedgerow along the road provided a sense of enclosure and intimacy.

What really inspired Clive McBain were the features reminiscent of old-fashioned cottage gardens. The gnarled old apple tree by the front door, its branches intertwined with climbing roses, was so lovely and suited the house so well that Clive used it as a focal point and a stylistic theme for the rest of the garden, what he called "the postcard version of a cottage garden."

That first fall, Clive, along with a couple of friends, scythed the lawn, pruned trees, and rebuilt fences. Also, they removed a narrow stone walk that made an awkward and most uninviting entrance to the house, relaying the stones in a graceful, sweeping curve.

In late July and August, various shades of pink phlox (Phlox paniculata) *are among the borders' major features.*

At one time there had been perennial borders on either side of the original stone walk, but weeds had taken over, and all but the sturdiest plants had been choked out. The idea of borders appealed to Clive. On either side of the new stone path, the shapes of the borders would frame the cottage and direct attention to the front door. Planted with old-fashioned plants such as hollyhocks and delphiniums, the borders would also provide a charming setting, in keeping with the cottage's simple, vernacular architecture. And if confined to the area either side of the path, the garden would be small enough that he could maintain it himself on weekends.

During the late autumn and mild winter weather, truckloads of well-rotted horse manure, washed rough sand, ground lime, mushroom compost, and coarse peat were forked into the borders to the depth of a foot. The addition of the horse manure and mushroom compost helped create humus to improve drainage, water retention, and air circulation of the very heavy clay soil.

That winter, when it was too cold to work in the garden, Clive did some study on cottage gardens and plants. Put off by the more conventional garden books, "with all their do's and don't's," he read and reread *The Cottage Garden,* by Anne Scott-James. Published in 1981, it is an enjoyable and at the same time somewhat scholarly account of the history of cottage gardens.

Another favorite was *The Cottage Homes of England,* by Steward Dick. First published in 1909 in London, Dick's book explores the history, architectural styles, and construction of cottages throughout England. The watercolor illustrations by Helen Allingham are soft, almost impressionistic sketches of country life, where doves coo in thatched roofs,

Brilliant orange montbretias (Crocosmia × crocosmiiflora) *are planted at several key spots at the bottom and the top of the borders and are dramatic focal points from July to September.*

roses wind around ancient brick chimneys, and cottage doors are surrounded by roses, hollyhocks, and delphiniums.

On winter evenings, in front of the fire, Clive began designing his garden. Rather than writing long lists of plants and elaborate successions of bloom, he drew up rough color sketches—quick, almost abstract designs of colors and shapes. Delphiniums became clusters of blue lines, coreopsis and heleniums were drawn as smudges of yellow and gold, peonies became splashes of red.

"I can't say that I sat down and planned it in great detail or knew that a certain yellow would work beautifully with a soft pink—none of that at all. That would work, in many ways, against the feeling of the sort of gardens in these books. I imagine the way they were created was the gardener managed to pick up a plant or

In late June, pink, yellow, purple, and red hybrid lupines and dark blue hybrid delphiniums are features toward the back of the borders. Mounds of salmon-pink Geranium endressii 'Wargrave Pink' edge the stone path to the front door. The spear-like foliage of bearded irises remains a feature throughout the growing season.

two, then put them in whatever little space there was."

Clive's actual selection of plants took place at the nursery that spring. "I just took a whacking great trolley and said I'll have that and that and that. I didn't know my plants by name very well. But I did know that a certain plant would grow to 6 feet and grow 2 feet wide or that plant was a low grower and would look good if it spread across a path."

By looking at the pictures on the plant labels and reading the descriptions, Clive recognized the plants he had read about. He then selected low-growing plants for the edges of the path and taller plants of various heights for the middle and rear of the borders. With a general idea of how tall each plant would grow and the spacing between them, as well as how much ground he had to fill, he selected 75 plants.

That afternoon he planted the borders. The first thing he did was organize all the different plants—pots of delphiniums in one spot, coreopsis in another, and so forth, along the entire length of the path. Using the plastic labels, with their color pictures as guides, he placed some of the taller-growing plants as features for each bloom period: lupines for May, delphiniums for June, false sunflowers and sneezeweed for July into September, and Michaelmas daisies for August through September. He then walked up and down the path trying to imagine what the effect would be like once the plants were in bloom. After a certain amount of shifting around, the positions of the feature plants were decided. He then arranged the rest of the pots, including mountain bluets (*Centaurea montana*) and columbines (*Aquilegia* hybrids) through the garden as fillers. Annuals were added later along the edges and to fill in gaps.

"I was interested in an overall impression, a feeling sort of like Impressionist painting," explained Clive of his impromptu planting technique. To help achieve the effect he

was after, plants like sneezeweed (*Helenium autumnale*) and tickseed (*Coreopsis grandiflora*) were repeated on either side of the path. "Most books say don't repeat yourself. I think that's nonsense. The books also say to plant in groups of three, then go on to the next group of three. I tended to buy seven or eight plants of each type, then decided to plant two there and three there and another two there, all within sight of each other."

As a result, certain plants, such as *Geranium endressii* 'Wargrave Pink', run like a theme throughout the borders. Planted on the lower right and left sides, then in selected spots, the repetition of this salmon-pink geranium leads the eye from one side to the other and up the path. Shasta

daisies (*Chrysanthemum × superbum*), pyrethrums (*Chrysanthemum coccineum*), and other daisylike flowers, including fleabane (*Erigeron hybridus*) and a threadleaf coreopsis (*Coreopsis verticillata* 'Moonbeam'), were also repeated. Clumps of montbretia (*Crocosmia × crocosmiiflora*) were planted as focal points at the beginning and top of the border close to the edge of the path. In these key positions, the montbretia's dramatic foliage and bright orange flowers helped balance the borders.

For all the spontaneity in its planning, Durbans' borders have a good succession of bloom, beginning in May with pink, yellow, and blue 'Russell Strain' lupines, foxgloves (*Digitalis purpurea*), and masses of blue or white forget-me-nots (*Myosotis* species). The foliage of emerging perennials, in a dozen different shades of green, provide the background.

Early in May, Clive does all his staking. Ranging from 6 to 10 inches tall, the perennials are still small enough for him to walk between them, and their stalks are still supple enough to be handled without breaking. Staking, like everything else at Durbans, developed through trial and error. The first spring Clive bought hundreds of bamboo stalks. He then surrounded each perennial with three

Soft pink G. sanguineum *var.* striatum *spill over and soften the edge of the path directly in front of the cottage.*

Columbines (Aquilegia *hybrids*) *in shades of pink, yellow, blue, and white are tucked in between various perennials close to the edge of the borders, where their delicate flowers can be appreciated.*

to six stakes and several yards of twine. After spending most of a Saturday erecting these elaborate constructions he stepped back, took a look at his handiwork, and dismantled everything.

"They looked awful. So I went around our hedgerows and cut branches and stripped them of all their leaves and put them in. The branches had quite a few twigs, so these helped support the plants. When I was through, it was very difficult to see that any of the plants had been staked at all." The following spring, he cut the hazel twigs before they had leafed out and stored them in a shed

till it was time to stake.

By June the perennials have leafed out and Durbans' first really big show of perennials is in full flower. Dozens of Pacific Coast hybrid delphiniums combined with peach-leaved bellflowers *(Campanula persicifolia)* and shasta daisies *(Chrysanthemum × superbum)* are features, along with large clumps of tickseed *(Coreopsis grandiflora)* and a threadleaf coreopsis *(C. verticillata* 'Moonbeam'). Along the edges of the path, a lovely mix of dark and pale pink, white, and lavender-flowered thymes alternate with the salmon-pink flowers of hardy geraniums *Geranium endressii* 'Wargrave Pink', magenta *G.*

sanguineum, and soft pink *G. sanguineum* var. *striatum.*

Foxgloves *(Digitalis purpurea)* are also a feature in June. A classic cottage plant, they have a long period of bloom. In May the flowers begin opening at the bottom of the stalk and continue opening along the stem till July. But by the time the last few flowers have opened, the stalks are so gawky and unattractive that most gardeners have gotten fed up and cut them back.

Although *D. purpurea* will occasionally winter over, at Durbans it is treated primarily as a biennial (a plant that flowers the second year from seed). To assure a continual display each year, Clive lets his plants self-seed. Rather than leaving the brown and dying stalks standing, he bends them in half (without breaking), then tucks them inconspicuously among the other border plants while the seeds mature. The seeds are then removed and strewn around the garden or left to fall around the base of the plant. If these little groups of seedlings are too thick, they are thinned and planted throughout the border.

Peak perennial display at Durbans continues into July, when perennials that began in June are joined by the old-fashioned single hollyhocks *(Alcea rosea,* or *Althaea rosea),* yellow, and white yarrows, astilbes, heleniums, and lavenders. *Coreopsis grandiflora* and *C. verticillata* 'Moonbeam' spread a haze of yellow through the border from June right into September.

In August, the borders feature summer phlox *(Phlox paniculata),* Michaelmas daisies or hardy asters (*Aster novae-angliae* hybrids and *A. novi-belgii* hybrids), and huge clumps of orange montbretia (*Crocosmia* × *crocosmiiflora).* Also in August, the delphiniums begin flowering a second time. These feature perennials are surrounded by annuals, including snapdragons, pink and white cosmos, and zinnias. At peak bloom in August, these annuals fill in the inevitable gaps and do a great job of hiding the bottom half of hardy asters and phlox when their lower leaves turn brown and dry in late summer.

Along the path, Clive has mixed pansies, fibrous-rooted begonias, nasturtiums, various shades of blue love-in-a-mist, white and purple alyssum, and lobelia between clumps of hardy geraniums, thymes, and various violas. The mixture of bright colors and varied leaf textures makes an informal cottage-style edging that retains its interest right up to hard frosts.

Some of these border perennials will continue to bloom all summer

without any special care, other than staking. But the majority, including the *Delphinium* hybrids, *Campanula persicifolia,* and *Coreopsis grandiflora,* need their faded flowers removed to encourage repeat blooms.

Deadheading can be time consuming, but it is not difficult. The trick is knowing how and when the various plants need to be cut back—information

In late June, a thatched bird house is surrounded by Shirley poppies (Papaver rhoeas), *hybrid delphiniums, and the young flowers of yellow yarrow* (Achillea filipendulina). *By mid-July, the hollyhocks will be in bloom with single red, pink, and yellow flowers.*

tion Clive acquired from gardening neighbors. Delphiniums are easy. After the flowers have faded, he cuts back the flower stalks to the nearest healthy leaves below the raceme to encourage the plants to put out side shoots. If the delphiniums are cut back to the crown after the side shoots bloom, the plants will often bloom again in late summer. These later blooms will tend to be smaller on shorter stems, but they are still a pretty good show.

Deadheading *Coreopsis grandiflora,* with all its small flowers, is a chore. If all the seed heads are just pulled off or clipped, the plant is left looking like a bunch of green twigs. To avoid this crew-cut look Clive cuts off the faded flowers individually where they meet the main stem. *Coreopsis verticillata* 'Moonbeam' seems to do fine without deadheading and continues to bloom right into September.

As for *Geranium endressii* 'Wargrave Pink', Clive is more interested in maintaining a continuous but modest flowering all summer. So rather than cutting the plants back after heavy June flowering (as some gardeners do to induce new growth and a heavy, second bloom), once the seeds are brown, he takes a handful of flower stalks and gently pulls them through his fist; this removes most of the seed heads but leaves the plants and their foliage intact.

Many of the border plants Clive selected, such as pyrethrums (*Chrysanthemum coccineum* hybrids), heleniums (*Helenium autumnale* 'Butterpat' and *H. autumnale* 'Wyndley'), and *Heliopsis helianthoides* 'Golden Plume', were inexpensive, fast growers. By midsummer of the first year, plants that had been tiny when planted that spring had flourished and become specimens a foot or more across—quick growth that shaded the ground around the plants so few weeds had a chance to get started.

By the second year, the majority of the plants had filled out and the borders had the look of a mature garden. The silver-edged thymes and *Geranium endressii* 'Wargrave Pink' softened the hard edges of the walk, while hundreds of both pink and salmon annual Shirley poppies *(Papaver rhoeas)* created the perfect foil for good-size clumps of blue Siberian irises and delphiniums and provided color from June to August. "Other than staking, I actually spent precious little time doing any gardening. The borders seemed to look after themselves quite well," recalled Clive.

At the end of the second growing season, it was also apparent that some changes were necessary. "I made some really terrible mistakes. Suddenly this 3-inch pot plant was 18 inches wide and 4 feet high. It comes as a surprise if you've never grown these plants before." The reverse also happened: a plant listed as 10 feet grew 3 feet tall instead. In some cases plants were placed too closely together, and others grew much faster than their neighbors. Along the edges of the path, various thymes, including *Thymus × citriodorus, T. serphyllum,* and *T. serphyllum* 'Album', were practically smothered by the exuberant growth of hardy geraniums.

Edgings are probably the most challenging area of a border for a new gardener. The rest of a border can be a pleasant mixture of different perennials and annual fillers, but its edgings remain an important focal point all season long. Creating a truly effective border edging of contrasting textures, form, and foliage is something few new gardeners can get right the first few years.

Ideally, a border's edges should be an interesting contrast of texture and color as well as different plant forms—soft, rounded clumps contrasted with spiky leaves and perhaps a taller, mid-border plant like Siberian iris *(Iris sibirica)* brought forward to vary the height. All this means is that you have to know how high, wide, and fast these potential edging plants grow. Knowing how well the plants and their foliage hold up throughout the season, as well as when (or if) they flop and get mildew, will all figure into planning a good edging. It takes a few seasons of observing plants growing to know whether a plant's foliage and overall form merit such a prominent position.

The edgings of a border are an excellent place to highlight contrasts of texture and plant forms, a plant's foliage, even the way the flowers are held on the stems. The sharp verticality of *Iris sibirica* at Durbans, for example, would be even more pronounced if seen along the edge, where the entire plant is visible from the ground up. So knowing what he didn't know, Clive planted a few low-growing perennials and herbs along the edge of the path, then filled in with annuals.

Like most new gardeners, Clive chose his perennials primarily for color and season of bloom. Foliage was something he hadn't even considered, and because he hadn't grown any of the plants before, he had no idea what they looked like before or after they had finished blooming. As a result, key areas of each border looked decidedly gappy when pyrethrums and shasta daisies had finished bloom-

(Opposite) In the border on the right side of the path, shasta daisies (Chrysanthemum × superbum) *mingle with salmon, pink, and crimson Shirley poppies* (Papaver rhoeas), Geranium endressii *'Wargrave Pink', and lavender.*

ing and were reduced to squat clumps of leaves.

At the end of the second year many of the borders' fast-growing perennials already needed dividing. By the third summer the slower-growing plants, including peonies and lavenders, were smothered by exuberant sprawls of heliopsis, heleniums, and chrysanthemums; it was obvious that in the fall approximately half the plants would require division.

Dividing perennials, like staking and deadheading, is a fairly simple procedure, but it can be very time consuming if most of a border requires division every few years. Some of the plants Clive selected on his whirlwind tour of the local nursery could be left for a number of years before they required or benefited from division. *Chrysanthemum coccineum,* for example, could remain three or four growing seasons till division became advisable. The *Iris sibirica,* planted as good-size divisions, might be left four or five years before the center of the plant died out. Various geraniums, including *Geranium endressii* and *G. sanguineum* and its varieties, could be left even longer. Most fortunate of all, oriental poppies and peonies preferred to be left undisturbed.

That fall, as Clive contemplated all the perennials that required dividing, it was apparent that some refinement of his planting scheme was in order. By this time he also knew a lot more about plants—how they grew and how they looked throughout the growing season. Foliage, he had learned, was important. So to reduce all the staking, deadheading, and dividing, and to help give the borders a framework of foliage that would last all season, he planned on replacing some of the weedier plants with perennials having long-lasting, attractive foliage—possibly false indigo *(Baptisia australis)*, gas plant *(Dictamnus albus* 'Purpureus')*, peonies, and perhaps a few perpetually blooming shrub roses. Japanese anemone *(Anemone × hybrida)*, and a mix of Michaelmas daisies *(Aster novae-angliae* hybrids and *A. novi-belgii* hybrids) combined with a few of the existing late yellow and gold flowers would carry the borders right through autumn.

With an abundance of blue flowers in May and June, mountain bluets (Centaurea montana) *are quick growing, inexpensive, and used throughout the garden as fillers.*

Durbans is a good beginning garden. It is fast, easy to grow, with a good succession of bloom, and inexpensive to plant. Because McBain did most of the work himself, the whole garden, including peat, sand, and rotted manure, cost about $800.

Probably the two most important factors in the initial success of McBain's garden were his willingness to experiment and his thorough soil preparation. Another was his refusal to believe everything he read. During one of his nursery visits he purchased a climbing rose with the idea of growing it up into the branches of a small plum tree by the gate. Before planting it, he did a bit of research on rose care. After wading through pages of do's and don't's, he got to the part where it said one should be very careful about planting roses close to a tree.

"So I said fine, I'll put it next to my tree. In two years, the rose totally covered that plum tree. It just goes to show, you can't generalize. Some things do and some things don't stick to the book. I think that's what's so exciting about gardening.

"I make it up as I go along. If something goes wrong and that accident benefits the whole garden, then terrific, I leave it. There isn't a master plan here, and that, I think, is the secret of this garden's charm."

Bearded irises are planted throughout the borders and are a feature of the garden in late May and early June.

CHAPTER 5

COTTAGE STYLE

(Opposite) Concrete sphinxes frame the entrance to the front door of Waystrode Manor. The chartreuse flowers of lady's mantle (Alchemilla mollis) *sprawl across the path, mingling with ferns and pansies planted around the stone wall. Stone pots with bright pink petunias and wire baskets with red pelargoniums provide spots of bright color.*

(Right) The distinctive leaves of the hardy crimson gloryvine (Vitis coignetiae) *frame a leaded window. The cement trough is planted with pelargoniums, petunias, and the silver-leaved* Helichrysum petiolatum.

COTTAGE GARDENING, while old-fashioned and full of romantic design elements, is a style adaptable to all sorts of sites and houses. Over a period of many years I visited hundreds of English cottage gardens, from tiny city back yards to country acres. Each was as unique as its owner, but all had something in common. In every garden, cottage-style plantings, when coupled with good design, transformed boring or problematic sites into beautiful and distinctly personal spaces. The following four gardens are some of the best and suggest how versatile cottage gardening can be.

23 BEECHCROFT

One of the smallest, yet most exciting cottage-style gardens was tucked behind a modest row house in the city of Oxford. As with several of the gardens in this book, I had heard about Beechcroft through an English gardening friend. After listening to him rave on about how wonderful the garden was, I called and arranged a time to see it.

Walking down the narrow, tree-less street and standing on the stoop of 23 Beechcroft I was curious but, having seen so many city gardens here in the United States, with their obligatory pachysandra and vinca, I wasn't harboring any great expectations. When Anne Dexter opened the door and led me through the hall into the drawing room, I was totally unprepared for what I was about to see.

The garden seen through the

French doors was like no city garden I had ever seen. Here was the most wonderful yet seemingly impossible profusion of roses and clematis wound through the branches of trees and cascading from walls. The stone path, practically hidden by flowers, was straight out of an English fairy tale.

The creation of this garden, as it turned out, was equally fantastic. When Anne moved into 23 Beechcroft, the only view of the back yard was through a small window at the end of a narrow, dark kitchen, and the only way into the yard was through the scullery, out a side door, and down a narrow, dark alley. All that didn't matter much because the only things growing in the garden were some bits of rough grass, a few raspberry and gooseberry bushes, and a large mountain ash stuck right in the middle. The whole arrangement was singularly unappealing and exceedingly dreary.

But Anne was set on having a garden, and if she was going to create a garden, she certainly wanted to be able to see it and enjoy it from inside the house as well as outside. With the help of a local contractor, the dark little kitchen was turned into a drawing room with a pair of French doors.

She then began the task of turning the barren rectangle into a garden, a task made all the more challenging because, by the time the renovations of the house were finished, the gardening budget was mighty small. To top it all off, absolutely everything—stones, soil, and plants—would have to be brought through the front door, down the hall, and out the kitchen door.

To create a bit of drama and make the most of the narrow back yard, she decided to create a vista. Stone steps to a false door set against the brick wall, surrounded by ferns and flowering shrubs, would create the focal point at the end of the garden. A stone path down the center would then be edged by two long borders on either side. The whole garden could then be viewed from a tiny stone terrace, just big enough for two or three chairs, outside the drawing room's glass doors.

The plan for Anne's garden was simple enough, but first the mountain ash had to be taken down and removed. The next trick was to get in the 38 yards of paving stone required for the path and terrace—delivered by wheelbarrow through the front door, down the hall, through kitchen and alley, and into the garden. She then laid the patio and the S-shaped stone path down the center of the garden.

Anne never drew out a plan, but she had a very clear idea of what she wanted and the plants needed to create the effects. Like many city back yards, Beechcroft didn't get a lot of sun. Although the yard faced south, it was hemmed in on two sides by brick walls. Each side received sun for only part of the day, so certain areas had to be planted as shade garden.

Privacy was a major priority. The 5-foot stone walls did nothing to hide neighboring clotheslines with their socks and sheets. Her solution to that problem was ingenious and cost practically nothing: using bamboo poles lashed together with old nylon stockings, she constructed a lattice along the right side of the garden. This increased the height of the wall by 3 feet and served as a framework for six espaliered flowering plum trees. Planted 3 feet apart, about 1 foot from the wall, these different prunus would grow about 20 feet high, eventually forming a kind of living lattice for climbing plants. The black-purple leaves and pink flowers of *Prunus cerasifera* 'Nigra' and the dark red young leaves (later turning purple), and pink-white flowers of *P. cerasifera* 'Atropurpurea' would also create an interesting background for the mix of evergreen and deciduous shrubs that would form the garden's framework.

Anne's selection of trees and shrubs consisted, for the most part, of common, inexpensive varieties. Except for a few larger specimens, everything was from 1 to 2 feet high. Part of this was the result of economic necessity, but the smaller sizes also allowed her to fit more in initially. Later she could prune them to keep them in balance.

The variegated or golden foliage of golden privet (*Ligustrum ovalifolium* 'Aureo-marginatum'), and golden-leaved, evergreen honeysuckle (*Lonicera nitida* 'Baggesen's Gold') became important accents and focal points in the partially shaded garden. The sharp contrasts of their yellow leaves against the dark green and purple leaves of the plum trees gave the borders an added sense of depth.

Roses were then planted as focal points for the garden's first big show in June. Because the garden was so small, it took only about a half a dozen to create the effect Anne wanted. Her choices included 'Golden Wings', a modern shrub rose with large, pale gold, sweetly scented flowers from June to October, and 'Buff Beauty', a hybrid musk with very full,

The vista through the garden at 23 Beech Croft to the French doors of the living room. On the left, the deep wine-red Clematis *'Madame Edouard Andre' is grown behind and through* Berberis *'Somerset'. On the right side of the path, the borders feature various berberis and* Euonymus *'Emerald and Gold'.*

The false door set against the brick wall at the end of Anne's garden is highlighted by flowering hydrangea, variegated hostas, or ornamental grasses, and ferns.

To achieve the longest season of interest in this narrow space, Anne created layers of bloom, beginning in early spring with white and pale blue muscari and groups of pink or white scillas, tucked in small groups under the shrubs. These were followed by a few narcissus, placed toward the rear of the border, so their messy, maturing foliage would be covered when the shrubs leafed out. Anne's collection of perennials that bloom throughout the summer and into fall includes, as she puts it, "a bit of everything," from hardy geraniums and Michaelmas daisies to artemisias and astrantias.

There is little space, so the hundreds of different perennials are crammed in more tightly than any gardening book would ever recommend. Some plants, of course, lose out to the competition; others thrive in the tangle. To prevent the garden from becoming an amorphous mass of different colors, or solid patches of fast-growing plants such as artemisia, requires a lot of thinning and pruning.

With so many different plants in such a small space, Anne's various combinations (what she calls pictures) create seasonal focal points. These combinations of foliage, color, and texture have a wonderful, jewel-like quality reminiscent of Persian minia-

apricot-colored blooms, with flowers throughout the summer. *Rosa rubrifolia,* or *R. glauca,* was chosen more for its distinctive gray-purple foliage than its small, single, reddish flowers. Given room, *R. rubrifolia* could reach 7 feet tall and 4 feet wide; here,

tightly sandwiched between other plants, its growth was more restrained and its foliage an accent. Although roses prefer full sun, as with many of the shrubs Anne planted, she discovered they would grow with less and still flower.

tures. In one section, for example, the blossoms of a pink rose might be draped like calligraphic scrawl across the branches of a red-leaved barberry bush, while in a deeply shaded corner a gold-edged hosta and silver-edged ivy create a vignette-like highlight.

Also important in this small garden is Anne's imaginative use of plants with large, bold leaves, such as variegated hostas, *Brunnera macrophylla, B. macrophylla* 'Variegata', and *Bergenia cordifolia.* Placed among the many smaller-leaved plants, they too create focal points and a significant contrast in scale, without taking up lots of room.

But the garden's main feature is its profusion of clematis. Winding their way through roses and into shrubs, they provide this tiny garden with bloom from May right into October. As with so many garden successes, this collection began with a single specimen. Planted over 20 years ago, Anne's *Clematis alpina* (one of the smaller-flowered, May-blooming species), with its cup-shaped violet-blue flowers, was so happy and grew so abundantly that Anne thought, "Why not plant a few more?" Now her collection contains over 40 different clematis, including May- and June-blooming *C. macropetala,* a small-flowered species with dark blue, bell-shaped flowers. In July several varieties of *C. viticella* (with bell-shaped, nodding flowers) begin blooming, along with the *C. texensis* hybrids rose-pink 'Duchess of Albany' and deep red 'Gravetye Beauty'. Both *C. viticella* and *C. texensis* will continue blooming through the summer. Some of the larger-flowered hybrids such as 'Victoria' (a soft heliotrope with buff stamens) and 'Perle d'Azur' (sky blue with green stamens) begin flowering in June and continue into September.

Years ago, when Anne was first beginning her collection of clematis, she spent days trying to come up with

The miniature rose 'Pour Toi' is a feature in a flower "picture" with red-leaved berberis and the dainty white flowers of Gillenia trifoliata.

a system of supports for these weak-stemmed shrubs and vines that would be cheap, space efficient, and easily constructed. After looking at several ready-made and rather costly supports, she came up with an ingenious solution. Anne figured trees would be the cheapest and probably the most effective supports, so she asked a friend with a country wood lot to cut some saplings, 4 inches in diameter, leaving the side branches as 8-inch stubs.

These 15 saplings were then sunk 3 feet into the ground, wrapped with wire netting, and wired to metal eye hooks in the brick wall. Strong rope was draped loosely between these posts, rather like Christmas garlands, and covered with wire netting to give the clematis something to cling to. The supports were so artfully done that now, when the clematis are in full foliage, there isn't a clue that chicken wire, rope, and dead trees are behind it all.

Another secret to her success with clematis was the actual planting. Careful not to disturb surrounding plants, Anne dug a hole for each clematis at least three times the size of the plant's root ball, loosened 6 inches of soil at the bottom, mixed in rotted manure, then added a thin layer of garden soil. Next, she mixed bone meal with the soil going back into the hole. Once the clematis was planted, more bone meal was worked around it. She also made it a point to plant each vine 2 inches below the soil level of its pot. That way, if clematis wilt killed back the plant, chances were pretty good it would sprout again.

Now, each autumn, she mulches all her clematis with well-rotted manure, careful to keep it 4–6 inches away from the stems to avoid rot. Sometimes she places a flat stone or two on top of the soil to help keep the roots moist. Because the thick foliage of surrounding plants prevents rain from reaching the clematis roots, watering is critical. If the weather is hot and dry for a few days in a row, she sets a soaker on the plants to assure deep and thorough watering.

As soon as the clematis start growing in the spring, Anne begins training them. If left to their own devices these vines would scramble wildly, covering plants or falling in a mass on top of themselves. Each morning, using a long stick where necessary, she pokes and arranged the new tendrils around plum trees and roses and across barberry bushes so the clematis flowers can be seen.

Although a very small garden— largely *because* it is so small—its maintenance takes about four hours a day, beginning in early May. Throughout the growing season, plants are carefully deadheaded and pruned so they don't overrun each other. The tight spacing of the plants also results in some pretty stiff competition for nutrients. To keep the soil fertile, Anne applies leaf compost gathered from the local parks and well-rotted manure brought back from the country in the trunk of her car.

In October, at the end of the growing season, the entire garden is cut down and hauled through the house in large plastic bags. With a single clematis filling a bag, it is a big job, but worth every bit of effort. As Anne cuts and stuffs, she often thinks back to the freshness of spring mornings and the quiet fullness of summer afternoons, the garden rich with the fragrance of honeysuckle and roses. Invariably she smiles when she remembers the looks of delighted surprise on visitors' faces as they walk into the drawing room and see her garden for the very first time.

A flower "picture" featuring the finely cut silver foliage of Artemisia *'Powis Castle' (to the left),* Filipendula rubra, *and* Artemisia ludoviciana.

WAYSTRODE MANOR

Many of the cottage gardens I photographed were created from scratch, whereas others were built on the foundations of existing gardens. I saw a good many larger cottage gardens, but Waystrode Manor in Kent provides one of the best examples of how cottage gardening could transform a stiff and formal garden into a setting with character and charm.

When Jill and Peter Wright bought Waystrode in 1963, the small, shingled manor house was an archaic delight. Begun about 1352 and added to century after century, it was rambling and whimsical, with huge chimneys and eccentric little doors and windows.

The various gardens surrounding the house, oddly enough, had nothing to do with the house; with their tight beds of annuals and finicky bits of mowed grass, they looked like a cross between a suburban lot and a badly designed public park. They were also, Jill quickly discovered, surprisingly time consuming to maintain. During their first year at Waystrode, she also observed that the basic framework of the various gardens was essentially sound. All they needed was to be rethought and replanted in a more spontaneous style, something that

Clematis 'Perle D'Azur' frames the back door with flowers from June to August. In the reconstructed stone urns the silver foliage of tender Helichrysum petiolatum provides a foil for white daisies. Pink perennial sweet peas (Lathyrus latifolius) flower from June to September and self-seed between the stones of the terrace.

would complement the house's idiosyncratic architecture.

Instead of drawing up plans, Jill first figured out what she liked and didn't like about the existing gardens—what features had to go, what would stay, and how those remaining could be made more interesting and (if possible) less work. In the front of the house, for example, the basic layout and dimensions of the walled, grass entry garden were fine, but the mower couldn't reach into all the tight corners or come close enough to the wall, so most of the trimming had to be done by hand. Figuring maintenance time could be better spent elsewhere, Jill and her part-time gardener, George, spent several days removing sod and laying down paving stones. The spaces between the stones were then planted with various low-growing campanulas and lady's mantle (*Alchemilla mollis*).

The wall separating the entry garden from the driveway was a lovely piece of rustic stonework with a smattering of spring-flowering rock plants in little pockets of soil between the stones; again, a good idea, but not much of a display. To highlight the entrance to the house, Jill decided to make the wall an important spring feature, so seeds and rooted cuttings of basket-of-gold (*Aurinia saxatilis,* or

Alyssum saxatile), white-flowered snow-in-summer (*Cerastium tomentosum),* along with purple rock cress (*Aubrieta deltoidea),* were planted between the stones. In a few years, the wall became a thick tapestry of gold, mauve, and lavender rock plants in April and May.

To make the entrance to the house even more dramatic, Jill had a local artisan cast a pair of concrete sphinxes, and she placed them to either side of the entrance through the wall. After a few winters these inexpensive statues had weathered and looked almost as venerable as the house.

The front garden is now simple to maintain. After the wall is finished blooming, the plants are cut back, and that is it for the season. The *A. mollis* between the stones of the entry garden is equally undemanding; after the plants have flowered, it, too, is cut back, a procedure that takes about 20 minutes. The leaves then remain an attractive feature right into autumn.

Once the front of the house was taken care of, Jill began on the rear garden. If ever there was an uninspired garden this was it: two long straight lines of yew hedges flanking a wide stone path edged with grass and annuals. The moment you walked into the garden it was obvious it didn't

contain a single surprise.

Though the garden was boring, the yew hedges were a truly handsome feature and the paving was good. Yew hedges such as these were also a valuable horticultural commodity that took years to mature, so there was no good reason to get rid of them. But it was obvious to Jill that something more had to happen, because a straight line of annuals wasn't going to lure anybody down through that garden.

She began by making a few relatively simple changes. One of the first was to train the yew's branches into arches over the paths leading out of the garden and along the main axis. In her imagination Jill also saw the hedge as the perfect background for perennial borders. To make the beds wide enough, she and George removed the grass edging and several feet of paving stones. These wider borders were then enriched with compost and manure and planted with a variety of old-fashioned perennials.

Inspired by the rose garden at Sissinghurst, Jill planted dozens of shrub roses as focal points, at the corners of paths and in the middle of the borders. Bearded and Siberian irises, peonies, phlox, and other feature plants provided additional focal points. Fast-growing perennials,

(Opposite) In the front garden at Waystrode Manor, lady's mantle (Alchemilla mollis), *with its sprawling masses of chartreuse flowers, is planted between the stones. After the lady's mantle is through blooming, its flower stalks are cut back and its distinctive leaves remain attractive right into autumn.*

including lady's mantle *(Alchemilla mollis)*, mountain bluet *(Centaurea montana)*, circle flower *(Lysimachia punctata)*, and half a dozen different hardy geraniums, including *Geranium psilostemon (G. armenum)*, were then planted around them.

One of the garden's most important features was added a few years after the borders were planted. Following the death of an old apple tree (the sole support for a tremendous white rose), Peter Wright replaced the tree with four metal arches. Jill then added a stone trough and an urn to create focal points along the stone path.

Each year spring bulbs and new perennials were added. Sometimes Jill saw a plant at a nursery or in a friend's garden and had a feeling it would be perfect next to a certain rose or combined with some foliage plant. About ten years ago she saw a yellow giant scabies *(Cephalaria gigantea)* in a friend's garden, and that, too, found a spot, combined with dark pink peonies, *Alchemilla mollis,* and *Geranium psilostemon.*

Bloom begins in early April with

In June, large sprawling clumps of lady's mantle (Alchemilla mollis) *and circle flower* (Lysimachia punctata) *create bright spots of color and soften the edges of the perennial borders featuring peonies, foxgloves, heucheras, monkshoods, hardy geraniums, including magenta-flowered* Geranium psilostemon, *and the tall, shaggy, yellow flowers of giant scabies* (Cephalaria gigantea).

small spring bulbs, including scilla and snowdrops. Sweeps of daffodils are surrounded by thick carpets of for-get-me-nots *(Myosotis alpestris)* and varieties of primroses *(Primula* species). In June the garden features peonies, irises, and foxgloves, along with dozens of different shrub and climbing roses. Later in the month delphiniums and the tall, yellow giant scabies *(C. gigantea)* are features. Along the edge of the border huge mounds of *Alchemilla mollis* sprawl into the path. In July and August there is a massive show of various phloxes, along with aconitums and, often, a second bloom of delphiniums.

The garden has no set color scheme except for the very end, where a little "room" (enclosed by clipped yew arches) features gray foliage plants and white flowers. Here, white daffodils, white-flowered lungwort *(Pulmonaria angustifolia),* and small-flowered white bleeding heart *(Dicen-tra eximia* 'Alba') are spring features. In June and July white clematis and potentilla are features, and various white-flowered dianthus create a mixture of soft blue-gray and gray-green foliage against a background of several different silver-leaved artemisias.

In early May the plants in the middle and rear of the borders are staked with dark green metal hoops, and by the end of the month the foliage is so thick the supports scarcely show. Twice a year, in early spring and late fall, dead foliage is cut back and plants are thinned or divided. Except for a persistent crop of the perennial weed ground elder *(Aegopodium podagraria)* that must be cleaned out periodically, the perennials are so thick that weeds don't have much chance to get started. About mid-December the hedge is trimmed, a job that is still a huge task, but one made easier by a 2-foot-wide path behind the border running the entire length of the garden, providing a place to stand while trimming.

Compared to the original plantings of annuals, Jill's yew garden requires surprisingly little maintenance. Now a continuous succession of plants assures that there is always something new in bloom to lure friends and guests down the garden's path.

Ferns and drifts of variegated apple mint (Mentha rotundifolia *'Variegata') soften the edges of stone steps and paths. In the background the fragrant shrub rose 'Adam Messerich' flowers throughout the summer with clusters of dark pink blooms.*

COBBLERS

Cobblers is nearly two acres, the largest garden featured in this book. With winding brick paths, old-fashioned shrub borders underplanted with flowering ground covers, and a pond edged with perennials and accented by white wooden benches, it is full of ideas and plant combinations for cottage-style gardens—large and small. (See Chapter 3, "Cottage Plants.")

For all of Cobblers' diversity, it is the areas surrounding the house, and where the driveway and garage meet, that offer some of the most interesting ideas, particularly for gardeners who want to turn these utilitarian architectural features into beautiful and intimate parts of their gardens.

In 1968, when Barbara and Martin Furniss bought Cobblers, the hillside with its gnarled old apple trees was waist high in weeds and wildflowers. The old farmhouse, built in the fourteenth century, was chock full of structural idiosyncracies, but it was the entrance area to the house and the driveway (some of the most unattractive spaces imaginable) that provided the greatest challenges.

As with so many landscapes, the driveway at Cobblers had been designed solely to get cars into and

out of the garage, with no thought to appearance. The driveway, a wide stretch of black macadam, filled the front yard, then cut straight up between the house and barn to a huge concrete garage in the middle of the back yard. As a result, the house and barn were totally cut off from one another and the property divided into several disjointed pieces.

A practicing architect at the time,

(Opposite) In late May the rectangular beds in front of the house at Cobblers in Sussex feature orange poppies, bright yellow wallflowers (Cheiranthus cheiri), and blue hardy geranium (Geranium 'Johnson's Blue'). Blue and white forget-me-nots have self-seeded in borders and the stones of the terrace. To the left, Spirea bumalda *'Gold Flame'.*

(Above) A handsome specimen of the climbing rose 'Albertine' is trained over the lych-gate connecting the house and the barn, framing one of the garden's most dramatic views.

Martin came up with a plan that was very simple but resulted in dramatic changes. As with most cottage gardens, the house was to be the heart of the garden. The area around the house would be planted with borders full of flowering perennials, shrubs, and vines, establishing the garden's style. The feeling would be very informal, but the underlying framework would be architectural, the strong lines helping to tie the house and barn together.

The first step was to tear down the ugly concrete garage behind the house. Martin then redesigned the barn for use as a garage. Working on weekends and holidays, he and Barbara altered the barn's roofline, added a cupola and doors for two cars, then finished the building with the same rustic roof tiles and siding used on the house. The old driveway was then torn up and rerouted in a graceful curve, following the contours of the hillside, around the south side of the barn. Edged with shrub borders and large sweeps of herbaceous plants, the gravel drive soon resembled a broad garden path.

The garden areas surrounding the house were laid out as a geometric framework of steps and rectangular lawns and borders. The hillside at the back was divided into two long, narrow borders separated by a brick path. A rectangular lawn next to the house repeated the lines of house and borders and created a pleasant place to sit and view the garden on summer evenings. (See Plan for Cobblers.)

The layout at the rear of the house, with its strong geometric lines, is rather formal. The informality of the plantings, however, softens any hard edges and provides a succession of bloom from early spring right through the summer. In the lower border, dozens of pink and red roses bloom from June to hard frost. In the upper border, peonies, lupines, and daisies are highlights. Sweeps of self-sown foxgloves, along with a few towering yellow mulleins, provide vertical accents.

Along the edge of this upper border, sprawling mounds of catmint (*Nepeta mussinii*) and lady's mantle (*Alchemilla mollis*), with chartreuse flowers from late June into July, spill over the edges. At the end of the path between the two borders a white wooden bench surrounded by various irises, red valerian (*Centranthus ruber*), and *A. mollis* provides the borders with a focal point.

The front of the house proved a much more challenging design problem. Here, the land fell in a steep bank to the driveway, leaving the house perched awkwardly above. To help bring the house and garden together, Martin designed a simple layout of stone steps, low retaining walls, and borders divided by a rectangular terrace. This geometric arrangement allowed easy access to the front door of the house and to the barn and established a stylistic unity with the rear garden. At the same time it created plenty of level planting area and good strong lines that helped make the entry area interesting all year. (See Plan for Cobblers.)

A gravel path was then laid between the house and barn to replace a section of the original macadam driveway. Stone steps linked the gravel path with the terrace in front of the house. A rustic, shingled lych-gate (or breezeway) built between the back doors of barn and house further strengthened the relationship between the two structures. The lych-gate

A statuesque clump of Geranium psilostemon *is a focal point at the end of a perennial border.*

eventually became one of the garden's most attractive features and a frame for the rear garden.

Although the architectural framework of the garden's entry area solved any number of practical design problems, it was the plantings of perennials, vines, and roses that gave the area its warm, welcoming atmosphere. The foundation plantings immediately in front of the house were particularly important in establishing the entry garden's style and in reinforcing the relationship between house and surrounding garden. For these borders, Martin wanted plants that would soften the hard edges of stone walls and perform the traditional role of foundation plantings without looking dull.

So instead of predictable and static rows of yews, rhododendrons, and 'Blue Rug' junipers, he started with a background of deciduous flowering shrubs and vines trained on wires attached to the house, then planted around them with masses of old fashioned cottage-style perennials and low-growing rock plants. These flowering shrubs and vines provide the border with structure and seasonal highlights. In winter the twiggy shapes of flowering quince (*Chaenomeles speciosa* hybrid) and *Hydrangea villosa* give an otherwise bare border

Behind the house, a brick path edged with clumps of Alchemilla mollis, Nepeta mussinii, *self-seeded verbascums, daisies, and roses leads to a bench surrounded with foxgloves* (Digitalis purpurea).

an interesting variety of shapes and textures. During the growing season several different clematis assure that the back of the border is in bloom from May through September.

Spiraea × *bumalda* 'Gold Flame' and other shrubs with colored foliage or distinctive forms are focal points. *Hypericum patulum* 'Hidcote' (just to the left of the front door) is a focal point in the foundation border from July to September. From 3 to 4 feet tall, 'Hidcote' is either deciduous or semi-evergreen, depending upon the severity of the winter. During very cold winters it dies back to the ground but in spring grows so quickly that by midsummer it is usually full size and covered with fragrant, golden yellow, cup-shaped flowers about 2 inches across.

To the right of the bay window Martin planted *Ceanothus* × 'Autumnal Blue', a vigorous but tender evergreen

Along the edge of the pond at Cobblers, a large clump of the ornamental grass 'Bowle's Golden Sedge' is a feature in a narrow border planted with Alchemilla mollis, Primula japonica, *and later-blooming* Lythrum salicaria.

shrub with panicles of small, soft blue flowers from July into autumn providing a particularly beautiful background for white summer phlox (*Phlox paniculata*) and the silvery seed pods of honesty (*Lunaria annua*).

The bloom in these borders was also planned around a succession of feature perennials. In June bearded and Siberian irises and fernleaf yarrow (*Achillea filipendulina*) are focal points, surrounded by dozens of different fillers, including beard tongues (*Penstemon* species), bellflowers (*Campanula* species and hybrids), and rose

campion (*Lychnis coronaria*). Honesty (*Lunaria annua*), with flowers reminiscent of wild phlox, has self-seeded so abundantly that its flowers make a lovely white haze throughout the borders, uniting its various colors. From mid- to late summer yellow daylilies (*Hemerocallis* hybrids), various goldenrod (*Solidago* hybrids), and white and pink summer phlox (*Phlox paniculata*) are features.

Throughout the growing season the borders' edges are a mixture of plants selected for flowers, foliage, and growth habit. In April they are

Blue and white Iris sibirica, *interplanted with orange, yellow, and dark pink* Primula japonica *and later-blooming astilbes, frame a homemade wooden bench at the edge of the brick path along the lower edge of the pond.*

thick with raucous clumps of yellow, orange, and red wallflowers (*Cheiranthus cheiri*). Sprawls of blue-flowered forget-me-nots (*Myosotis alpestris*), purple rock cress (*Aubrieta deltoidea*), and pink and white saxifrage (*Saxifraga* species) spill over the walls and edges of the gravel driveway. In May and early June self-seeded columbines (*Aquilegia* hybrids), both pink and blue, grow so thickly along the gravel path beside the house and barn that it is impossible to tell where the garden ends and the driveway begins. In June large clumps of silver-gray lavender (*Lavandula angustifolia*) provide contrast for mounds of pink-flowered *Geranium endressii* and rock roses (*Helianthemum nummularium*), with semi-evergreen leaves and translucent yellow, orange, and pink flowers. Catmint (*Nepeta mussinii*), with its gray-green leaves and spiky blue flowers (from June to September, depending upon whether or when it is cut back), is planted in several key spots along the edges.

Red valerian (*Centranthus ruber*), a sprawling perennial with large terminal clusters of tiny, reddish-pink flowers, is another prominent edging plant used to soften the edges of stone walls and steps. Encouraged to self-seed, it has spread along the edges of the driveway and up along the narrow path between the house and barn. Here it remains a feature from late June right through the summer.

Borders along the barn's east wall and to either side of the gravel path were designed to soften the hard lines of house and barn and to help link the two structures. Plants with bold forms or distinctive, long-lasting foliage, such as hostas, ferns, *Centranthus ruber,* and bigleaf goldenray *(Ligularia dentata),* were selected to give these borders an interesting background without taking up a lot of space. Low-growing rock plants, including various saxifrages and hardy geraniums, softened the edges of the border and provided seasonal highlights.

One of the entry garden's most important features is the barn's east wall. The first thing you see once inside the front gate, it is large, flat, and boring. Because it was impossible to ignore, Martin decided to play it up and make its weathered wooden door a focal point. Planted with half a dozen different vines and perennials (in layers one behind the other), the wall became an asset, as well as a fine lesson for planting small, tight spaces.

Just six plants made the door an attractive feature from May right into October. To the left of the door, a euphorbia with yellowish green flower

bracts in May to June is combined with *Centranthus ruber.* Behind them, the gold-edged ivy *Hedera* 'Goldheart' and hybrid *Clematis* 'Scartho Gem' (with pink flowers from June to September) are trained up the wall and onto wires on the roof. To the right side of the door, *Abelia × grandiflora,* an evergreen shrub with bronze

In June, a border at the edge of a path at Cobblers is a colorful tangle of perennials, including Japanese primroses, daisies, violas, and saxifrages. A bold mass of yellow flag (Iris pseudacorus) *gives the border a dramatic background.*

foliage and pink tubular flowers (from July into October), seems to grow right out of the center of a huge clump of variegated hosta.

The borders around the south and west side of the barn are very different in character. Instead of the strong, straight lines that give the entry garden its framework, these beds are

rounded, slightly raised, and edged with cobble-shaped stones. Set within the curve of the driveway, they are more like informal country borders and are full of perennials and roses. Surrounded by this picturesque sprawl of perennials and covered with great swags of climbing roses, the garage looks exactly like a charming summerhouse.

The border on the barn's west side was planned for a lengthy succession of bloom but is particularly lovely in June, when pink hardy *Geranium endressii,* white-flowered saxifrage, and spiky mounds of silver-leaved dianthus sprawl over the edges, softening the line between borders and driveway, so that in many places the two are inseparable.

In June the barn border also features some of the most eclectic combinations of colors and plant forms. In one section, apricot and peach-colored bearded irises, pink penstemons, blue *Campanula persicifolia,* and the yellow flower spikes of *Sisyrinchium striatum* and various mulleins (*Verbascum* species and hybrids) are combined. A more dramatic combination features dark red *Paeonia officinalis,* blue-purple *Geranium grandiflorum,* and sulphur-yellow *Achillea filipendulina.*

Various fillers, including the biennials *Hesperis matronalis* and *Lunaria*

A barn door is framed by variegated and flowering vines—to the left Hedera 'Goldheart' and to the right Abelia × grandiflora. Trained up wires and along the roof, Clematis 'Scartho Gem' blooms from June to September. To the left, the greenish-yellow flower bracts of a euphorbia provide a dramatic accent in May and June, along with summer blooming red valerian (Centranthus ruber).

In the front of the barn, a raised border features bearded irises, peonies, and achilleas; hardy geraniums (including Geranium endressii) and mounds of dianthus sprawl and soften the edges of the gravel driveway.

annua (self-seeded in bare spots throughout the border), help unite all the various-colored perennials. *Alchemilla mollis,* planted in several spots, seems to go with just about everything. As an underplanting for dark red *Paeonia officinalis,* its sprawling chartreuse flowers provide contrast, and along the edges of the border the flowers of *A. mollis* complement the soft pinks of tender erodiums, hardy geraniums, and several different saxifrages.

Roses are also a feature in June. 'Albertine', an old-fashioned rambler with fragrant, lobster-pink flowers, and 'Arthur Hillier', with small clusters of single, rosy-crimson blooms, are trained against the barn walls and across the roof. 'Complicata', a vigorous rose with single pink flowers and prominent gold stamens, fills the branches of a flowering crab apple.

Planted at the rear of the border,

this flowering crab tree makes a wonderful rose trellis and in the process helps hide the barn's west wall. Like so many of Martin's combinations, it shows how just a few plants can be combined to create dramatic focal points with interest from early spring right into autumn.

In April the crab apple becomes a cloud of purple-crimson flowers, and the border's most important feature. Then, in May and June, it provides support for a wild tangle of *Clematis macropetala.* Planted next to the rose at the base of the tree, this small-flowered species clematis with its blue, bell-shaped flowers provides a wonderful complement to the crab's dark purple leaves.

Toward the end of August, most of the flowers in this border are past, and it is the contrast of foliage and plant forms that provides interest till hard frost. By the end of the summer, *C. macropetala* has been transformed into an extravagant, silvery haze of fluffy seed pods: intertwined amid the crab apple's bronze foliage and purple-bronze fruit, it carries the entire border. The rose 'Arthur Hillier' also has assumed its autumn guise: a glorious cascade of fiery red hips, it remains a spectacle till birds strip it of that glory and winter transforms it yet again with ice crystals.

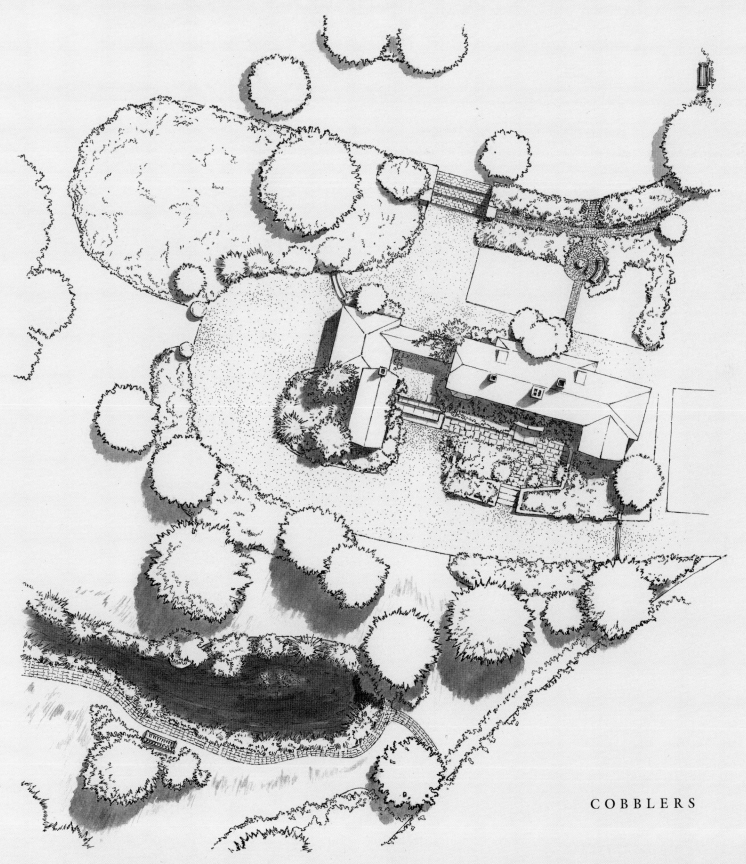

COBBLERS

KINGHAY

When Mollie and Joe Thorne first saw Kinghay, they weren't interested in the architectural merits of the house—which was lucky, since the unfinished, one-story bungalow didn't have any.

At first glance, the land surrounding the bungalow didn't look like much either, but as they pushed their way through the thick underbrush of hazel and hawthorn, Mollie realized it had tremendous potential. Bordered by fields and quiet country roads, the oddly shaped acre had hedgerows full of roses and honeysuckles, a small stream, and 18 mature oaks. Mollie fell in love with the place and decided this was where she would make her new garden.

"I didn't even look inside the house," she recalls. "The oak trees looked so lovely against the sky, I said to Joe, 'We can plant our own ornamentals, but we'd never get oak trees like that.' I could see that they would make a sort of backdrop—like a theater—for all the other plants."

The land had potential, but it had also been neglected for years. By the time Mollie and Joe bought it, it was an almost impenetrable mass of hazel and hawthorn. One of their first projects was to chop down the underbrush and clear around the front of the house so they could finish its construction and lay out the driveway.

Next the area alongside the drive was cleared; this became their first border. Here various shrubs, including philadelphus, deutzias, and barberries, were planted, and at the very back of the border white poplars (*Populus alba*) were planted for their silvery leaves.

The backbone of the border in place, Mollie then filled in with whatever perennials she could find that were fast-growing (but noninvasive) and cheap. Huge clumps of hardy geraniums, including *Geranium platypetalum,* and masterwort (*Astrantia major),* picked up at local plant sales for the equivalent of a dollar, soon covered the bare ground and kept weeds from taking over. These "stopgap plants," as Mollie called them, also gave her time to think out the plant combinations and color schemes she really wanted. Gradually, these initial perennial fillers were removed and replaced, and the gravel driveway became one of the most attractive areas of the garden.

The rest of the garden evolved in slow stages. In fact, the area beyond the pond was nicknamed Outer Mongolia, because they didn't even set foot in it for years. Beginning on the areas nearest the house and driveway, Mollie and Joe gradually chopped down small trees and cleared the underbrush with a machete. The rough ground was then leveled with a large old rotary mower. Repeated mowings eventually got rid of the brambles, then sections of rough grass appeared, which were later turned into lawn and paths or removed to make borders.

While they cleared the underbrush, Mollie began to imagine the design for her garden. Instead of drawing a plan on paper, then imposing it upon the landscape, she observed existing conditions (including sun and shade), then let these, in large part, determine the placement of paths and borders. Unlike most cottage gardens, the house was never meant as a focal point. Instead, the garden developed

(Opposite) "I like fatness and generosity," states Mollie, *"but if you're going to have all this burgeoning of plants, you've got to have a lot of hard lines. And that's why I have the paving, square lines and square shapes which sort of counteract all the burgeoning shapes of plants."*

A rectangular bed surrounded by gravel is thickly planted with alliums, campanulas, dianthus, and species delphinium. Behind the bed, the bright golden leaves of a variety of honey locust (Gleditsia triacanthos 'Sunburst') create a focal point that can be appreciated from different areas of the garden.

around the most distinctive features of the property. The oak trees and stream (widened in one spot to a small pool) provided the garden with its framework.

Once the ground was cleared and leveled, Mollie and Joe began laying out paths and digging borders out of the rough grass. A keen plantswoman, Mollie had no interest in large areas of grass. "I hate grass," she stated. "Lawns are a nuisance. I consider them the housekeeping of gardening." To keep her "housekeeping" at a minimum, only small areas of grass were left for sitting areas or for a better view of the pond. In some areas, small squares of grass and paving were also

laid out as a kind of geometric framework for the profusion of plants.

The rest of the garden became a series of variously shaped borders with gravel or grass paths winding among them. Each new bed dug out of the rough sod was outlined with brick or concrete. Poured into heavy cardboard forms, the wet concrete was then banged with a rough board to create a textured surface. Scored with a trowel at 1- or 2-foot intervals, the concrete resembled separate paving stones while creating a continuous barrier to prevent the surrounding rough grass from spreading into the new borders. By the following year the concrete had weathered and the

perennials had spread over the edges, softening the whole effect.

Small trees and shrubs were then planted in various borders to help establish the garden's framework. Unlike many cottage gardeners, Mollie planted many different evergreen shrubs. As a result, what she calls her naturalistic cottage garden is just as interesting in winter as it is in the height of summer.

"You've got to have your backbone," she explains. "In winter, the garden is full of life—all green, golden, and yellow, and different shades of gray. There are also a lot of trees and shrubs, and each has its own beautiful outline. *Rosa* × *macrantha* is all arms and legs, and the alder's red catkins are absolutely gorgeous against the winter sky."

Because the location of these trees and shrubs played such an important role in creating and defining the garden's spaces, Mollie sometimes spent hours deciding where certain specimens would be planted. "I never put a plant in anywhere—that was going to be of any stature—without putting in a stake where I thought it should go." She would then walk around the garden looking at the stake from every possible angle. "If I wanted to look at it from ten different places, I sometimes asked my husband to stand

A garden bench, surrounded by shrub and climbing roses, is placed at the edge of the lawn for a view of the pond and to emphasize a turn in the path. To the right, a large clump of pulmonaria spills over the edge of the gravel path, and the creamy flower spikes of Aruncus dioicus *combine with pink shrub roses underplanted with iris and campanulas.*

where I thought it should go and I would say '2 feet to the left,' or '2 feet farther back.' A couple of feet can make a tremendous difference."

Trees and a variety of shrubs also were key elements in creating the backbone of Mollie's mixed borders, their form and branch structure, as well as the color texture and shape of their leaves, contrasting or complementing the plants around them. "All the beds have some shrubs because I like all the plants mixed up together. I think putting all herbaceous things in one great big bed never pays off, chiefly because you've got one season where everything looks nice for five minutes and then you've got a lot of deadheads and spaces. With shrubs you've got a shape even when your herbaceous stuff is finished."

Flowering shrubs, along with shrub and species roses, were also features in the borders in front of the house. Underplanted with species delphiniums, old-fashioned cottage pinks, and varieties of peach-leaved bellflower, they softened or hid the bungalow's hard, square lines. 'Charles de Mills', a vigorous rose with deep red flowers and dark green foliage, along with *Rosa rubrifolia,* or *R. glauca,* with small reddish flowers and gray-green foliage, became dramatic foliage accents. 'Golden Wings', another

At Kinghay in Wiltshire, white birch frame the bungalow surrounded by old-fashioned shrub roses.

shrub rose selected for its foliage and large, sweetly scented golden yellow flowers, became a focal point from June to October.

In June, the rest of the garden features almost a hundred varieties of old roses. Mollie does not grow hybrid tea roses. "They're horrible things. Once you've seen one, you've seen them all. And in winter, beds of hybrid tea roses are nothing but a few dirty little sticks."

Like so many cottage gardeners, Mollie prefers the more graceful, fuller forms of shrub roses. "I love the old ones. They may be fleeting, but they are so beautiful. A lot of people who visit say, 'Oh, but they only flower once.' That makes me cross. So I say, 'You don't expect your lilacs or prunus to flower twice. Why the dickens should you expect your roses to flower twice?' If it is as beautiful as

this"—she points to a huge 'Nevada' covered with fragrant cream-colored flowers—"for perhaps another three weeks, what more could you ask?

"I do have a few modern roses that fit in with my color schemes. But they have to be treated as ordinary plants. Roses treated as madonnas and put on pedestals are awkward, forced, and uncomfortable."

Roses, old and new, also create strong seasonal focal points in borders along the drive and beside paths. Underplanted and surrounded with sprawling herbaceous perennials such as horned violets (*Viola cornuta*) and hardy geraniums (*Geranium* species and hybrids), even Mollie's modern roses look old-fashioned. *Viola cornuta,* planted along the edges of paths or under the taller-stemmed plants such as peonies, is an important filler throughout the garden. With flowers like small pansies, it is easy to grow and will thrive in a wide variety of conditions from full sun to partial shade.

"I couldn't garden without *Viola cornuta,*" Mollie says. "They're all over the place and clamber right up the stems of other plants. The whites and dark blues are gorgeous, and they all flower from May till frost. They also self-seed true and fill in any bare spaces."

In a border along the edge of the gravel drive, the pink-purple flower spikes of gas plant (Dictamnus albus 'purpureus') *and a voluminous pink-flowered weigelia are features in June. To the right, a red-leaved berberis provides a striking contrast. Blue spikes of* Nepeta mussinii *and the chartreuse flowers of* Alchemilla mollis *spill over and soften the brick edging.*

Mollie's collection of hardy geraniums includes over two dozen different varieties and species. Like the violas, the majority of hardy geraniums are easy to grow and will thrive in a wide range of conditions. Most bloom in May or June and, with few exceptions, don't require staking. Planted around perennials such as *Iris sibirica* and the species peonies *Paeonia obouata* and *P. tenuifolia* (a single red with threadlike leaves), various hardy geraniums help create seasonal focal points with foliage that remains attractive right into September. (See Chapter 10, "Spontaneity, Combinations, and Magic in My Garden.")

Geranium renardii, with velvety, gray-green foliage and pale pink flowers in midsummer, and forms of *G.*

macrorrhizum are planted in masses alongside paths. Combined with the bergenias *Bergenia cordifolia* and *B. ligulata,* these and other geraniums are also particularly useful in low-maintenance areas of the garden or in those tricky transition areas between sun and shade.

Although Mollie's garden is a succession of colorful bloom from spring to frost, one of her favorite colors is green. She loves the interplay of all the different hues, shapes, and textures of leaves, and she delights in creating unusual combinations. Plants with variegated foliage, including various pulmonarias, are favorites. Along the edges of partially shady paths named varieties of *Pulmonaria angustifolia,* as well as *P. saccharata* 'Mrs. Moon' and *P. officinalis* 'Sissinghurst White', are featured in bold masses. Various pulmonarias are also combined with bold groupings of variegated *Brunnera macrophylla* (with sprays of forget-me-not–like flowers in early spring) to accent shady corners.

One of the most unusual features of Mollie's garden is her collection of fragrant plants. Throughout the garden these fragrant trees, shrubs, roses, vines, and perennials are used as seasonal accents. The particular quality of a plant's fragrance, as well as how far

it carries, plays an important part in deciding where it is placed.

"Some plants are fast with their scent," explains Mollie. "The scents of other plants waft. The rose 'Sander's White' carries quite a long ways. Most roses don't. Shade-tolerant 'Mme Isaac Pereire' is very sweet, one of the most beautifully scented roses there is. But you have to stick your nose into it."

As a result some plants, especially the shrub roses, are planted close to the edge of the paths, whereas those whose perfumes carry are placed in the middle of borders or at a far corner of the garden.

"All round the garden there are lots of 'Sweet Briar' *(Rosa eglanteria),"* Mollie points out. "There is one by the garage, and on a sort of warmish, damp day, the smell is absolutely gorgeous—as long as you keep clipping them, because it's the new foliage that smells. *Clematis flammula*, a tender fall-blooming, Mediterranean species grown up a plum tree, is another. When that is out it's like a pot of warm honey."

Like many cottage gardeners, Mollie often lets her plants self-seed. The more common, easily grown fillers, such as *Viola cornuta* and various astrantias, including *Astrantia major,* are left to their own devices. But Mollie collects the seeds of the rarer or more unusual plants to assure successful propagation. Throughout the growing season she keeps an eye on these plants, watching and waiting till their seeds are just right to pick.

"If it's a plant whose seeds I particularly want, I take the seeds when they are really ripe, when the pod is on the verge of exploding. Different seeds are ready at different times. It depends upon the year. If you've got a hot season or a late season, it can make a difference of six weeks. But if you're about the garden you're sort of looking all the time."

Mollie is also careful to store the seeds properly. "First of all, I dry them in a paper bag, hung up by different lengths of string, in a dry place. Then, when they are thoroughly dry, I put them in little envelopes in a screw-top jar in the refrigerator.

"Before I sow my seeds I always soak them overnight. If seeds don't sink you can be pretty sure they're nonviable. Even a tiny little seed will sink if it's got any life in it."

These seeds are then sown and grown on in the greenhouse that winter. The following spring thousands of small plants are then set out in the cold frames, ready to sell for charity on days the garden is open to the public for the benefit of the National Gardens Scheme, a 60-year-old charitable trust. (Each year under the auspices of the Garden Scheme, almost 2,000 privately owned gardens are open to the public, with the proceeds from entrance fees and plant sales going to various causes, including the Queen's Nursing Institute and the Gardener's Royal Benevolent Society.)

Because Mollie offers so many unusual plants, including species delphiniums and hellebores, on open days there is often a line waiting for her to unlatch the gate. Some people come each year, hoping to add to their own collections or to purchase a plant they missed buying the year before.

Although she loves rare and unusual plants and is constantly adding to her collection, if Mollie likes a plant or sees a place where its color or texture will complement one of her planting schemes, she doesn't care if it's a wild roadside plant, not a rarity.

"I have people who actually come here and turn their noses up at something because it is common or a British native. I tell them, 'If those plants were fetched from the farthest Himalayas you'd be breaking your back to get hold of them.' I can't bear snobbishness in any form, let alone in gardening, and that's why I like this cottage gardening thing—because people are still being themselves. They just like plants."

Along the edge of a path, Potentilla *'Yellow Queen' is underplanted with scarlet-orange* Geum *'Mrs. Bradshaw' to create a striking combination of bright colors.*

Planted in a partial shade, variegated Siberian bugloss (Brunnera macrophylla *'Variegata') makes a striking specimen. In spring brunnera blooms with sprays of flowers resembling blue forget-me-nots held above the foliage.*

CHAPTER 6

ROSES COTTAGE STYLE

(Opposite) The rambler rose 'Goldfinch' is trained over a rustic wooden arbor framing the path into the main borders at Chilcombe House. In the foreground, the dark, purple-blue flower spikes of Salvia × superba *mingle with the silver flower spikes of lamb's ears* (Stachys byzantina) *and pink rock rose* (Helianthemum nummularium), *and white* Chrysanthemum parthenium *'White Bonnet'.*

(Right) In June, 'Goldfinch' blooms with clusters of fragrant golden-yellow flowers that fade to cream.

DURING THE YEARS I spent exploring the villages and country lanes of England, I saw hundreds of cottage gardens. Although no two were alike, many featured roses, framing doorways and windows or rambling along white picket fences. These simple effects often transformed the most ordinary front yards into distinctive cottage gardens.

Occasionally, I discovered a cottage garden planted almost exclusively with old-fashioned shrub and climbing roses, but surprisingly few were well designed or had interesting plant combinations. In most, roses were treated as bedding plants—in squares and circles, underplanted with the most ordinary annuals.

Since roses can play such an important part in establishing a cottage garden's character, I wanted to devote an entire chapter to the subject. The trick was to find a garden (perhaps even two) where roses and good design were brought together.

One day, very much by chance, I discovered just the garden I was looking for in a tiny Somerset village. Surrounded by fifteenth-century farm buildings, it was the most idyllic site imaginable. Planned entirely around roses, the garden at East End Farm was also rich in ideas for combining shrub and climbing roses with perennials and old-fashioned flowering shrubs.

A short time later, I found another cottage-style rose garden high atop a

Roses 'Goldfinch' (left) and 'Tour de Malakoff' (right) frame a rustic wooden arbor and a vista down the lavender-lined grass path.

hill in Dorset. A wild and romantic spot with rustic wooden arbors covered in honeysuckle and clematis, its paths lined with old-fashioned perennials and lavender, Chilcombe House was also full of good design ideas—and roses.

Built on very dissimilar sites, the gardens at Chilcombe House and East End Farm are beautifully designed. In both, roses are important elements. Trained up arbors, climbing roses frame views, define each garden's various spaces, and become focal points at the ends of vistas. In borders, shrub roses help create the full-to-overflowing look so characteristic of cottage gardens.

CHILCOMBE HOUSE

In 1969, when John and Caryl Hubbard bought Chilcombe, the gardens were in ruins. Years of neglect had turned lawns to hayfields and reduced a once beautiful walled garden to piles of rubble and waist-high weeds.

Although the site had disadvantages, it also had one of the loveliest views in Dorset: from the house you could see for miles across the downs, and on misty afternoons farms in neighboring valleys appeared so close it seemed you could almost touch the cows on their way to milking. As lovely as it was, the view provided a real design challenge. Both John and Caryl wanted an old-fashioned cottage garden with rose-covered arbors and intimate, quite spaces. The view, unless skillfully handled, would easily overwhelm a simple garden.

Another difficulty was the distance between the house and the garden. In most cottage gardens, the house is the central feature, but at Chilcombe the house was about 50 feet up the hill from the walled garden. The challenge was to design a layout that would relate the garden to the house, give the bare hillside a sense of enclosure, and make the view part of the garden—all within the foundations of the existing walled garden.

The first task was to cut back the underbrush and rebuild the garden's walls and steps. Once the ground was clear, it was rototilled and heavily manured. Following the advice of an old farmer, John then planted potatoes. A traditional English farming practice, this is one of the easiest and surest ways of cleaning out perennial weeds, including couch grass, nettles, and dock.

"With potatoes you're always working the soil," John explains. "Each time you ridge up the potatoes, it kills weeds. Then there are the potatoes themselves. If you get a good crop, the tops smother everything."

That winter, John and Caryl ate a lot of potatoes and worked on the garden's plan. To give the windswept hillside a sense of intimacy, they devised a layout of paths and borders that divided the garden into "rooms." Separated by hedges, walls, and paths, these areas, with their geometric arrangement, repeated the shape of the house. From many vantage points, the lines of the garden and the house would appear to be part of the same composition.

In the lower half, the area to the left was reserved for vegetables, and the remains of an old orchard to the right became a lush spring garden

A rustic wooden gate set in an ivy-covered stone wall creates an intimate entrance to Chilcombe House. Beyond the house is the spectacular view of the Dorset countryside.

The climbing rose 'Sea Gull', with its large clusters of richly scented flowers, can grow up to 25 feet high and is an excellent choice for training up trees or a north wall.

with daffodils and primula in the grass beneath the apple trees. The upper half eventually became a flower garden, where rustic wooden arbors were draped with roses and clematis and the most wonderful combinations of herbs and perennials.

To help protect the upper half of the garden from heavy coastal winds, a hedge of copper beech, English yew, and various hollies was planted across the middle of the hill. As it grew, it became an important part of the garden's framework and an attractive year-round feature. The upper half of the hillside was then terraced using railroad ties. To hide the ties, the Hubbards planted ivy. In a few years, the vines had grown so high and thick that the walls disappeared.

Next, paths and steps were laid out. Although they had the whole hillside to work with, in the beginning they deliberately kept the flower garden small, so it could be more easily maintained. They then devised a simple trick that made it seem larger.

Instead of placing the main path in a straight line through the doorway in the wall, with an unobstructed view downhill to the end of the garden, they blocked the view with an espaliered pear, turning the path to the right. About 10 feet farther along the path and to the left, the garden's most dramatic vista (through the center of the garden) would then appear as a total surprise. As the garden evolved, the secondary paths and their steps were also arranged so the countryside would appear in glimpses around corners and through arbors—all of which helped the view to become an integral part of the garden without overwhelming it. (See Plan of Chilcombe House for locations of doorway and main path.)

Once the garden's basic framework was established, John drew a rough plan for the borders to either side of the main path. Framed by fastigiate Irish yews at the top and bottom corners and planted with shrub roses, these borders would become the garden's highlight in June. Shrub roses of various sizes would also help give these rather large borders (approximately 10 feet wide and 60 feet long) the mass and height their dimensions demanded.

A few of these roses were selected directly from nursery catalogs, but having grown roses in their previous garden, John and Caryl found that most of what they read on the subject had little to do with their gardening experience. Many catalogs created glorified pictures of the plants they were trying to sell or, just as misleading, omitted important details on their growth.

In June, the main border is overflowing with old-fashioned shrub and climbing roses. An old stone wall and a hedge of copper beech, English yew, and various hollies help give the garden its framework and a sense of enclosure. Fastigiate Irish yews create dramatic vertical accents and remain an important year-round feature in a garden otherwise devoid of trees.

Throughout the garden, climbing roses and flowering vines are trained up arbors or stone walls as features or as background for various combinations of plants. Here, the climbing rose 'Fantin Latour' gives extra depth to a simple combination of poten-tilla, daylilies, hardy geranium (Geranium pratense *'Double Violet'*) *and evening primrose* (Oenothera missouriensis).

"By the time we came here, we had gotten through the stage of believing catalogs," John recalls.

To help separate fact from fanciful catalog descriptions, Caryl and John visited gardens famous for their rose collections. At Charleston Manor in Sussex and Cranborne Manor in Dorset they compared the growth habits of real roses with descriptions in books and catalogs.

'Blanc Double du Coubert', a white *Rosa rugosa* hybrid, and 'Felicia', a well-shaped hybrid musk with rich, pink flowers, were chosen as features toward the rear of the border. Here

they would provide fairly continuous bloom throughout the summer while their attractive foliage created a varied background for a succession of perennials. In autumn the thick, dark green leaves of 'Blanc Double du Coubert' had the added advantage of turning a lovely mixture of red and yellow. Some roses such as 'Ispahan', a fragrant, light pink damask, and 'Nathalie Nypels', a perpetual flowering floribunda with clusters of semi-double, silvery pink flowers, were planted as minor events.

Yet not everything, they discovered, went according to plan. In the

rose books John and Caryl had read, 'Ispahan' was supposed to grow about 3 feet tall and 4 feet wide. One did. But the other just kept on growing. Eventually, it reached 8 feet tall and 10 feet wide. "Now it takes up practically the whole of that section," John points out. "But I like it. It's a great, mad, wonderful thing."

To support this beautiful, rambling mound, John has used everything from wooden frames to posts with wire wrapped around them. "I've tried lots of different methods, but I find if I just attach it to itself, that works best."

Although the borders were designed to feature roses, an eclectic mix of old-fashioned cottage plants and unusual perennials plays an important secondary role. John is an artist, and in these borders (as throughout the garden) he uses perennials to create rich, often complex combinations of foliage textures and color. The effects may appear almost riotous at times, but invariably there is a sense of underlying harmony—created by repeating colors, foliage textures, or masses of plants.

Because the hillside is so windy and cold in early spring, the borders were designed to begin blooming in May. Then, pink lungwort *(Pulmonaria officinalis)*, with its white-spotted, heart-shaped leaves, purple pasqueflower *(Anemone pulsatilla)*, and both blue and white horned violets *(Viola cornuta)* are among the first plants to flower.

To help create a sense of symmetry among the border's four sections, these and other edging perennials are planted at regularly spaced intervals. In June, after the flower stalks of *P. officinalis* are cut back, clumps of spotted dead-nettle *(Lamium maculatum* 'Album') and the silver stalks of lamb's ears *(Stachys byzantina,* or *S. lanata)* become accents. These same plants, with their attractive, long-lasting

At the end of the lavender-lined path, a wild white froth of Crambe cordifolia *resembles a gigantic baby's breath. To the left, the spiky, silver stalks of* Onopordon arabicum *create a dramatic complement.*

foliage, keep the edges interesting right through summer.

As a general rule, taller plants are placed toward the rear of the borders and shorter perennials toward the front, but to help create a pleasing variety of heights, lavenders, potentillas, and some of the taller hardy geraniums are brought close to the edge and combined with the small, pansy-like flowers of *Viola cornuta,* which bloom from April to November.

Delphiniums *(Delphinium* hybrids), foxgloves *(Digitalis purpurea),* and giant scabies *(Cephalaria gigantea)* are featured in the middle of the borders, for early and mid-summer bloom. Large groupings of *Geranium pratense,* with its small, violet-blue flowers, are repeated on the left and right

sides of the borders and combined with yellow-flowered evening primroses (*Oenothera* species). In August, 3-foot stalks of clary (*Salvia sclarea* var. *turkestaniana*), a hardy biennial or perennial with white and pale blue or lilac flowers and striking yellow or purple-blue bracts, are a feature.

At the rear of the borders, hollyhocks (*Alcea rosea*), various meadow rues (*Thalictrum* species), and large masses of later-blooming globe thistles (*Echinops* hybrids) and monkshoods (*Aconitum* species) are featured. Here their distinctive forms and foliage provide a background for a succession of spring- and summer-flowering perennials. In bloom in August and September, with dark blue flowers on 4- to 6-foot stalks, aconitums also become a handsome complement to late-blooming roses and Michaelmas daisies.

On the original plan, John drew a rough shape indicating the approximate size and placement for each group of plants. Taking their growth rates and habits into account, he then figured how many plants were needed to create certain effects. Although the borders have changed over the years, the scale and the size of key plantings established in the original plan have remained much the same.

Some of the border's changes were planned; others were purely accidental. Selected plants, including foxglove (*Digitalis purpurea*) and wild parsnip (*Angelica archangelica*), a statuesque plant, 6–10 feet tall with rounded umbels of yellow-green flowers, were allowed to self-seed. Sometimes they popped up in spots John would never have thought of. One year *A. archangelica* appeared in the middle of the border amid clumps of Japanese anemone (*Anemone × hybrida*) and delphiniums (*Delphinium* hybrids). The effect was so dramatic and so wonderfully unexpected that he left them.

The character of Chilcombe's other areas, or "rooms," evolved over a period of years. Sometimes the effects were simple. The grassy area to the left of the main border, for example, was divided by a stone path lined with lavender and catmint. In late June and July, a wild white froth of colewort (*Crambe cordifolia*) and the spiky, silver stalks of *Onopordon arabicum* provide a dramatic focal point at the top of a thyme-covered bank at the end of the path. Although not the kind of thing you'd expect to find combined with herbs, as a contrast for masses of traditional purple lavender they help give the garden its wonderful, idiosyncratic style.

Some areas, such as the cobble garden to the right of the main border,

became delightfully complex arrangements of texture and color. For years this corner was a vegetable plot with rows of lettuce and cabbage, but eventually John ran out of places to plant things, and it, too, became flower garden. Section by section, the vegetables were replaced with perennials and herbs.

The area to its far right (behind a pergola covered with climbing roses, honeysuckle, and clematis) was designated for plant propagation and wildflowers. Using existing paths as a starting point, John and Caryl divided the rest of this garden into eight squares. Additional paths were laid out and eventually paved with brick and with stones collected from the beach a few miles away.

Each area of the garden now contains different plantings. By mixing perennials, herbs, roses, even fruit trees, John gave each a different character. In the lower half of the garden, an old fruit tree provides the focal point for masses of perennials. Here hardy geraniums and tradescantias create a striking mix of textures and plant forms. At the end of the path, a rustic wooden bench acts as a focal point.

In the upper half of the garden, the flower spikes of various salvias, including the mauve-blue *Salvia haematodes* and the dark, purple-blue of

(Opposite) In the cobble garden, paths made of beach stones and bricks and rectangular beds provide the framework for an exuberant mixture of perennials and herbs, including masses of rose-purple chives (Allium schoenoprasum) *and the violet-blue panicles of garden sage* (Salvia officinalis).

Climbing rose 'Fantin Latour' and a Chilean potato-tree (Solanum crispum *'Glasnevin Variety') spill over and soften a stone wall.*

S. × *superba,* are contrasted with mounds of both yellow and pink rock rose *(Helianthemum nummularium)* and clipped globes of southernwood *(Artemisia abrotanum).* Against a background of dark blue, lavender, and green, the splashes of bright pink and yellow create an almost electric contrast. White daisies and silver-leaved foliage act as background colors to tie the whole composition together.

In the cobble garden, as with the rest of the garden, roses are an important design element. Trained up pergolas and homemade wooden arbors and through the wooden frames supporting espaliered fruit trees, roses help provide the garden with height, background, and a sense of enclosure.

In June, the pergola (over the path along the far right side of the garden) is festooned with fragrant roses, including 'Francis E. Lester', 'Félicité et Perpétue', and 'Mme Alice Garnier'—providing a decorative screen for the wildflower area and enclosing that end of the garden. In autumn, 'Francis E. Lester' decorates the pergola again with clusters of small red hips.

Along the north and east sides of the garden, roses and clematis (trained against the frames of espaliered fruit trees) provide a background for perennials. Other roses have been placed as accents. Next to the rustic wooden arbor leading to the main borders, 'Goldfinch', a climbing rose with clusters of fragrant, pale yellow flowers, was planted entirely by accident. "Up till then," explains John, "we had an idiotic prejudice against yellow. But it's a very good rose for arbors because it doesn't get too big and it goes well with almost any color."

Each spring, John takes a break from his painting and spends about two weeks working in his garden, cleaning up borders, tying up roses, and separating self-sown seedlings. Because the hillside is so windy, many perennials require staking with "pea sticks." Two to three feet tall, these multibranched twigs (usually hazel) are cut before the trees leaf out. The twigs are then placed around perennials when they are 6–12 inches tall. Once the plants leaf out, these supports are practically invisible amid the foliage.

For the rest of the growing season, John spends about an hour each day maintaining the garden. Weeding, rather surprisingly, isn't a big job. By June, the tightly planted perennials are so dense that he can't get into the borders without stepping all over everything.

His attitude is philosophical. "Occasionally, I crash into them—but if I can't get in there, weeds can't either."

For years, John did his own mowing, hauling the mower up and down the garden's various stairways. Recently he gave it up without any regrets. Now chores such as mowing, hedge trimming, and leaf raking— "the housework of the garden"—are left to a part-time gardener, who also maintains the vegetable garden.

In autumn John is back in the garden full time for another two weeks. Although the borders appear as a wild and romantic tangle, a fine balance has to be maintained. Perennials that have gotten too large and are crowding out their smaller neighbors are divided and self-sown seedlings are thinned and transplanted.

During that time, John also refines the design of his borders and experiments with colors and textures by adding plants or moving existing specimens. His best combinations have a spontaneous, impressionistic quality, with layers upon layers of different colors. To get these effects, he doesn't bother sketching ideas or trying to scribble additions to the plan originally drawn on paper. Instead, he finds it much more effective to do his designing right in the garden.

A cloud of Crambe cordifolia *and the climbing rose 'Crimson Conquest' help create a "garden room" around a pair of bamboo chairs tucked into a corner of the stone wall. The variegated foliage of yellow archangel* (Lamiastrum galeobdolon) *provides light and texture at the base of the wall.*

At the end of the main borders, Irish yews frame the view of the orchard and the surrounding countryside. The left border features roses 'Ispahan' and 'Yesterday' underplanted with masses of Geranium pratense *'Double Violet' and the tall yellow giant scabies* (Cephalaria gigantea). *Pink and purple foxgloves* (Digitalis purpurea) *provide vertical accents. Clumps of silver-leaved lamb's ears* (Stachys byzantina) *accent the edges of both borders.*

A good many combinations result from observations made during the growing season. As John walks through the garden, he often finds himself imagining different plants together. Sometimes he sees a plant in one area, then another some distance away. He then moves one or the other, or finds a location where the new combination will become a feature or complement existing plantings.

Sometimes, individual plants or particularly effective combinations are repeated in different areas of the garden or a border. One year, for example, noticing how well *Geranium pratense* 'Double Violet' looked with a variety of plants in different areas of the main border, John decided it was just the right thing to use as a background color. Plants were lifted, divided, and replanted. Now, large masses of *G. p.* 'Double Violet' unify the border's four sections.

A few years ago, a well-known English gardening writer visited Chilcombe. Entranced with the garden, she wanted to know exactly how John came up with his distinctive color combinations and style of plantings.

"She talked about 'logical groupings,' " says John, "and I didn't know what she meant. Then she explained that an awful lot of people have a blue border, a yellow border, an autumn border, a spring border, or they grow all one sort of thing. It never crossed my mind to work that way. I work instinctively, in a rather improvisational manner, and I think *that* is the way most cottage gardens evolve."

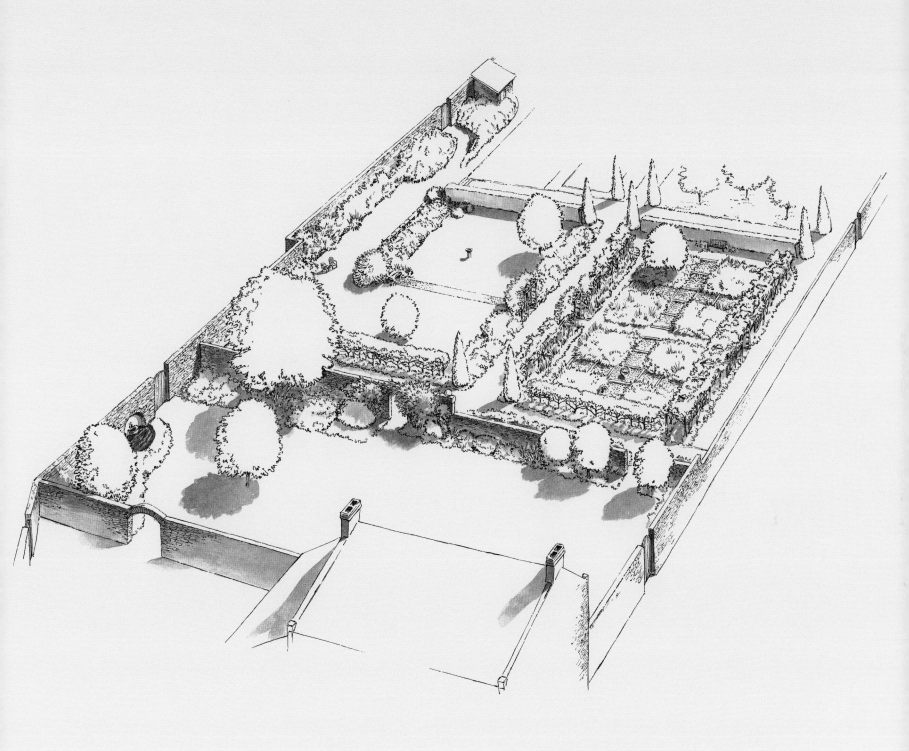

CHILCOMBE HOUSE

EAST END FARM

In 1946, when Margaret Wray first saw East End Farm, the garden contained nothing but a few perennials and an *allée* of old apple trees. With its worn-out grass and dying trees, the garden was so bare it was difficult to think of it as a garden at all. But walking around the farmyard, with its stone walls and beautiful old barns, she knew she had found the perfect setting for the old-fashioned roses she had known as a child. In her imagination, she could see the bare stone walls and barns covered with climbing roses.

For the first few years, most of Margaret's gardening was in her imagination. When she wasn't chasing after her three young children, tending a large vegetable garden, or milking cows, she planted a few perennials, pulled weeds, and thought about the design for her rose garden.

As with most gardeners in this book, her gardening budget was limited, so her design had to make the most of existing features. The old walls and stone barns were, of course, a wonderful asset, but these same walls also cut off views of the village and the surrounding countryside. As a result, the enclosed back yard seemed slightly claustrophobic, even smaller

than it really was. The trick would be to come up with a layout that would give the flat garden a bit of drama and make it seem larger.

For a while she thought of tearing out the apples, putting down grass, and starting from scratch. Then one day she saw the apple trees from a

(Opposite) The view down through the main borders in June. The bird bath creates a focal point and the apple trees and stone path a framework for borders overflowing with old-fashioned perennials and shrub roses in dozens of shades of pink, red, cream, and gold. To the right, blue catmint (Nepeta mussinii), *yellow circle flower* (Lysimachia punctata), *and magenta* Geranium psilostemon *are combined to fill in around the bare lower canes of shrub roses.*

(Above) 'Madame Hardy' blooms in June with sumptuous, pure white flowers having a small green eye at the center and a slightly lemony or smooth, buttery fragrance—depending upon the time of day, the temperature, the humidity, and the person smelling it. The foliage is light, bright green (when young), on bushes about 5 feet tall.

fresh viewpoint. Here, she realized was the framework for her rose garden: if the apple trees were left and the borders beneath them widened, she could plant her favorite old shrub roses and surround them with perennials. The resulting vista down through the middle of the back yard would also help the garden seem larger and deeper.

With the help of a neighbor, the narrow borders were widened. Gradually weeds were removed and wheelbarrow-loads of cow manure added to the rocky soil. Not one for plans, Margaret never sat down with pencil and paper to draw out her borders with specific roses in set locations. A good many of the roses were purchased first, then their locations decided.

She planted some roses in the center of the borders as focal points. 'Honorine de Brabant', a very old rose with large, cupped blossoms striped with delicate shades of lilac and pink, accomplished this in the right border; a bushy shrub with lush foliage, it would grow about 6 feet tall and 5 feet wide. 'Queen of Denmark' or 'Königin von Dänemark', another large shrub with deep pink, ruffled petals and grayish-green leaves, did the same in the middle of the left border.

At East End Farm, the rambler rose 'New Dawn' is trained against the front of the thatched stone cottage and over the top of the stone wall surrounding the dooryard. With clusters of fragrant, blush-pink flowers from June to October and glossy, dark green foliage, 'New Dawn' is an excellent choice for the north side of a house or partially shaded arbor.

'Mme Hardy', a rose Margaret describes as the most beautiful of all whites, was planted on the edge of the right border. Here its graceful forms and fragrance could be more easily appreciated. 'Goldfinch', another particularly fragrant rose, was also planted at the edge of the border; an 8-foot climber with clusters of small, primrose-yellow flowers, its scent is sweet, with minty undertones, never overwhelming but powerful enough to be appreciated several feet away.

Over the years, Margaret has added to and altered her collection of roses. Some that required richer, deeper soil died and were replaced, but the majority of her choices thrived in the garden's rocky soil—helped, no doubt, by yearly dressings of well-rotted cow manure.

'Russelliana' or 'Russell's Cottage Rose', a good-size bush with dark green foliage and clusters of dainty, crimson and pale purple flowers, proved so tolerant of poor soil and partial shade that she planted it in five different locations. To minimize repetition, each 'Russelliana' was surrounded by different combinations of perennials. Under one, Margaret planted masses of white daisies, blue

Siberian iris *(Iris sibirica)*, and catmint *(Nepeta mussinii)*. Another was surrounded by *Geranium endressii* 'Wargrave Pink', pale pink summer phlox *(Phlox paniculata)*, and cottage pinks *(Dianthus plumarius)*.

Throughout the borders, old-fashioned perennials have played a practical as well as an aesthetic role. Massed around newly planted roses, perennials cover the bare ground till the roses fill out, and in the process they act as a kind of living mulch to keep weeds from getting started.

As with the selection of roses, Margaret's placement and combinations of various perennials evolved, over a period of years. Many were gifts from friends and relatives. Others were purchased at church fêtes or at the gates of country cottages. Some were unusual, but the majority were common and easily grown. Most of these perennials were chosen also for their June flowering. Some, if cut back, could be brought into a second flush of bloom, but their main purpose was as a complement to the roses.

Like so many cottage gardeners, Margaret has made good use of catmint *(Nepeta mussinii)*. Along the borders' edges, it is combined with lamb's ears *(Stachys byzantina,* or *S. lanata)*, *Veronica* 'Crater Lake', and *Geranium endressii* 'Wargrave Pink'. Toward the middle of the border, *N. mussinii* is combined with various artemisias, delphiniums, and blue Siberian irises, as a subtle complement to several *Rosa rugosa* hybrids, including the silver-pink 'Conrad Ferdinand Meyer' and deep pink 'Roseraie de l'Hay'. Combined with mounds of magenta-flowered *Geranium psilostemon (G. armenum)* and lavender-purple *G. platypetalum, N. mussinii* is an effective filler for the middle of the borders, where it does a wonderful job of hiding the bare bottom canes of many varieties of shrub roses.

In the middle of the borders, taller perennials are also planted quite near the roses and allowed to grow right up through the canes. Surrounded by silver-leaved southernwood *(Artemisia abrotanum)*, delphiniums *(Delphinium* hybrids), mauve-blue *Salvia haematodes,* and airy, mauve sprays of meadow rue *(Thalictrum aquilegifolium),* the warm pink blossoms of the rose 'Kazanlik' look like a huge Victorian bouquet.

"It's really things that are quiet and don't get in the way of the roses," Margaret says of her combinations. "You can't have terribly strong colors next to roses. The annual red salvia is murder. But yellow, particularly the more sulphury, gentle color, is absolutely essential in a garden."

'Queen of Denmark' or 'Königin von Dänemark' will grow about five feet tall and four feet wide and is very winter-hardy and disease resistant, and an excellent choice for a partially shaded shrub border or woodland planting. In June and early July, 'Königin von Dänemark' blooms with a heavy flush of wonderfully scented, distinctly quartered, pink flowers.

'American Pillar', with single, reddish-pink flowers, and 'Alberic Barbier', with semi-double, creamy-white flowers, frame a barn door.

To lighten up shady corners and give life to red and pink roses, Margaret uses circle flower *(Lysimachia punctata),* a weedy member of the loosestrife family with vertical spikes of small, yellow flowers. Fernleaf yarrow *(Achillea filipendulina),* with its flat umbels of sulphury yellow flowers, is also used as an accent—a brilliant foil for dark blue Italian bugloss *(Anchusa azurea)* and light blue peach-leaved bellflower *(Campanula*

persicifolia) and a striking contrast to the chartreuse flowers of lady's mantle *(Alchemilla mollis)*.

After the roses are past, pink and white summer phlox *(Phlox paniculata),* the silvery seed pods of honesty *(Lunaria annua),* and later-blooming lavender and rose-colored Michaelmas daisies *(Aster novae-angliae* hybrids and *A. novi-belgii* hybrids) give the borders a bit of color. But mostly it is old-fashioned annuals such as nicotianas, love-in-a-mist, bachelor's buttons, and pink and yellow Shirley poppies that carry the show through July and August. Grown on the windowsills during the winter, each spring these annuals are transplanted by the hundreds into the garden.

These borders, with their annuals, perennials, and roses, are the garden's main feature, but roses mixed with big, billowing, June-flowering shrubs including pink-flowered weigelas and various philadelphus also play an important part in establishing the cottage style of the rest of the garden.

Some of the most beautiful combinations feature the mock orange *Philadelphus × lemoinei* 'Belle Etoile', with its pure fragrance reminiscent of orange blossoms. Several 'Belle Etoile', 6 feet tall and about as wide, are planted through the garden in borders and against stone walls, their sweeping branches covered with white, camellia-like flowers—a most graceful complement to pale pink and dark red roses.

To give a bit of color to the barn walls, Margaret planted dozens of different climbing roses. Although "climbing," these roses need support, so wire grids with horizontal wires every 1–2 feet and vertical wires every 3 feet were attached to large screweyes sunk into the stone or mortar. As

the roses grew, Margaret placed the young canes and tied them into position with soft twine. When the roses bloom, the wire grids practically disappear.

Margaret also planted roses to highlight the rustic wooden pergola at the end of the borders. Some are highly scented, such as 'Emily Grey', a

double yellow with 15-foot canes, and 'Sea Gull', with large clusters of white flowers on 25-foot canes. Others are highly visible, such as 'Paul's Scarlet Climber', with its clusters of brilliant scarlet flowers on 10-foot canes. All grew tall enough to be trained up the posts and over the top.

Other climbing roses were chosen

The stone garden shed, where tools and wheelbarrows are stored.

to grow into the branches of trees. Color and style of bloom were considerations; also important, however, were a rose's growth habit, the length of its canes, and its tolerance for shade. If a tree was alive and healthy, Margaret planted a less vigorous rose; but if the tree was dead or dying, she selected a particularly dense grower such as 'May Queen', with its clusters of semidouble, lilac-pink flowers and dark green foliage on canes up to 15 feet long.

Initially, the canes of climbing and rambling roses such as 'Paul's Himalayan Musk', 'Moonlight', and 'Bobbie James' were tied to tree trunks, but once the canes reached into the tree's branches, they usually managed to stay there without additional help.

The roses and trees were, in most cases, well matched. An exception was *Rosa filipes* 'Kiftsgate'. Planted at the base of an old apple tree, its canes eventually covered that tree, another nearby, and the roof of the barn. Each June, however, 'Kiftsgate' was such a spectacular event, with its thousands of single white flowers, that Margaret didn't have the heart to get rid of it.

The apple trees eventually died, and in a few years their rotten trunks threatened to collapse beneath the weight of the rose. If 'Kiftsgate' ever fell down, there would be no getting

A stone path cuts through the border to the bird bath and a billowing specimen of the shrub rose 'Moonlight'. To the left, the deliciously scented, pink-mauve flowers of 'Belle de Crecy' and the fragrant, creamy-white clusters of 'Goldfinch' spill over the path. To the right is a cane of white-flowered 'Mme Hardy'.

it back up again. In an effort to save it, Margaret had the local blacksmith weld a circle of steel spokes, about 6 feet across, to the top of a 20-foot pole, the post was set in a base of poured concrete and the rose canes tied to the pole. In a few years, when the apple trees finally gave way, 'Kiftsgate' was left standing.

Like most gardeners, Margaret started her rose garden without a lot of knowledge. The majority of her expertise came out of trial and error. Although she read about things such as pruning, even the best written advice could serve only as a guideline. Pruning, she discovered, depends upon the rose. Since most climbers

flower on current season's growth, they are pruned in early spring, just after growth begins or when plants are still dormant. Ramblers usually flower once, on previous year's growth, produced from ground level. Periodically, the old woody canes of climbers and ramblers are pruned out and new growth trained onto the grid of wires.

The species and old shrub roses require little pruning, except the removal of straggly growth and dead wood in early spring. (No matter how healthy a rose is, there is invariably some dead wood underneath.) Because many of the species and shrub roses flower on previous year's

Throughout the garden, roses are underplanted with perennials and annuals selected for their different growth habits, foliage textures, and flower colors. To the left, 'Fantin Latour', a very old, very winter-hardy shrub rose with delicately fragrant, blush-pink flowers in June, is underplanted with a pretty scramble of hybrid delphiniums, iris, Shirley poppies (Papaver rhoeas), *magenta-flowered* Geranium psilostemon, *and lady's mantle* (Alchemilla mollis).

growth, if pruning is necessary, it is generally done just after flowering.

Relatively few of these old roses were self-supporting, so for years many of the shrub roses were held up by a haphazard collection of wooden stakes, metal poles, and odd bits of bailing wire. 'Ispahan' had grown so enormous that half a dozen large posts were needed to keep it upright.

Finally, Margaret's daughter, Marni (who now lives with her and helps maintain the garden), discovered the solution on a visit to Sissinghurst, a National Trust garden in Kent renowned for its collection of old shrub roses. Here, the gardeners had surrounded the roses with rather formidable wooden cages, some as large as 5 feet across. In June, when the shrubs are in full leaf and flower, these

supports are scarcely noticeable.

That winter Ronald, their one-day-a-week gardener, improvised a collection of wooden supports. From a nearby woods, he and Marni collected saplings about 2 inches in diameter. The saplings (their bark still intact) were then cut to the proper lengths and nailed together into square and triangular frames. These frames were then nailed to 4-inch–diameter posts sunk into the ground.

The individual rose determined the angle of the posts, as well as the height of the cross-bars connecting them. Some—depending on their height, width, and shape—looked better in triangular frames, others in squares. Once the cages were adjusted to the proper height, the canes of 'Ispahan' and various roses, including

'Tour de Malakoff', 'Duchess de Montabello', and 'Kazanlik', were arranged so they spilled gracefully over the top, then tied to the cages with strong, soft twine.

Margaret's collection now includes almost a hundred different roses. Most are what she calls old roses, introduced around or before 1900. Although her collection is notable, Margaret's choice of roses is far more spontaneous than systematic. She planted many of the roses, including 'Charles de Mills', because she had known them as a child, others simply because she liked the fragrance, color, and shape of their flowers.

A good many shrub and climbing roses are French, with colors ranging from the blush-white and distinctly quartered blooms of 'Souvenir de la Malmaison' to the camellia-like bright rose-pink blooms of 'Louise Odier', and 'Commandant Beaurepaire', with its large, crimson flowers streaked with purple and pink and splashed with white. Some, such as 'Moonlight', with its creamy white, almost-single flowers, are English. 'American Pillar', with its clusters of reddish-pink flowers, and 'New Dawn', with its semidouble, blush-pink flowers, are American introductions.

A small number, including 'Commandant Beaurepaire', are repeat bloomers. Even fewer ('New Dawn' is an example) provide continuous bloom from June to October. Most bloom only from mid-June into early July, depending upon the year and the weather. For these few weeks, the garden is "unbelievably beautiful," according to visitors who see it at its peak. "And so short-lived," they invariably add with a sigh.

For Margaret and Marni, who grow it, the excitement of a rose garden begins in early spring, when the first leaves break from bare, brown canes. Slowly, inexorably, the buds emerge, becoming fuller and fuller until at last they cannot contain themselves. Some explode in an instant; others unfold petal by petal, their fragrance ripening like fruit in the sun. Far more quickly than they began, roses fade and petals fall. Soon the paths are strewn with an aftermath of pink and gold and scarlet. A walk through the garden is both lovely and sad.

Three or four weeks is a mere moment in the life of a garden, but perhaps this is nature's way of assuring us that there is no time to become satiated, and no chance that roses as beautiful as 'Queen of Denmark' or 'Mme Hardy' will ever be taken for granted.

A very fragrant rugosa hybrid, 'Roseraie de l'Hay', becomes a dense shrub with dark green foliage and flowers throughout the summer. Shade tolerant, it also has attractive autumn foliage.

CHAPTER 7

GABLES: A WOODLAND COTTAGE GARDEN

(Opposite) From above it is easy to see how the entry garden, with its embracing shape, wooden garden benches, and mixture of evergreens and flowers, creates a sense of welcome. To the right, an old apple tree is covered with the June-flowering rambling rose 'Paul's Himalayan Musk', with graceful sprays of small, blush-pink flowers on supple canes up to 30 feet long.

(Right) The white, button-like flowers and dark green foliage of bridalwreath (Spirea prunifolia) *provide a background for the dark lavender-blue flower spikes of* Nepeta *'Six Hills Giant' and blue peach-leaved bellflower* (Campanula persicifolia).

GABLES is a mixture of surprise and illusion, a place where paths seem to disappear in the distance and neighbor's back yards are all but invisible. Located on the edge of a small Gloucestershire village, it is a wonderful assortment of garden "rooms" with rustic benches, ponds, and roses.

In many ways, Gables is the classic cottage garden, with climbing roses, perennial borders, and paths overflowing with lady's mantle, but there are also wild mixes of plants you'd never expect to find in a cottage garden. Here is a bog garden of astilbes and ornamental grasses, and there a woodland with narrow winding paths and low-maintenance ground covers. Deep within the woods, tiny pools are surrounded by primulas, wild irises, and gunneras with leaves almost 4 feet across.

For all its diversity, Gables doesn't feel crowded or disjointed. Each area, however different in style or character, has some logical and pleasing relationship to those around it. The result is a garden with a unique sense of unity and style.

When Tom Savery first saw Gables in 1974, the property looked like a bomb had been dropped on it. The soil around the house was so badly compacted not even the toughest weeds could grow. The rest of the property was hidden under a jungle of brambles and trash accumulated over years. As for the house, the owners lived in one half and bred chickens and pheasants in the other. Without

(Above) In June, the entrance to the woodland behind the house is a mass of white-flowered snow-in-summer (Cerastium tomentosum) grown between the cracks of the stone steps. Along the right, the blue spikes of Nepeta 'Six Hills Giant' practically fill the path, while deeper into the woodland, pink and white peonies and a white shrub rose create bright focal points against a background of green trees.

(Right) A weathered garden bench is framed by Nepeta 'Six Hills Giant' and the graceful flower spikes of Campanula persicifolia.

giving it too much thought, Tom put in a ridiculously low bid. "Much to my horror, I got the place," he recalls. "But once I recovered from the shock, I began to see that it had a lot of possibilities."

While the house was being cleared of chicken feathers and made livable, work began on the garden. With the help of friends, the hillside behind the house was cleared, and 30 years of tin cans, rusty bedsprings, and rotten lumber hauled away. Once the trash was cleared, it became easier to see what they had to work with. It also became easier to see neighbors' back yards, with their clotheslines, garages, and barbecue grills. Lacking any large trees or shrubs, the property was exposed on all four sides. The footpath running along the western boundary and the pub across the road made the front yard a public event.

After years of living in London, Tom wanted a garden with privacy, a secluded place where friends could join him for tea and informal dinner parties on summer evenings. "I also wanted to create the illusion it was much bigger and wilder than it really was," he says, "and I wanted the garden to relate as closely as possible to the house, because I think house and garden should be as one."

To begin, Tom envisioned the gar-den as a series of separate areas, each with its own distinctive character. Around the house, the garden would have a somewhat formal feeling; the farther away from the house, the more informal it would become. Gravel paths and honey-colored Cotswold stone walls would serve as the garden's framework and help tie the various areas together.

Not exactly sure how to create all this, Tom asked some friends to collaborate with him on the design. Their first effort resulted in an elaborate plan with long terraces and steps cut into the hillside. On paper it looked great, but once they began work in the garden Tom realized it was excessively complex and did nothing to relate the house to the land surrounding it.

The real beginning for the garden's design came with the removal of a huge mound of dirt against the back of the house. Once the soil around the house was leveled, the design seemed to unfold. Planted as lawn, edged with stone paving, and surrounded by low stone walls, the area outside the back door would become like an outdoor room, an effective transition between house and garden. From the lawn, two sets of steps would lead up to a long, L-shaped, gravel terrace. Retaining walls would then separate the terrace from the woodland on the hillside above it. Once the basic layout was agreed upon, the location of terraces, steps, and paved areas were laid out with stakes and string. (See Plan of Gables.)

While digging the foundations for the walls surrounding the lawn, Tom and his friends found that each hole immediately filled with water. Evidently the water table was just below the surface. Faced with the prospect of a perpetually soggy lawn, Tom decided a drainage ditch would be the solution—and that was the beginning of the bog garden.

As with the rest of the garden, the woodland garden on the hillside behind the house began with a few simple design ideas and a good bit of imagination. In his mind, Tom saw the ugly, barren hillside as a romantic, spring woodland, where narrow paths wound through dappled shade. Planted with ground covers and shrubs, this would be the wildest part of the garden, and if properly screened from the lawn at the back of the house, it would be a total surprise to anyone visiting for the first time.

One of the earliest and most important design decisions for this woodland was the placement of the main path. To help make the garden seem larger, Tom realized this path should cut across the hill's longest diagonal. The secondary paths could then weave among a few existing trees and large mounds of earth. Once the route of the main path was decided, topsoil was brought in and dumped in several long mounds 15–25 feet long and about 5 feet high. Planted with small trees and deciduous shrubs, these berms of earth created a series of interesting spaces and visually separated the woodland from the more formal areas around the house.

Some of the shrubs on these mounds, including the *Viburnum opulus* 'Compactum', *V. × juddii* and *V. × bodnantense,* were planted in masses to create a dense background. Several *V. plicatum* 'Mariesii', with their distinctive horizontal branching and flat, lacy, white flowers, were planted in prominent positions as focal points. Other shrubs, including *Cotinus coggygria,* the 15-foot smoke-tree with its pinkish-gray flower panicles, and a tender tree aster *(Olearia × haastii),* with grayish-green evergreen leaves and white, fragrant, daisylike flowers, were also used as specimens.

A good many of the shrubs were selected for their flowers. *Syringa microphylla* and half a dozen other varieties of lilac would assure a succession of bloom from early May into

(Above) Enclosed by stone walls and a low, clipped box hedge, a newly planted rose garden is laid out in a formal pattern around an old stone sundial. Lavender and catmint (Nepeta 'Six Hills Giant') *spill over the edge of the stone paths.*

(Opposite) Sprawling mounds of lady's mantle (Alchemilla mollis) *spill over the edges of the gravel path to the front door. To the left, white peonies and goatsbeard (Aruncus dioicus), with creamy-white plumes, are underplanted with* Geranium endressii *'Wargrave Pink'.*

June. Various shrub roses, including *Rosa rubrifolia,* or *R. glauca,* with its small, single, pink flowers and chocolate-colored leaves, would continue the flowering into early July.

Sometimes, shrubs and small trees were chosen to meet the particular needs of the site. In wet ground, along the west and south boundaries of the lot, Tom planted several *Salix matsudana* 'Tortuosa'. During the growing season, these fast-growing,

shrubby willows would create privacy. In winter, their curious corkscrew branches would become an interesting background feature.

Unlike many gardeners who immediately think of rhododendrons (with their leathery, dark green leaves) for a winter garden, Tom liked the sparse, twiggy look of the Cotswold woods in winter and wanted to create a similar feel in his back-yard woodland, so he selected shrubs with interesting

branch structure and combined them for a variety of effects. *Viburnum plicatum* 'Mariesii', for example, was planted to complement the graceful, drooping branches of the weeping pear (*Pyrus salicifolia* 'Pendula'). In a few years, they had assumed their characteristic forms, and on a sunny morning, after a January ice storm, this and other shrub combinations looked like wild and fanciful sculptures.

To help give the hillside the feeling of a woodland garden, Tom planted bold masses and sweeps of ground covers (chosen for different textures and shapes) among the shrubs. Many of the plants used in the woodland (and throughout the garden) were gifts from friends and neighbors. Once word had gone around the village that the fellow at Gables was starting a garden from scratch, total strangers began arriving with card-board boxes full of plants.

"People were extremely generous. But I was never quite sure what was going to come through the front gate. Often people would come by with a strange bit of wilted greenery and I'd have to wait till the next year to find out what it was. And that made getting one's combinations right, first time round, very difficult."

Tom also brought a lot of plants from nurseries. That summer was the

In the woodland, a gnarled apple tree is underplanted with bold masses of hosta, Siberian bugloss (Brunnera macrophylla) *and the quick-growing cypress spurge* (Euphorbia cyparissias) *with lime-green leaves and yellowish bracts. Blue peach-leaved bellflower* (Campanula persicifolia) *provide spots of color.*

driest England had experienced in many decades. The mighty Thames was reduced to a muddy trickle, and nurseries were unloading their stock at cut-rate prices. For about ten pounds, Tom could buy hundreds of plants, filling the front and back seats and the trunk of his car.

With so many plants and so much bare ground to cover, there wasn't time to think about creating effective combinations: shady plants went in shade, sunny plants in sun. The second year, with most of the ground covered and weeds more or less under control, Tom began moving plants around to refine his combinations.

Along the edges of paths and in bold masses around the bases of shrub roses he planted lady's mantle (*Alchemilla mollis*), Siberian bugloss (*Brunnera macrophylla*), *Pulmonaria officinalis*, and a favorite catmint (*Nepeta* 'Six Hills Giant'). Hardy geraniums, hostas, and various foamflowers, including *Tiarella cordifolia, T. wherryi,* and *T. trifoliata,* also became staples throughout the garden.

Cypress spurge (*Euphorbia cyparissias*) was another quick-growing ground cover. The only problem was its enthusiasm; spreading by underground stolons, in a few years it became a real weed. But its lime-green foliage and yellowish bracts were such

an effective foil for the pink hardy geranium *Geranium endressii* and blue peach-leaved bellflower (*Campanula persicifolia*) that Tom decided to leave it in selected spots. Once it crept outside its boundaries, however, it was pulled out along with weeds.

Not one for tidy little groups of plants, Tom planted in long sweeps and masses, sometimes two or three dozen of the same plant. To create interest with a limited selection of plants, he also varied the size and shape of these groupings. Some of the ground covers, including the various barrenworts *Epimedium grandiflorum, E. × versicolor,* and *E. × versicolor* 'Sulphureum', were slower growers, so these were planted in small groups as subtle accents or as contrast for the large, distinctive leaves of variegated hostas and *Bergenia cordifolia*.

Unlike many owners of small gardens, who plant solely with miniature evergreens and dainty herbaceous plants with delicate foliage, Tom understood the importance of contrasting scale. Also, he wasn't a plant snob. If a plant had attractive or dramatic foliage and promised not to be invasive, he didn't care how common it was.

The second year, for example, one of the plants he had been given as a gift matured into a handsome speci-

men of garden rhubarb with bright red stems and crinkled, dark-green leaves almost 2 feet across. Thinking it would look fantastic combined with peonies, Tom moved it into the partial shade beneath an old apple tree. It looked so good that he planted several more as dramatic focal points throughout the garden.

In the partial shade of a fruit tree, the blue flower spikes and silver-green foliage of the ever useful Nepeta *'Six Hills Giant' create a delicate background for hosta and orange and white oriental poppies* (Papaver orientale).

Heartleaf bergenia (*Bergenia cordifolia*), with squat spikes of rose-colored flowers and large, leathery green leaves, was another herbaceous plant Tom used as an accent. Planted at strategic points along the edge of the path, it emphasizes a turn and relieves long stretches of *Nepeta* 'Six Hills Giant'.

A steep stone path leading from the woodland to the lawn behind the house is accented by variegated hosta and the foliage of bearded irises. A vigorous sprawl of Nepeta 'Six Hill's Giant' cascades over the wall. To the left, the foliage of artemisias and the silver flower stalks of lamb's ears (Stachys lanata) punctuate plantings and create highlights along the edge of the path. At the base of the stone wall, Cerastium tomentosum has self-seeded.

Although the woodland was planned primarily as a green garden, many of these ground covers also flower. In April, *Pulmonaria officinalis* blooms with small, pink and blue flowers. Along the edges of paths, its light green leaves splotched with white become a subtle accent when combined with the new shoots of Siberian iris *(Iris sibirica)* and fresh green leaves of *Geranium sanguineum* var. *striatum (G. sanguineum lancastriense)*. Planted with white daffodils and clusters of red kaufmanniana tulips, large clumps of *P. officinalis* became a focal point under an old apple tree.

Another spring foliage and flower combination is blue-flowered *Brunnera macrophylla* and late-flowering white daffodils, planted in the partial shade of the hazelnut trees. In May and early June, the brunnera's forget-me-not–like flowers are held slightly above small, heart-shaped leaves. By mid-June, its leaves mushroom to 8– 10 inches across. Combined with the graceful spears of *Iris sibirica* and the flowering spikes of *Nepeta* 'Six Hills Giant', it too makes a bold accent.

Gradually, Tom added flowering perennials as color accents. Amid masses of *B. macrophylla* beneath the old apple tree, he planted pink peonies *(Paeonia* hybrids) and orange ori-

ental poppies *(Papaver orientale)*. Viewed from the steps at the beginning of the woodland, their bright colors (against a background of deep green foliage) drew the eye and gave the garden a sense of greater depth.

Sometimes the combinations of texture and flower color were carefully thought out, but just as often plants such as *Brunnera macrophylla, Alchemilla mollis,* and mountain bluet *(Centaurea montana)* self-seeded and were found coming up in far corners of the garden. Sometimes, Tom left these self-sown plants where they were; sometimes they were used to fill in gaps beneath shrubs or along paths.

Because he had so many of the same plant, Tom invented different combinations to vary their effects. *Nepeta* 'Six Hills Giant', for example, was used in many different settings throughout the garden. Planted with snow-in-summer *(Cerastium tomentosum),* it helped soften the stone steps and create an informal, even somewhat mysterious, entrance to the woodland. Tom also used *Nepeta* 'Six Hills Giant' as an edging for paths, but instead of planting it in solid lines, he gave the path visual continuity by planting a big clump on the right (backed by *Iris sibirica* and *Brunnera macrophylla*) and another clump farther up, on the left side of the path,

this time in combination with hostas, *Geranium endressii,* and *Alchemilla mollis.*

Another staple throughout the garden is *Alchemilla mollis.* Something of a chameleon like *Nepeta* 'Six Hills Giant', its character changes depending on its surroundings. Combined with epimediums, brunneras, and hardy geraniums along the edges of paths or under shrubs, it looks the perfect woodland plant. With astilbes and ornamental grasses, it appears perfectly at home around the edge of a small pond. Planted with peonies, bearded irises, and aruncus along the front walk, it becomes a border plant. For most of the growing season, *A. mollis,* with lightly tomentose, kidney-shaped leaves, is a foliage plant, but in late June and July it becomes an important color accent. Along the front walk, its froth of chartreuse flowers combines well with everything from roses and aruncus to peonies and irises.

As with the woodland, this entry area began as an all-green garden, the shapes, forms, and contrasting textures of various small-leaved evergreen and deciduous shrubs creating year-round interest. Here, as in most of his garden, Tom doesn't rely on an elaborate succession of bloom. Instead, seasonal features give the area color. In early June, several varieties of water-loving irises are features in the shallow pool. In mid-June and early July, roses, peonies, and aruncus become highlights. Along the edges of the path and at strategic corners, hardy geraniums and lady's mantle are planted in masses and as bold accents.

Typically of Gables, this entry garden requires surprisingly little maintenance. The shrubs, unlike a good many flowering perennials, don't require continual deadheading to keep them attractive, and because these and other plants are so closely spaced, with little or no bare ground between them, weeds don't have enough light to get started. This tight planting of perennials to either side of the front walk also helps minimize staking.

In this entry area and throughout the garden, Tom has tried to avoid staking whenever he can. Plants such as *Campanula persicifolia* and *Papaver orientale*, for example, are surrounded by masses of *Geranium endressii, Brunnera macrophylla,* and *Nepeta* 'Six Hills Giant'; with all the plants intertwining and mingling, there is a minimum of flopping. Plants such as delphiniums, dahlias, and gladioli, requiring more substantial support, are usually planted in the kitchen garden, where they can be staked with stout sticks and look right at home with bush

A vigorous rose with large clusters of single, reddish-pink blooms, with off-white centers, 'American Pillar' flowers from mid-June to the end of July.

beans and tomatoes.

Tom grows relatively few perennials solely for their flowers, so deadheading is not a major task. When various ground covers are through blooming, their spent flowers aren't all that noticeable; nor will the plants go into a serious decline if he doesn't get around to removing their faded blossoms.

To keep the garden looking fresh, Tom does deadhead some ground

covers and perennials, using techniques he has refined over the years. In May, after the *Brunnera macrophylla* has finished blooming, he grabs the flower stalks by the handful, close to the crown, then gives them a good twist. Most of the brunneras are planted in drifts, so he can move quickly through each section. When the heavy June bloom of hardy geraniums is past, leaving the plants covered with small brown seed pods, Tom

Throughout the garden, climbing roses are trained onto trees and up the sides of buildings and walls. Here, the stone barn behind the house is draped with the rose 'American Pillar'.

cuts them right back to the crown. By mid-July, the flowers of *Alchemilla mollis* and *Nepeta* 'Six Hills Giant' are usually sprawling and flattened by the rain and also ready to be cut back.

For about a week, the garden looks a bit bare, but with the warm weather of midsummer, new leaves grow quickly. By the beginning of August, *A. mollis* is back, bright and green.

About the middle of August, *Nepeta* 'Six Hills Giant', *Geranium endressii*, and *G. sanguineum* var. *striatum* are in bud. By the beginning of September, the garden is in bloom once again.

In early October, the first hard frosts have hit and the foliage has begun to turn. Around the front yard, the lindens have turned golden, and in the woodland, viburnums and shrub

roses are now crimson and gold. Many of the herbaceous perennials and ground covers have taken on subtle, autumn colors. Along the paths, the reds and oranges of *Geranium sanguineum* var. *striatum* combine with the rich, golden yellow of *Iris sibirica*. Too lovely to disturb, they will be cut back to the crown later in the month.

Some of the more tender-leaved

A grassy woodland path is edged with various hostas, Siberian bugloss (Brunnera macrophylla), with large, heart-shaped leaves and forget-me-not-like flowers in spring, and broad sweeps of Alchemilla mollis. To the left, the shrub rose 'Nevada' blooms with large, creamy-white flowers in late May and early June and intermittently throughout the summer, often with a heavy flush of bloom again in late summer or autumn. To the right, the shrub rose 'Geranium', a moyesii hybrid with single, orange-red flowers followed by large, deep red hips, is well suited for partial shade.

ground covers, such as brunneras and hostas, are black or bedraggled after the frosts, so these are cut back. But beneath the apple tree, the leaves of *Bergenia cordifolia* have turned a deep, brown-maroon. Nearby, the heart-shaped leaves of the epimediums have also assumed their winter hues of rich, chocolate-burgundy. Like the bergenia, the epimediums are essentially evergreen, and the plants will retain their shapes till matted down by snow.

On misty autumn mornings, the woodland is lovely with its faded golds and scarlets. But, all too soon, the rain and winds strip the trees. When the last leaves have fallen, Tom sets aside a weekend for cleanup and bulb planting. Dressed in old tweeds and Wellingtons, he piles up the wheelbarrow with rakes, shears, and bushel baskets and heads out into the garden.

Instead of raking the leaves out of the entire woods (a task that would take days), Tom lets them lie around the trees and shrubs. Next year they will act as a mulch and will gradually break down to enrich the soil. After the herbaceous perennials are all cut back, the paths are raked and all the leaves dumped on the compost pile. By Sunday noon the garden is prepared for winter and Tom is planting bulbs, already looking forward to spring.

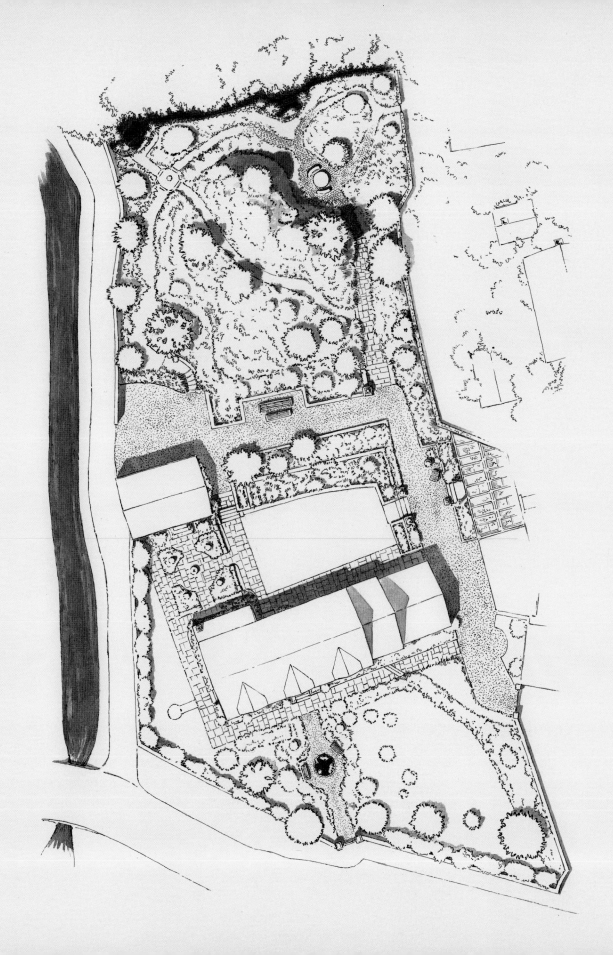

GABLES

129

CHAPTER 8

YEW TREE COTTAGE

(Right) Scattered throughout the borders of Yew Tree Cottage, plants of Campanula persicifolia *grow from two to three feet tall and are a delicate and graceful filler beneath shrub roses and climbing roses.*

*(Opposite) The graceful sweep of the curved borders frames the lawn and leads the eye to the weeping willow. To the right of the summer house, a blue Atlantic cedar (*Cedrus atlantica *'Glauca') gives the garden a magnificent background and dispels the myth that small gardens must have small trees.*

As A CHILD, I knew an elderly and very eccentric English gardener. Her garden was lovely and wild, with plants poking out of steps, sprawling across paths, and wrapped around everything from statues to trees. Behind all these flowers and vines were what she called, "some mighty fine bones." These, she insisted, were what made a garden. "Without bones, you just don't have the framework that makes a good garden."

Now bones were a mystery to me. I never saw any in her garden. But she made mighty fine chocolate chip cookies, and I didn't want to sound ignorant. It wasn't until years later, when I visited Yew Tree Cottage, that I finally understood what she meant.

The first time I saw Yew Tree Cottage was on a very gray autumn day. The frosts had come, so the garden was looking pretty bare, but as I walked along the grass paths, around corners, and down what I imagined to be vistas of flowers, it was apparent that Yew Tree had "good bones." I added it to my list of gardens to visit the following year.

When I returned the next June, the garden was in full bloom, with roses cascading over walls and delphiniums 6 feet high. Yew Tree's basic design was formal, almost classical, a geometric arrangement of grass paths and borders, vistas and formal lawn. The rest was pure cottage garden—a wonderful, whimsical mix of homegrown topiary and masses of old-fashioned flowers, irises mingling with delphiniums, and lady's mantle mixed with everything from catmint to shrub roses and campanulas.

The plantings were effusive, the combinations eclectic. Floral vignettes had an almost medieval character. Pink peonies flowing over crenellated box hedges were straight from the pages of illuminated manuscripts. Topiary pheasants and jam pots gave the garden a delightful sense of whimsy. Beautiful details, including stone walls, wrought iron gates, and rustic wooden benches made of gnarled tree branches, accented and completed the garden's design.

For all its diversity, Yew Tree isn't cluttered. The garden's plan has purpose and direction, and the layout of open and enclosed spaces has a simple, graceful logic. There are shady places to sit and sunny places to walk, intimate enclosures and wide open lawn. Grass paths direct the eye down vistas ending in garden seats and gates. It is hard to believe that the whole garden is only 80 by 90 feet.

One of the main reasons for Yew Tree's particular success is that its creator, Jean Sinfield, never thought of it as a small garden. From the beginning, she wanted a dramatic garden, with the high style of some of England's finest manor gardens—a place where she could play with big ideas. She also wanted a cottage-style garden, however, a romantic fantasy with masses of spring bulbs and old-fashioned flowers. The trick was to combine the two styles so the result-

ing garden became the best of both.

When Jean and George Sinfield bought their tiny cottage in 1956, it had been derelict for years. The land beside the cottage (where the garden now stands) belonged to the pub next door. A jungle of brambles and nettles, the vacant lot had been used as a dumping ground for everything from tires to old refrigerators. Appalled at all the ground going to waste, Jean asked the proprietor of the pub if she might use it for a garden. No doubt thinking her a bit mad, he rented it for a token rent of one pound a year. "Some people thought I was the biggest idiot in the world. The land didn't belong to me, but I couldn't resist. I was determined to make a garden."

With far more imagination than money, Jean set out to make her garden. Outfitted in Wellies and old tweeds, each morning she waded into the nettles with her shovel and wheelbarrow.

"I didn't think of time at all," she recalls. "I didn't even have a watch. Half past seven I'd be out there. I'd know the time when the schoolchildren came by in the afternoon. Then I'd dash in and get the meal. I'm afraid I didn't do much housework—I was all the time staring out the window and planning something."

On weekends her husband, George, helped her clear, pulling out things such as truck axles and old refrigerators, but mostly she worked alone, using an old wooden wheelbarrow to haul out debris and move soil.

Once the trash had been cleared, the next task—and probably the most challenging—was to level the uneven ground with its clods of earth and hummocks of couch grass. Once the rough ground was turned to lawn, the garden's framework of paths and borders could be planned and sections of the grass dug out.

Never having cleared a garden before, Jean figured the best method (and certainly the most affordable, with her infinitesimal garden budget) would be to drag their old gasoline mower through the nettles and tall grass. Slowly and laboriously she mowed the weeds and scraped down the mounds of earth. Where the ground was too rough, sod was lifted, subsoil removed, and the sod replaced, level with the surrounding ground.

"Gradually," Jean recalls, "the thing came to a lawn. But with my knowledge today I could do it in a week. I'd turn it over with a spade, working backwards in a line. That would level it, then the grass would grow up through."

Bearded irises edge a grass path to the front door of Yew Tree Cottage in Surrey. A Rosa moyesii *'Geranium' (grown as a standard) and a cement urn planted with sedums and accented with a sprawl of blue-flowered* Nepeta mussinii *help frame the entrance.*

The actual design for the garden began with a pair of borders near the cottage. From the house the only view into her would-be garden was through the kitchen windows. Jean wanted to see flowers from her kitchen for as many months of the year as possible. Color was important, but so were the shape of the borders, which would provide interest from October to February, when there were no flowers.

It was also important that the borders be an integral and pleasing part of the garden's design—when viewed from within the garden as well as from the kitchen. To help her determine the position and shape of the borders, Jean walked around the rough lawn and looked back at the cottage. She observed that, from several vantage points, the existing willow was a natural focal point. If laid out in a sweeping curve, the borders would lead the eye to the willow, emphasizing its position. The borders (in combination with the willow) would also help shape that end of the garden and frame the entrance to the courtyard located behind the cottage. (See Plan of Yew Tree Cottage.)

The shapes for these borders, as well as for the rest of the garden's paths and borders, were never drawn out on paper. Nothing was ever measured. Instead, Jean scratched a line with a stick, then pegged the outline with stakes and string. She then tried a number of different shapes till she got an outline that looked good from every vantage point.

The plantings in these first borders were a rather helter-skelter collection of spring bulbs and perennials, a mixture of plants that Jean had propagated or been given. The bearded irises were rescued from a friend's compost pile. Over the years most of the original plants in these borders were replaced, but those irises remained. Propagated many times over, they—along with dozens of named varieties—are now the garden's

major display in late May and early June.

The rest of the garden's design evolved in stages. Sometimes existing features—a stone wall uncovered beneath a pile of rubble, the willow, or a line of seven Lawson cypresses

In late June and July, blue and white peach-leaved bellflowers (Campanula persicifolia) *are a feature in the curved beds outside the kitchen window. Clumps of pink-flowered* Geranium endressii *'Wargrave Pink' and lady's mantle* (Alchemilla mollis) *sprawl over the borders' edges and help create a feeling of informality. At the end of the borders (nearest the house), peonies create strong foliage accents that last all season.*

alongside the cottage—gave Jean ideas. Both the willow and the cypresses were important as part of the garden's framework and textural background, and they also taught Jean some important lessons about scale and contrasting spatial relationships.

New and experienced gardeners alike often make the mistake of think-

ing small in a small garden. They bemoan the fact that their property measures in feet instead of acres, then go out and buy a book on miniature shrubs. The end result often looks like a clutter of plants in a scale-model parody of an English landscape.

When Jean began gardening, the willow was already a good-sized tree and would obviously get much larger. While the willow's ultimate height was certainly a consideration in the small garden, it offered so much—enclosure, privacy, texture, and seasonal color variations—that there was no question of chopping it down.

The idea of large trees also appealed to Jean's sense of the dramatic. For years she had wanted a blue Atlantic cedar (*Cedrus atlantica* 'Glauca'). Generally used as a specimen tree in rather grand English gardens and landscapes, the cedar would eventually reach a height of 120 feet and a spread of 90 feet. After a bit of soul searching, the tree was bought and planted.

Now, over 30 years later, the cedar, not surprisingly, is one of the garden's most spectacular and useful year-round highlights. It is big, but its exaggerated scale doesn't make the garden seem smaller. Just the opposite. The deep shadows and textures of its branches give the garden depth. In winter the combination of the willow and cedar branches swaying and rippling in the wind give life and color to an otherwise brown and barren garden. In early spring the cedar's grand sweep of feathery, blue-green branches is a magnificent complement to the willow's sinewy, yellow branches. Beginning in May, the cedar's blue-green foliage becomes a dark, dramatic background for the perennial borders.

An equally bold tree that Jean planted is *Catalpa bignonioides* 'Aurea', with a mature height of 45 feet and the most brilliant yellow-green leaves. Unlike the willow and blue cedar, it is not allowed to grow unrestrained: each spring it is cut back sharply to keep it in scale with the surrounding perennial borders. With its large leaves and huge, white panicles spotted yellow and purple, the catalpa resembles a raucous flowering shrub and provides a dramatic foil for delphiniums and roses. (See Plan of Yew Tree Cottage for placement.)

As the garden grew, so did Jean's ideas on design and plants. A good many inspirations came from books, photographs, and trips to well-known gardens. *The Great Gardens of Britain* by Peter Coats, which features some of Britain's more elaborate stately homes, was a major source. Other

inspirations came from newspaper and magazine articles.

Certainly a major influence on the garden's development was an article on topiary in the British edition of *House and Garden*. Enthralled with the idea, Jean decided she wanted a formal garden with clipped yew trees. In her imagination she could see a collection of evergreen shrubs pruned as peacocks and chessmen. Used as accents and as focal points, topiary could help define and articulate the

garden's framework of paths and borders, yet be totally in character with the garden's cottage style.

Jean's technique for shaping these fanciful creations developed through trial and error. Although she had no experience with topiary, she began by studying each plant—the position and shape of its branches, as well as noting in which direction the growth seemed strongest.

"A yew tree shows you its shape. You think, 'All right, I'll make that

The narrow grass paths between Jean's exuberant borders help create a feeling of intimacy and romantic enclosure in this area of the garden—a wonderful contrast to the areas of open lawn. To the right, the creamy flower spikes of Yucca recurvifolia *give the borders additional height and make a dramatic focal point through the summer.*

the tail and that the head.' You can see it right from the start. With the jam pot, when it was small, I decided it was going to be round, with a knob on top. I started when it was young, say about 18 or 20 inches, and just cut 'round the base slightly. But you can't get the second shape until the tree has grown a bit more. To do a ball on top takes about two years—for that much to grow. A yew tree makes the shape itself. You've just got to find it."

A bus trip to Hidcote, a romantic National Trust garden in Gloucestershire, was another important turning point for Jean in the garden's design. With its cottage flowers contrasted against a backbone of hedges and its various garden rooms placed on strong axial lines, Hidcote was very much the sort of garden Jean had in mind at Yew Tree.

"I was very impressed with the yew hedges and topiary," says Jean. "And all of a sudden I went mad on vistas. Everywhere I turned I wanted to be able to look at something ahead of me, a focal point at every angle."

Vistas, Jean learned, were not the sole prerogative of large English landscapes. A vista, even in a small garden, could create a sense of distance and depth, so the space seemed much larger. To get the greatest effect, Jean ran some of her paths the entire length or width of the garden.

There was no point in creating a vista, Jean reasoned, without something at the end. A vista, even on a miniature scale, must have a purpose. So she placed rustic, homemade

(Above) The climbing rose 'Bantry Bay' (trained up a wooden post) is surrounded by achilleas, campanulas, hardy geraniums, and delphiniums, including the Pacific hybrid 'Summer Skies'. With fragrant, deep pink flowers through the summer, 'Bantry Bay' will remain the highlight of this narrow border for almost four months.

(Opposite) In July, the main borders at Yew Tree Cottage feature dark pink Phlox paniculata, Achillea filipendulina, *delphinium, roses, and the creamy flower spikes of* Yucca recurvifolia. *The yellow-green leaves of* Catalpa bigonioioides *'Aurea' provide the borders with a brilliant background, while whimsical yew topiary, placed as accents, help give the garden its framework.*

benches and wrought iron gates—given to her by friends—as focal points.

An effective counterpoint to Yew Tree's formal vistas and geometric layout of paths are the perennial borders spilling over with old-fashioned cottage-style plants. In designing these borders, Jean flouted what a good many gardeners consider hard-and-fast rules. Never, say some, should a border be less than twice the width of its tallest plant—but Jean's narrow borders are in scale with the overall size of the garden, and they give it the rich detailing of lace. Full of hybrid delphiniums and climbing roses, these narrow borders, separated by equally narrow grass paths, create intimate, secret enclosures.

The border's succession of bloom begins in early spring and continues right into September. Maintaining the tight succession of bloom in these borders, none of which exceeds 4 or 5 feet in width, is a real art. There is so little depth that no plant can hide behind another. Once a plant is through blooming, it must still play its part for the rest of the season, or fade gracefully out of sight.

When the garden was in its infancy, Jean filled her borders with plants grown from seed or divisions and with cuttings from friends' gardens.

In late May and early June, bearded irises (many of their names lost over the years) are the garden's main show. Planted along the edge of borders, their spear-shaped foliage remains an attractive feature throughout the growing season.

Yucca recurvifolia, pulled out of someone's compost pile, grew so well that it and its offspring became major features in several borders. Easily grown cottage plants such as candytuft (*Iberis sempervirens*), lamb's ears (*Stachys byzantina,* or *S. lanata*), and fernleaf yarrow (*Achillea filipendulina*) became staples. Columbines (*Aquilegia* hybrids), hardy geraniums (*Geranium* species and hybrids), catmint (*Nepeta mussinii*), lady's mantle (*Alchemilla mollis*), pyrethrums (*Chrysanthemum coccineum*), and even delphiniums

(*Delphinium* hybrids) self-seeded in the light soil. Pricked out and grown on in a tiny nursery area, when large enough they were planted in new borders.

Many of these original plants appear again and again throughout the garden. Over the years dozens of named and unnamed varieties of bearded irises, in shades of yellow, lavender, white, pink, and maroon, have become the garden's major feature in June. Although there are lots of irises, they are never repetitious.

Used in various combinations, they create widely differing effects. For example, in front of the cottage, deep purple irises are silhouetted against dark green, clipped box. In the curved borders nearest the cottage, pink and cream-colored bearded irises are combined with peonies, *Geranium endressii* 'Wargrave Pink', and *Alchemilla mollis*.

"I place things—it doesn't look like it, but I do. I try to make colors blend and complement each other. Campanulas, peonies, and catmint, I think, are a lovely combination with irises, and *Geranium endressii* 'Wargrave Pink' looks very well with the irises and alchemilla."

Planted densely in the main parallel borders and in the small squares beyond the gazebo, the foliage of bearded irises remains an important texture in the perennial borders throughout the season. "I like the iris foliage almost as much as the flowers, and that is why they are in the foreground," says Jean. "Also, they support anything that is coming up at the back."

Grown in well-drained, sandy loam, in full sun, Jean's bearded irises are practically luxuriant, with foliage that remains attractive till frost. "They must have their rhizomes in the sun and cannot be planted too deeply. A little bone meal is all they require. You just sprinkle a bit around and rake it in like general fertilizer. About every three years you divide, and if you're sensible you give away the centers. Any gardener knows you don't give the outside away."

In June the main parallel borders are full of light blue, violet-blue, and white hybrid delphiniums. Pink roses are grown on posts, many of them placed against the dark green of clipped yews for contrast. This show is then followed in July by summer

phlox *(Phlox paniculata),* lilies, and a combination of shrub and climbing roses. Various veronicas, dianthus, lychnis, campanulas, nepetas, hostas, stachys, and alliums are used as fillers in the borders.

No cottage garden would be complete without roses, and Jean's collection of shrub and climbing roses includes more than 60 kinds. Beginning about the middle of June, roses are a feature, with an emphasis on old-fashioned varieties such as 'Penelope', a continually flowering shrub rose with pink, musk-scented blooms. 'Complicata', a single pink with bright-golden stamens, is another favorite. Many of the roses around the Victorian gazebo, across fences and walls, and up posts in borders are perpetual bloomers, so they remain a feature right through the end of summer. Jean also grows a carefully edited group of modern shrub roses, including perpetually flowering 'Nevada', whose arching canes and large, ivory white flowers festoon the walled garden behind the cottage.

The rich, sandy loam at Yew Tree and its airy, sunny site make ideal growing conditions for roses. Jean also makes sure that each newly planted rose and cutting receives an extra bit of attention.

"I give them a cup of tea now and

again," she explained. "If it's a young plant, I always empty the tea leaves on it—loose tea, not tea bags. We try all sorts of tea, but we're drinking Earl Grey at the moment."

During the first ten years of Jean's garden, most of her plants were common and easy to grow, but as her gardening skills matured she learned more about plants, and added to her collection.

"I got reading more books, and

In several spots Jean has planted bearded irises in front of yew hedges and topiary. Here their flowers (and later their foliage) are strikingly silhouetted against the dark green foliage.

seeing better plants at Chelsea Flower Show, and I got wanting the best I could manage to buy. Now I buy a lot of plants from Wisley, the Garden of the Royal Horticultural Society."

In the borders at the eastern end of the garden, Jean has planted some unusual and rather flamboyant herbaceous perennials as features for extended bloom. Various blue-flowered agapanthus (*Agapanthus* species) flower from July into September, along with 8-foot Matilija poppy (*Romneya coulteri*), a Southern California native, with single, white, poppylike blooms. Bear's-breeches (*Acanthus spinosissimus*), with its large, deeply cut leaves, flowers in July and August with spikes of purple flowers. Winter temperatures at Yew Tree (excluding particularly severe winters) rarely drop below 30°F., so these and other tender plants are left in the ground.

The placement of Jean's plants, as with everything else in her garden, has evolved from a combination of plan and inspiration. "Sometimes I have no intention of doing anything, but things come to me. A tree or a flower sparks it off. Sometimes if I see a lovely flower in one corner and another in another corner I say, 'Oh, they'd look lovely together.' So then it's a question of being brave and

moving one plant to enhance the other. If I'm quite certain it's not going to die, I sometimes move things in full bloom, in the right weather, in a warm rain. It isn't planned; it happens. I'm not knowledgeable. I do study books and care what I do, but mostly it's trial and error. You learn as you go along—you make mistakes, but you don't make them twice."

Yew Tree Cottage is not a low-maintenance garden, nor was it ever conceived as one. From the beginning it was an act of love, and it very quickly became a lovely and demanding obsession. Over the years, it has been a continuing source of satisfaction and delight for Jean and George, both for itself and for the pleasure it gives those who visit.

Jean and George (now that he is retired) each spend about four hours a day maintaining the garden. A good bit of time is spent trimming topiary and hedges and keeping the roses tied and deadheaded. The majority of Jean's herbaceous plant combinations are not in themselves labor-intensive, but some do need deadheading, as well as periodic division.

Maintaining the health of soil and lawns is an ongoing procedure. Although the garden started off with very rich soil, Jean and George top-

dress the borders each fall with well-rotted compost and leaf mold. A strong advocate of bone meal, Jean places a small amount under everything she plants.

During the growing season George cuts the grass weekly and leaves the cuttings on the lawn to decompose. The lawn is also fed two or three times a year with a commercially prepared lawn fertilizer. In early spring, and periodically throughout the summer, the borders are edged to keep grass from encroaching. Using a pair of long-handled edging shears, Jean can edge an 18- by 5-foot border in about 5 minutes.

A garden chore Jean has turned into an artistic ritual is the maintenance of her topiary collection. When she started her jam pots and pheasants, she wasn't used to large shears, so she did her pruning with a pair of large sewing scissors. In recent years, George has occasionally trimmed the topiary with power clippers, but these bruise the leaves, so when she has time, Jean uses scissors to get the close, even cut she prefers. Something of an expert, she can now trim a three-tiered jam pot in about 45 minutes.

While obviously not low-maintenance, Yew Tree offers a good many design and planting ideas that can be adapted for gardeners interested in a

(Above) In the rear of the cottage a homemade concrete pool helps shape a tiny garden seen through the kitchen window. Antique chimney pots (rescued from the demolition of a nearby house) create distinctive focal points and supports for climbing roses. To the left, the chimney pot and former outhouse (transformed with the help of secondhand windows) is draped with the climbing rose 'Mme Gregoire Staechelin'. To the right, the recurrent blooming rose 'Nevada', with slightly blowsy, creamy-white flowers, and once-blooming 'Maigold', with fragrant, golden-yellow blooms flushed-orange, are trained across the wall.

(Left) A chimney pot, its base surrounded by hydrangea and Bergenia crassifolia, is framed by the recurrent blooming rose 'Penelope', a hybrid musk with clusters of fragrant, creamy-pink blooms turning white.

A low hedge of clipped box (Buxus sempervirens) *provides the perfect foil for a voluptuous sprawl of pink peonies.*

past, and many of the perennials have been cut to the ground. Through the winter Jean and George clean up the garden, repair benches, paint gates, and plant bulbs. They also spend a fair amount of time on the telephone organizing the upcoming schedule of garden visitors—everyone from local garden clubs, to design instructors with their students, to European horticultural societies.

First open to the public in 1973, for the charities of the National Gardens Scheme, Yew Tree has become an inspiration for thousands of visitors. Many come yearly and have told friends who have told friends until visiting days now resemble a neighborhood party. Early in the morning, members of a local garden club set up chairs and tables, arrange plates of homemade cakes and scones, and prepare to serve tea to as many as two and three hundred people.

"We both enjoy the garden," says George Sinfield. "We could sit here and do nothing, but who wants that?"

"It's our life and that's it," adds Jean, who, like George, is in her seventies. "Old age? I can't be bothered to worry about it. I'm still gardening."

Postscript: In 1986, the Sinfields purchased their garden next to Yew Tree Cottage.

combination of classic formality and cottage-style exuberance but who haven't the time or the passion to make gardening their life. All these borders, for example, are narrow enough so every plant can be reached from either side. While this may not actually reduce the amount of work required to stake delphiniums, it does make the job more accessible. Jean's use of seasonal themes can also be adapted by planning borders around predominantly lower-maintenance plants, perennials whose staking, deadheading, and division requirements are nominal. (See Cultural Chart for maintenance requirements.)

By October, Yew Tree's show is

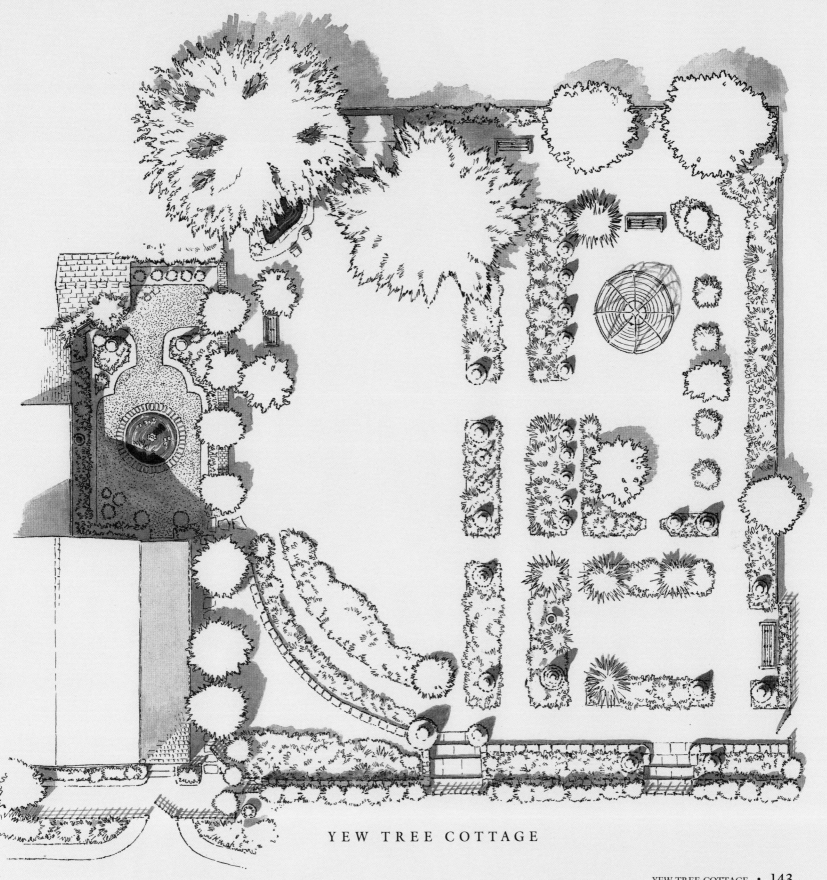

YEW TREE COTTAGE

CHAPTER 9

AMERICAN COTTAGE GARDENS: CITY AND COUNTRY

(Opposite) In late April and early May the meadow below Corgi Cottage is filled with sweeps of naturalized daffodils.

(Right) Daffodils are also a feature in a shady foundation border next to the cottage. Late-flowering Narcissus 'Thalia' *is combined with clusters of apricot-colored tulips and clumps of blue pansies, among the foliage of later-blooming violets and forget-me-nots.*

OVER THE YEARS I have discovered dozens of the most wonderful cottage gardens here in the United States, every sort from tiny dooryards on Martha's Vineyard and Cape Cod to Midwestern back yards and San Francisco terraces.

Sometimes these gardens are no more than a sunny path lined with bearded irises, cottage pinks, and old-fashioned roses; others are the most elaborate creations, with stone steps and walls and white painted arbors covered with clematis and honeysuckle. Each garden is as different from the others as its geographic location and its owner's personal style, and many were designed to meet the needs of particularly demanding sites, but all have the romantic, slightly overgrown look so characteristic of cottage gardens.

With so many appealing cottage gardens to choose from, I wondered how to write a chapter on American cottage gardening that would be truly useful for American gardeners. One approach would have been to touch briefly on as many different kinds of gardens around the country as space would allow, then mention a few key plants and combinations in each. The more I thought about these gardens, however, the more I realized how much their basic elements had in common and how easily the principles underlying their designs could be adapted to different areas of the country.

Effusive perennial or mixed borders, trees, and shrubs often played key roles in establishing the framework of each garden's design. The plants varied from one area of the country to another, nevertheless their basic design functions were often sim-

At Blue Flower Cottage, the granite gate posts and the weathered picket gate are framed by a flowering crab tree. Just inside the front gate is a tiny woodland garden, then an exuberant country-style border followed by a diminutive formal courtyard. This city garden is small, but divided into several "rooms," it seems much larger. Flowering shrubs, perennials, and ground covers give each area a distinctly different character.

BLUE FLOWER COTTAGE

Over the years, this tiny garden has become a much-loved part of the neighborhood, a place where neighbors stop to talk about the weather and the merits of this year's apple blossoms. Even business people and students—clearly in a hurry—cannot seem to resist taking a moment to lean over the wooden gate to see what's in bloom and to chat with Nancy Aiello as she sweeps the walk.

Unlike so many city gardens, with their boring borders of pachysandra and ivy, this garden is in bloom from spring to frost. Beginning in early April, its borders flower with delicate sweeps of blue squill and species daffodils. By May, the sweet scent of apple blossoms and lilacs perfume the air, and in June the perennial border along the front walk is in full flower.

When Nancy and Lloyd Aiello moved into Blue Flower Cottage almost 20 years ago, the cottage was practically hidden behind a huge lilac hedge. The tiny yard suggested a certain wild charm, but it was weedy and overgrown in some areas, threadbare in others, with no clearly defined paths or sitting areas. Any design that might have given the garden a framework had been lost long ago to benign neglect.

ilar. In a small California garden, for example, various tree asters (*Olearia* species) might be planted to provide seasonal focal points at the end of a path, beside a door, or as part of a foundation planting, whereas in New England, the lilacs *Syringa vulgaris* or *S. microphylla* might serve the same purpose.

I concluded that the most useful approach would be to feature two gardens apparently very different from each other, exploring how the placement of basic elements such as shrubs and trees, as well as paths, walls or fences, and borders, played similar roles in creating the garden's basic framework and shaping its distinctive spaces.

Blue Flower Cottage is a surprising mixture of woodland and country-style gardens, all the more surprising because it is right in the middle of a city in Massachusetts. With its flowering trees, picket fence, and rustic wooden gate, it has all the quiet charm of a pretty country dooryard, with some exciting design ideas for making the most of a small city or suburban yard.

Corgi Cottage, home of the children's book illustrator Tasha Tudor, is the site of a much larger garden. Created from a wooded hillside in southern Vermont, it is divided into several levels by stone walls and terraces, its sections drawn together by an intricate maze of grass paths and steps, and it is chock full of hollyhocks, roses, and delphiniums.

Together, these two gardens provide a host of ideas for cottage-style plantings and some imaginative solutions to some of the common landscape problems confronting American homeowners.

For the first two years, while the Aiellos rented the house, Nancy pulled weeds, discovered some of the property's various idiosyncracies, and imagined what she would do if it were hers. By the time the opportunity came to buy the house, she had begun to envision the yard as a garden with several distinct areas, each of a different size, shape, and character. This, she thought, would create variety and help the small area seem much larger than it actually was.

The development of the garden's design was a combination of planning on paper and working directly in the garden. As a first step, she drew a simple plan of the yard on graph paper. Drawn to scale, one square equaling one foot, this plan helped her to be more realistic in evaluating how much space she had for paths, trees, and shrubs. As she cleared the yard of overgrown shrubs and rooted out their stumps, Nancy imagined the shape and size of different areas and the placement of various shrubs— being careful to keep in mind their full height and width at maturity. She then sketched out her ideas on the rough plan.

Sometimes, the existing features or dimensions of the yard determined the size and shape of an area and helped create the basic design. A pair

of granite gate posts, for example, decided the exact location of the garden's main path. Nancy liked the idea of walking through a flower garden to reach the front door, so she decided the partially sunny strip along the left side of the path would become a perennial border. In addition to creating a colorful and inviting entrance, a perennial border offered a practical solution to an unavoidable problem:

due to the steep pitch of the roof, huge piles of snow slid off that side of the house after winter storms. The usual foundation shrubs would have been broken and crushed, but perennials, because they die back to the ground each year, would remain unharmed.

At the end of the straight entry path, in the area surrounding the front door, Nancy laid out a small,

Five leaf akebia (Akebia quinata) *is trained along the top of the rustic picket fence separating the front garden from the sidewalk. Its exuberant growth is kept in check by pruning several times during the growing season. In mid- to late spring it flowers with clusters of deep wine-colored flowers.*

circular courtyard. Later planted with grass and encircled by Baltic ivy and a variegated euonymus, it became the most formal part of the garden. The largest area, at the rear of the garden, was left open as a place for her two young children to play and for the adults to entertain or to sit quietly after the children had gone to bed. (See Plan of Blue Flower Cottage.)

Nancy's gardening budget was very limited, so she decided to get the slowest-growing plants in first, as they would be of a good size by the time the garden was completed. Once the basic shapes of the different areas were outlined, she began buying shrubs and trees. Their selection was based on a mixture of factors—design, practical considerations such as sun and shade, and pure nostalgia.

"I had such happy memories of growing up," she explained, "that when I came to have my own garden, I knew there were certain plants I just had to have. Planting these shrubs and trees—the weeping cherry, for example—was a nice way to regenerate those memories."

To decide the best positions for these plants, Nancy spent hours looking out windows onto the garden area and walking through the garden. The tiny garden was surrounded by neighboring houses and a hotel, so she wanted to enclose it to create privacy. Many new gardeners would have planted their selection of shrubs as a solid hedge along the boundary of the yard, but Nancy wanted to avoid the boxed-in feeling that characterizes and makes claustrophobic so many city gardens. So some shrubs were placed to screen neighboring yards selectively; others were planted to help shape the different areas and provide seasonal focal points to lure one through the garden.

The weeping cherry, planted just outside the living room window—at the end of the perennial border, where the path turns left to the front door—provides a striking example. Throughout the year, the cherry's graceful branch structure gives the path a most distinctive focal point, but when viewed from the garden's entrance in

The weathered wooden arbor is framed by a pair of Viburnum carlesii, *with sweetly scented, pinkish-white flowers in May. Planted on either side of the arbor, the viburnums frame an attractive view (into a neighbor's yard) over a low section of picket fence. To the left is globe flower* Kerria japonica *'Pleniflora'.*

late April, its delicate cascade of pink flowers transforms the narrow bluestone walk into the most delightful and compelling vista. (See Plan of Blue Flower Cottage for location.)

Nancy's selection of trees and shrubs was instrumental, also, in establishing the style of the garden's several areas. One of her most unusual choices was the Japanese umbrella pine (*Sciadopitys verticillata*). Planted just inside the front gate, the pine, with its distinctive conical shape and clusters of long, dark-green needles, makes a striking winter combination with the strong horizontal branching of the neighboring dogwood (*Cornus kousa*). During the growing season the pine, underplanted with a variety of ground covers, helps give the entry its slightly wild, woodland character.

Other shrubs were planted to help shape the garden's areas. Nancy placed dwarf Korean lilac (*Syringa patula,* or *S. palibiniana*), for example, with small, dark green leaves and fragrant panicles of light, lilac-colored flowers in mid-May, at the corner of the house. Pruned so it remained a compact, rounded shape about 6 feet tall and 5 feet wide, it helps to enclose and define the tiny entry area and separate it from the section of path along the perennial border.

Two larger flowering shrubs were

A blue-flower lacecap hydrangea is a focal point along the path in summer and helps divide the tiny woodland entrance garden from the perennial border along the side of the house. To the right is the silver foliage of artemisia; along the left side of the path, a line of rugged sensitive fern (Onoclea sensibilis) creates a lacy effect—its invasive tendencies held in check by the bluestone paving.

selected as seasonal accents to enclose the courtyard (outside the front door) and frame the narrow path from the courtyard to the lawn at the rear of the garden. Like the cherry tree and the dogwood, both shrubs were also planted so they created dramatic seasonal pictures when seen from inside the cottage. On the right, the hybrid cherry *Prunus* × 'Halle Jolivette' is pruned to a dense, rounded shape

about 8 feet tall. From mid-April to early May, its leafless branches are covered with small, semidouble white flowers. In autumn, its finely shaped, dark green leaves turn bronze-gold. To the left of the path is rose-of-Sharon (*Hibiscus syriacus*). More often seen as an ungainly shrub stuck awkwardly in the middle of a large lawn, Nancy's has been pruned so that its branches grow long and upright. Over the years it has assumed a large but compact and rounded form, and it provides an extravagant display of hundreds of semidouble rose-pink flowers (reminiscent of large, single hollyhocks) in August and early September. Like the prunus, its distinctive form and branch structure make it an interesting feature even in winter. (See plan for location of prunus and hibiscus.)

The lawn area, at the far end of the garden, comes as a total surprise. It is so completely hidden by borders planted with evergreen and deciduous flowering shrubs, you don't even know it is there till you're standing in the middle of the small grass courtyard by the front door. Barely 60 by 30 feet, the lawn seems much larger than it really is. Part of this effect, of course, is due to the contrast with the rest of the garden's narrow spaces and dense plantings. Equally important, however, is the way Nancy chose to enclose it.

To separate the lawn from neighboring back yards, Nancy erected wooden fences of various heights and styles. Along sections next to driveways and dumpsters, the fences were tall and solid. Covered with shade-tolerant vines, including *Hydrangea anomala petiolaris* and *Actinidia kolomikta,* with its dark green, heart-shaped leaves marked with pink and white, the fences became a distinctive part of the garden instead of a boring barrier.

Along other sections of the property line, where views into neighboring back yards are attractive, low picket fences were installed. One sees over them, so instead of ending at the fence, the garden seems to continue. Similar to the Japanese use of "borrowed scenery," these "borrowed" views into neighboring yards played a major role, giving the garden the illusion of greater depth and making it seem larger.

Nancy next dug a border (fairly wide in some spots, narrower in others) around the perimeter of the lawn. Then, instead of a straight wall of evergreens, she planted shade-tolerant deciduous flowering shrubs selected for their varied foliage, branch structures, and growth habits.

The placement of these shrubs was critical. To shape the lawn area and to break up the straight line and hard angles of the fence, Nancy arranged the shrubs in different size groupings or as specimens for seasonal highlights. Viburnums, including *Viburnum carlesii* 'Compactum', oakleaf hydrangea (*Hydrangea quercifolia*), *Kerria japonica* 'Aureo-variegata', and other shrubs that Nancy chose were then underplanted with deciduous and evergreen ground covers. *Vinca minor* 'Alba', *V. minor* 'Bowles Variety', with its large, deep blue flowers, *Hedera helix* 'Baltica' (one of the hardiest ivies), and low-growing variegated euonymus were planted in sweeping masses. Groupings of hosta and ferns and areas of European ginger (*Asarum europaeum*), with shiny, kidney-shaped leaves, created additional contrasts of shape and texture.

Ground covers, both evergreen and deciduous, are used throughout the garden, and like the trees and shrubs, they play a major role in establishing the character of its different areas. The entry area, for example, has the look of a slightly wild and woodsy country garden—partly, of course, due to the picket fence and the trees, particularly the flowering crab apple that frames the wooden gate.

Just as important are the ferns and succession of flowering ground covers planted in thick masses along the edges of the bluestone walk and beneath the umbrella pine and flowering dogwood. In early May, the masses of tiny, fragrant white flowers of sweet woodruff (*Galium odoratum*) combine with blue and white violets, the periwinkle blue flowers of *Vinca minor,* and the tiny, pink, heart-shaped flowers of fringed bleeding heart (*Dicentra eximia*). In June, *Geranium sanguineum,* with its small, magenta flowers, and *G. sanguineum* 'Album' flower along the edge of the path.

To lighten up shady corners, Nancy planted several variegated ground covers. "A lot of people say they don't like variegated plants," she says, "but some of them certainly have a wonderful place in the garden—the variegated pachysandra, for example, planted under the dogwood. During the summer the shade is very dense and it gives the garden a little extra lift. The *Lamium maculatum* I planted along the left side of the bluestone path gives a dappled effect, like sunlight, even on cloudy days."

In the partial shade along the edge of the perennial border, Nancy planted lungwort (*Pulmonaria saccharata*), with its dark green, heart-shaped leaves mottled with white spots. Dur-

In mid-July, the view across the lawn at the back of the house features oak-leaved hydrangea (Hydrangea quercifolia) *underplanted with various ground covers including European ginger* (Asarum europeaum), Vinca minor, *and* Hedera helix 'Baltica', *one of the hardiest ivies.*

ing April its tiny new leaves and drooping clusters of bluish, trumpet-shaped flowers mingle with species daffodils and bright red species tulips. After it is through blooming, its heart-shaped leaves remain a handsome foliage accent right through the summer.

As is so often the case with cottage-style perennial borders, Nancy's developed gradually, over a period of years. Instead of drawing a plan on paper, she began by poking in plants given to her by friends and relatives or dug from her mother's garden. Other perennials were chosen for fragrance,

cutting, or drying.

In her first attempts to recreate her idea of an old-fashioned, English country border, Nancy began by planting varieties of sun-loving perennials, including hollyhocks and hybrid delphiniums, but because the border received at most about five hours of

Planted in partial shade, Kerria japonica *'Pleni- flora' provides a bright spot of color in May. A self- seeded purple- flowered honesty* (Lunaria annua) *creates a striking contrast.*

sun a day (even at the height of sum- mer), these and other plants struggled for a few years, then died out. Rather than giving up and throwing in the trowel, she kept on trying new and different plants—some she would never have thought of in the first place. She found that as the garden changed, so did her ideas on which plants would create the garden of her dreams. After several years of trial and error, the border began to assume its present form, with a core of peren- nials such as bleeding heart (*Dicentra spectabilis*), Siberian iris (*Iris sibirica*), and various daylilies (*Hemerocallis* hybrids) that thrive in the partially shady location.

Over the years, she also discovered that a good many plants usually listed in catalogs as requiring full sun suc- ceed with less. Gas plant (*Dictamnus*

albus) and *Artemisia ludoviciana albula* 'Silver Queen', for example, thrived. Combined with yellow daylilies and the blue-flowered spikes of false indigo (*Baptisia australis*), they became important features in June. In July, bee balms *Monarda didyma* and *M. didyma* 'Croftway Pink' are high- lights, along with globe thistle (*Echi- nops ritro*) and bright yellow daylilies. The bee balm, planted in clumps close to the edge and toward the middle of the border, continues blooming well into August with shaggy red or pink flowers on 2½- to 3-foot stems.

The maintenance for this border is low, largely because it is small and the majority of the plants don't need stak- ing or frequent division. In fact, *Bap- tisia australis, Dicentra spectabilis,* and *Dictamnus albus* actually resent distur- bance and are much happier left

alone. The hemerocallis can be left undivided indefinitely, whereas the *I. sibirica* seem to do best if divided about every four or five years.

A few of Nancy's border plants, including *Artemisia ludoviciana albula* 'Silver Queen' and *Monarda didyma,* spread by underground roots and can be a bit rampant. The artemisia's silver foliage, however, is such a valuable filler and complement to all the bor- der's pink and blue flowers, Nancy just pulls it out when and where it begins to invade the root balls of nearby plants. As for the bee balm, a favorite of hummingbirds, if it spreads a bit, it too is easy enough to yank out.

Nancy is equally philosophical about plants self-sowing. Some self- sown seedlings, such as phlox and hibiscus, are weeded out, but most plants, including honesty (*Lunaria annua*), a feature of the border's April and June display, are allowed, even encouraged, to self-seed.

"Because I want the border to be very informal, I let plants grow where they select to grow," Nancy says. "I put them in where I want them, ini- tially, but if they seed somewhere else I figure that's exactly where they should be."

BLUE FLOWER COTTAGE

CORGI COTTAGE

Deep within the woods of southern Vermont, Tasha Tudor has created a most romantic cottage-style garden, with apple trees and lilacs and borders spilling over with peonies and pinks. Chock full of shrub roses and fragrant, flowering shrubs, as well as dozens of varieties of old-fashioned perennials, it represents American cottage gardening at its best.

Begun over 15 years ago, the garden surrounding Corgi Cottage has gradually developed into a delightfully complex arrangement of variously styled "garden rooms," each with a unique character. Stone walls built of local field stone divide the area immediately surrounding the cottage, and the hillside below, into two long terraces. Planted with borders of different styles, these terraces form the garden's central framework. Built into the walls are secret stone stairways (nearly hidden by old-fashioned flowering shrubs) and narrow stone steps leading to honeysuckle-covered arbors and intimate little gardens.

The entire garden is full of interesting and helpful ideas for Americans interested in cottage gardening. Along the front of the cottage, for example, Tasha's foundation borders create a series of distinctive little gardens that establish a most intimate connection between the cottage and garden. Instead of the usual straight lines of yews and rhododendrons that so often create a barricade between American homes and the surrounding landscape, her borders are laid out in graceful curves and planted with deciduous flowering shrubs and roses and underplanted with spring bulbs, perennials, and herbs.

(Above) Pots and window boxes of annuals including pink pelargoniums and richly fragrant, purple-flowered heliotrope provide color from June to frost on the front porch outside the kitchen door.

(Opposite) The foundation borders along the front of the house feature old-fashioned lilacs (Syringa vulgaris), *box* (Buxus sempervirens), *and masses of sprawling, white-flowered valerian* (Valeriana officinalis).

These foundation borders provide a delightful succession of bloom and fragrance, beginning in early spring with common lilacs *(Syringa vulgaris)*, one of Tasha's favorite plants, remembered from the gardens of her childhood. Planted in half a dozen key spots, beside doorways and windows, so their fragrance wafts through the cottage on spring afternoons, lilacs are one of the garden's highlights. In the partially shady border where cottage and barn meet, two gnarled and knobby *S. vulgaris* are a distinctive year-round feature, but they are really at their best in May, when in bloom with deep purple flowers and underplanted with the most delicate combinations of bleeding heart *(Dicentra spectabilis)*, spring bulbs, and dozens of different violets, including *Viola cornuta*.

By June, the borders surrounding the lilacs have changed character completely—the lilacs have faded into the background, and light green and yellow-edged hostas and the dark green leaves of *D. spectabilis* create a dense fabric of contrasting textures. Spikes of pink and purple foxgloves *(Digitalis purpurea)* provide color. Later in the summer, the borders bloom again—this time with the blue and white flowers of hostas.

Old-fashioned shrubs mock orange

(*Philadelphus* hybrids), deutzia (*Deutzia* hybrids), and beautybush (*Kolkwitzia amabilis*), all selected for their fragrant flowers and loosely branched growth habits, highlight various corners of the foundation border in June. Planted as accents to soften the corners of the house and barn, philadelphus, with its white flowers shaped like small camellias, deutzia, with its cascades of small white flowers, and kolkwitzia, with small, pink, trumpet-shaped blooms, are pruned sparingly, mostly to remove dead wood. Left to assume their natural shapes, they are now almost 10 feet tall, a bit gangly but full of personality, their branches arching over the path. (See Plan of Corgi Cottage for location.)

In the sunny border along the back of the cottage, the rose 'Mme Plantier' is another June feature. A vigorous and versatile grower that will also tolerate a certain amount of shade, it can reach up to 20 feet if trained into the branches of a small tree. Here, 'Mme Plantier' is a loose mound, however, about 5 feet tall and 6 feet wide, its arching canes covered with large clusters of fragrant, pale, creamy white flowers from June to about the end of July. A dark purple clematis intertwines among the rose's grayish-green leaves and continues to keep that corner of the border colorful right into

Along the front of the cottage, a gnarled and lichen-covered lilac is underplanted with white-flowered valerian (Valeriana officinalis) *and later-blooming asters.*

September.

In the border surrounding 'Mme Plantier', white foxgloves (*Digitalis purpurea* 'Alba') and valerian (*Valeriana officinalis*) with umbels of white flowers on 5-foot stems create a lacy yet pleasingly exuberant combination. When valerian is through blooming it is cut back, and its dark green, pinnate leaves remain an attractive background for late-blooming summer phlox (*Phlox paniculata*) and the annuals nicotiana and white alyssum.

At the far end of this border, Tasha planted 'Cuisse de Nymphe', a very old rose dating back to the fifteenth

century. Placed at the corner of the house so its canes would arch gracefully over the path, 'Cuisse de Nymphe' blooms from June to the end of July with fragrant, blush-pink flowers set amid blue-green leaves. One of the first roses Tasha planted, it has proved hardy during the coldest, snowless winters, when temperatures dropped to −20°F.

Any doubts I had about growing shrub roses (old and new) in colder areas of the United States were certainly alleviated as I walked around Tasha's garden. Not only were the roses large and healthy, but a good many, such as 'Mme Hardy', 'Queen of Denmark', *Rosa rubrifolia,* or *Rosa glauca,* 'Tour de Malakoff', and 'Rosa Mundi', a very old Gallica with light crimson and white stripes, were the very ones I'd seen in English cottage gardens.

Roses, I discovered in England, are among the most important features of a well-designed cottage garden. Planted next to a house or cottage, roses can highlight or soften architectural details. Combined with either deciduous or evergreen shrubs, roses can transform even the most traditional foundation plantings.

Shrub and climbing roses planted along the edges of paths or over arbors help make intimate, inviting

spaces. Placed as focal points at the end of a path, at the corners of a house, or beside a doorway, they emphasize important points in the landscape and help create a garden's framework. As Tasha so aptly put it, "Placement is everything."

Corgi Cottage features dozens of old-fashioned shrub roses everywhere, from foundation plantings to the vegetable garden. Roses are also highlights in the plantings surrounding a

(Above) The shrub rose 'Mme Hardy' frames the door and provides an emphatic statement at the end of the border full of sprawling Valeriana officinalis. *At the end of the house, the delicately perfumed, pink rose 'Cuisse de Nymphe' was planted to arch over the path and steps leading to the lower terrace.*

(Left) With fragrant, pink flowers and grayish-green foliage, 'Cuisse de Nymphe', also known as 'Maiden's Blush', flowers in June and July.

(Above) *In the partial shade beneath an old apple tree,* Digitalis purpurea, Aquilegia *hybrids, and* Hesperis matronalis *have self-seeded. In the foreground grows a clump of the biennial sweet William (*Dianthus barbatus *'Newport Pink').*

(Opposite) *The borders along the edge of the grass terrace in front of the cottage feature white-flowered perennials, including gas plant (*Dictamnus albus*), peonies, bearded irises, and dianthus, set against a background of pale, silvergreen foliage of annual opium poppies (*Papaver somniferum*). Self-seeded blue and white forget-me-nots (*Myosotis palustris*), pink and yellow columbines (*Aquilegia *hybrids), and blue peachleaved bellflowers (*Campanula persicifolia*) are fillers. Beginning later in June, the pale pink and crushed raspberry* Papaver somniferum *are features, followed by* Phlox paniculata.

little sitting area beneath an arbor where Tasha serves tea. Here, a rose Tasha calls 'Father Hugo's Rose' *(R. hugonis)* blooms in May in combination with *Dicentra spectabilis* 'Alba'

and blue forget-me-nots (*Myosotis* species). "It is the earliest-blooming rose I know of, and I think, one of the loveliest," Tasha says. "Very dainty and very vigorous, with delicate green foliage."

In the same sitting area, Tasha has also planted 'Agnes', a non-recurrent rugosa hybrid with dark green, crinkled leaves and fragrant, amber-yellow flowers, a color Tasha describes as "delicious."

For a long season of interest Tasha planted the species rose *Rosa rubrifolia*. In June, it blooms with clusters of small, soft mauve-pink flowers set against purple stems and foliage. Roses are not usually planted for their foliage, but *R. rubrifolia* is one of the exceptions. Excellent for use as a hedge or against a north wall, it is planted on a bank in Tasha's garden, where its deep plum-colored autumn foliage and clusters of deep reddish-purple hips are seen from the upper terrace and the lower garden.

For years, *R. rubrifolia* was surrounded by masses of white madonna lilies *(Lilium candidum)*, a most delicate combination, but over the years the lilies died out and last spring the rose was underplanted with masses of *Hosta plantaginea,* with dark green leaves and fragrant white flower stalks in late summer. Planted about 12

years ago, the *R. rubrifolia* has weathered some hard winters, but the winter of 1988–1989 (a very cold one, without the usual protecting snow cover) proved almost too much. Killed back to the ground, it began its comeback last spring with bright, copper-red new growth.

When Tasha first started planting roses, she ordered a good many from a nursery specializing in old roses. Several, including one planted in the border at the base of the stone steps, turned out to be wrongly labeled. Instead of yanking it out, she waited to see what it would do. Now, many years later, this still-unnamed rose towers 15 feet above the border, gnarled and knotted, like some idiosyncratic garden sculpture. The pink flowers are small and pretty, but not very showy. "But it has the most beautiful orange hips that last all winter long," explains Tasha, "and it is so lovely in the white snow, its hips covered with ice and the sun shining through."

Roses are also features in the main perennial border along the terrace below the cottage. Trained up pillars and allowed to grow into large, bushy mounds, a variety of roses create important seasonal accents in scale with this large border and the luxuriant, slightly billowy look characteris-

tic of cottage-style borders.

At the far end of the border, near the stone steps, Tasha planted the rose 'Reine des Violettes', or 'Queen of the Violets'. This hybrid perpetual rose will often bloom throughout the summer, but in June it is really at its peak—a wonderful wild mound of soft gray-green foliage with hundreds of the richest violet flowers touched faintly with cerise.

A longer-blooming rose is 'Nevada'. A vigorous, dense shrub that can grow about 8 feet tall and almost as wide, it flowers heavily in June, and it usually will flower intermittently throughout the summer months, then put on another good display in autumn. Planted against the stone wall at the rear of the perennial border, its large, loose, single, cream-colored flowers with dark gold stamens create a lovely background for the electric blue Italian bugloss

Anchusa azurea 'Dropmore' and the purple flower sprays of meadow rues (*Thalictrum* species).

"Looking down at her from the upper terrace, she is ravishing," says Tasha of 'Nevada'.

The border itself is a lovely, slightly mad jumble, with plants sprawling over the edges and each other. The colors are mostly pale pinks, roses, mauves, and dozens of different blues, with an occasional bold splash of red for contrast. Almost 100 feet long and 8 feet deep, the border is the garden's *pièce de résistance* in June and July; as is the case with any really good perennial border, the placement and combinations of its plants have evolved over the years.

"I've never made a garden plan," Tasha says. "I see it in my head then just stick the plants in."

Like many cottage gardeners with whom I talked, Tasha plants perennials as seasonal features, to create groupings—or what she calls pictures. In May, for example, foxgloves (*Digitalis purpurea*), globe flowers (*Trollius* species), and Siberian irises (*Iris sibirica*) are features, surrounded by columbines (*Aquilegia* hybrids), Johnny-jump-ups (*Viola tricolor*), and lush sweeps of blue forget-me-nots (*Myosotis* species).

In June the borders feature roses,

In the golden light of a spring afternoon, the main perennial border (on the terrace below the house) is full of the promise of June, with red peony shoots and the fresh green foliage of Siberian irises and delphiniums.

red and white peonies, bearded irises, foxgloves, and lupines in various shades of blue, purple, and pink, surrounded by purple and white honesty *(Lunaria annua)* and a dozen different campanulas, including *C. carpatica* and *C. persicifolia.*

Pink and white dianthus, lavender, and lady's mantle *(Alchemilla mollis)* spill over the edges. Planted at more or less regular intervals, these edging plants maintain the border's soft, informal look, and their various textures and foliage forms give the edge a distinct yet subtle rhythm that is sustained throughout the season.

Walking along Tasha's border late one June afternoon, it occurred to me that her style of maintenance and her unique horticultural practices play a large part in establishing her garden's distinctive character. In most gardens, for example, peonies are held upright with metal hoops. As a result, "properly staked" peonies often become beautiful, well-mannered, but isolated specimens. Many of Tasha's peonies, on the other hand, are not staked but are left to bow gracefully beneath the weight of their blooms. In the main border the combination of red and white peonies lying low amid violas and campanulas creates a contrast as beautiful as it is unlikely.

For a number of years, Tasha also

In June, the main border is a delightful sprawl of old-fashioned perennials, including Valeriana officinalis. *The spikes of foxgloves* (Digitalis purpurea) *and lupines* (Lupinus *hybrids) provide vertical accents.*

planted peonies in the border along the edge of the top terrace for a totally different effect. Placed close to the edge of the wall and left unstaked, the peonies cascaded over the wall. From the middle terrace one looked up into their large, sensuous blooms—a most unexpected and delightful way to view peonies.

In late June and July the main border features white, dark blue, and lavender Japanese irises *(Iris ensata)* combined with orange-gold globeflower *(Trollius* hybrids) and large clumps of blue, pink, and mauve delphiniums *(Delphinium* hybrids). *Delphinium* 'Guinevere', a lovely mauvepink, is one of Tasha's favorites, both in bud and in bloom. Planted in several places throughout the border, 'Guinevere' is also combined with

large groups of white martagon lilies *(Lilium martagon* var. *album)*, the white form of the turk's-cap lily.

The spaces surrounding delphiniums, peonies, and other feature perennials are packed solid with fillers, including horned violets *(Viola cornuta)*, fragrant white and mauve sweet rocket *(Hesperis matronalis)*, and sweet William 'Newport Pink'. The foliage of various artemisias and dianthus creates silver highlights that illumine the border with an almost ethereal quality.

Single and double hollyhocks *(Alcea rosea,* or *Althaea rosea)* are features toward the rear of the border. Originally grown from seeds collected in her mother's garden and from Tasha's old garden in New Hampshire, these single hollyhocks range in color from hot reds and yellows to soft apricot and a lovely "watermelon pink." Planted in groups of 6–12 plants roughly 8 inches apart, they begin blooming in July and continue into August as the flowers open higher and higher up the 7-foot stalks. Although usually classified as biennials, sometimes plants (particularly the singles, which Tasha describes as more vigorous than the doubles) will live for several years. Each year Tasha lets selected hollyhocks set seed to assure a steady supply of seedlings.

One major drawback to hollyhocks is their susceptibility to rust, a disease that begins as orange spore cases on the leaves and eventually turns them brown. Tasha, who is keenly aware of the natural ecological balance in her garden, doesn't like to spray with chemicals; instead, she plants things such as a variety of hollyhock mallow, *Malva alcea* 'Fastigiata', in front of the hollyhocks to hide their rusted foliage. About 3 1/2–4 feet tall with a bushy, branching habit, this plant blooms in July with pink, translucent flowers shaped very much like miniature single hollyhocks, and if the faded flower stalks are cut back to the main stalk before they have gone to seed, the plant will continue flowering right through August in combination with summer phlox (*Phlox paniculata*) and several different monkshood (*Aconitum* hybrids).

This succession of feature perennials helps give the border its structure by highlighting specific areas or creating strong splashes of color. But it is the small details, the delicate intermingling of various perennial and biennial fillers, that play an even larger part, perhaps, in giving Tasha's border its romantic style.

Among her favorite fillers are the hardy geraniums. Throughout the garden she grows about a dozen different kinds, their growth habits ranging from the dense, mounded masses of soft pink *Geranium sanguineum* var. *striatum* (*G. sanguineum lancastriense*) to the loose sprawling habits of *G. sanguineum* 'Album' and *G.* 'Johnson's Blue'. Most of these hardy geraniums bloom heavily in late May and June and are combined with other June-blooming plants including daisies, campanulas, roses, and peonies. The pink-flowered *G. sanguineum* var. *striatum*, unlike the other hardy geraniums in Tasha's garden, frequently will continue to flower intermittently right into September, when it pro-

The voluptuous blooms of peony 'Sarah Bernhardt' cascade into a lovely tangle of blue-flowered Geranium 'Johnson's Blue'.

duces another flush of bloom. (See Chapters 3 and 10 for more on hardy geraniums.)

Baby's breath *(Gypsophila paniculata)*, another perennial filler, is planted throughout the border to create the soft, almost impressionistic quality of which Tasha is so fond. To achieve this effect, Tasha doesn't wrap her plants with a cat's cradle of stakes and twine so they end up looking like big white beach balls when they bloom. Instead, she leaves her *G. paniculata* plants to sprawl luxuriantly through the borders, their airy sprays of white flowers mingling with blue *Campanula carpatica* and *Viola cornuta*. Unfortunately, *G. paniculata* is not reliably winter hardy in this border, with its damp soil, so each spring Tasha investigates to see how many plants made it through the winter, then she fills the inevitable gaps with young plants grown from seed and wintered over in pots in the cold frames.

A good many of Tasha's fillers are prolific self-seeders. This usually assures a steady supply of plants, but it can also require a bit of forbearance. In May and early June, for example, forget-me-nots envelop the border in a lovely and delicate froth of pale blue, but forget-me-nots can be as ephemeral as they are delicate. They

(Top) In June, the west end of the main border features red and white peonies against a background of budding delphiniums and candidum lilies and valerian. On the upper terrace, an old-fashioned beauty bush (Kolkwitzia amabilis) *arches over the path in a fountain of pink and yellow-throated flowers.*

(Above) Along the border's edge, regularly spaced clumps of pink-flowered dianthus and lady's mantle (Alchemilla mollis) *help give the voluminous planting a framework and pleasing sense of rhythm.*

do not reliably winter over, so to assure a steady crop from year to year Tasha leaves the plants till they look quite disreputable. Then when they have withered and seed pods are mature, the plants are finally cut back or pulled out, and any remaining seeds scattered in bare spaces among perennials.

Most self-seeders in this main border (and throughout the garden) don't really have any designated spaces. Instead, they are allowed to sow where they will and are thinned out if need be. The plants of *Viola tri-color* and *V. cornuta*, for example, were planted years ago. Now they are so abundant they have become like a ground cover, twining their lank stems around peonies, campanulas, and everything else.

Another of Tasha's favorite fillers, the biennial Sweet William 'Newport Pink' (a particularly lovely shade of apricot-pink) self-seeds true to color, so each year a few plants are left till the flower heads are dry and brown. The seeds are then either scattered in the border or planted in a specially prepared seed bed in the vegetable garden.

This propagating area is vital to the success of Tasha's border. Carefully orchestrated sowings of various seeds assures a steady supply of biennials, perennials that don't necessarily winter over, and smaller, filler perennials such as campanulas. When large enough to compete, the young plants are transplanted into the tightly planted borders.

"I like a nice scrambled garden," Tasha says. To give her borders their full, overflowing look, she spaces plants much more tightly than anything recommended in gardening books. "I believe in quantity. If I buy things, instead of buying two I'll buy six, and overplant. I find if you have an abundance of flowers, if there's a

(Above) A rustic wooden arbor set against the stone wall provides support for wisteria, honeysuckle, and climbing roses. To the right, a hedge of box (Buxus sempervirens) *edges the path.*

(Top) Bold spikes of self-seeded verbascum create a dramatic feature beside the door to Tasha's barn.

failure one year, at least you have something planted close by to fill in."

The plants are so tightly placed that there is stiff competition for available nutrients, so to help keep them healthy the borders are fed twice a year. In the autumn, after the heavy frosts, the plants are cut back and the borders are fed with 10/10/10 prepared organic fertilizer and lots of well-rotted manure. In spring, when the emerging perennials are still small (so working around them doesn't damage the tender new shoots), the same nutrients are again worked into all the borders.

Except for fertilizing, Tasha's style of gardening keeps her borders from being too labor-intensive. Many plants are often left to self-seed, so deadheading isn't as time-consuming as it might be, and since plants are so tightly spaced, and since self-seeding plants such as *Viola tricolor, V. cornuta,* and *Hesperis matronalis* quickly fill in any bare ground available to them, weeding is reduced.

During the past 20 years, Tasha has experimented extensively in her garden. She has not been one to follow blindly the advice of gardening magazines, books, or nursery catalogs as if they were some sort of gospel. She has found that nurseries tend to be overzealous in their descriptions of

In front of Tasha's greenhouse, rock walls spill over with yellow-flowered Corydalis lutea *and fragrant herbs mingle with dianthus and white-flowered snow-in-summer* (Cerastium tomentosum).

(Below) Along the edge of the border, the bold flowers of biennial Canterbury bells (Campanula medium) *contrast with sprawling mounds of* Geranium *'Johnson's Blue'.*

what a plant has to offer and tend to the conservative side (for their own protection, no doubt) when it comes to zone ratings.

Although Tasha has certainly read her share of gardening books, her knowledge of gardening is the result of trial and error. From wildly successful plantings to deeply mourned losses of favorite plants, she has come to know her garden intimately. She knows the sunny, protected corners where the snow melts first in spring, and she knows where the soil is damp

In August hundreds of hybrid lilies are the main feature of Tasha's garden.

very cold. Apart from the wind chill factor, temperatures can drop as low as -15–$20°F$, Zone 5, according to the U.S. Department of Agriculture. Tasha says that, just because a plant is listed for Zone 6 or 7 and she is in Zone 5, "That doesn't necessarily mean that you can't grow certain things. Because if you find just the right spot, you can. I've done it."

Box *(Buxus sempervirens)*, for example, is often listed as winter hardy only to Zone 7, but Tasha has planted it in several locations throughout the garden, both as a low hedge and as a specimen plant. Those outside the back door are over 10 years old and stand about 3 1/2 feet tall and about as wide. Pruned as loose balls, each winter they are protected with a wooden frame covered in burlap, and they come through the toughest winters unscathed.

Tasha also grows wisteria in a protected spot over a rustic wooden arbor. Most years it is simply an attractive mass of dark green leaves, but if the winter is mild and the temperature doesn't fall below $-10°$, the wisteria will be covered with deeply scented purple racemes. Those occasional springs when the wisteria does bloom, its fragrance perfuming the garden is a most generous reward for all those years of waiting.

or quick-draining. She has become, too, something of an expert on the garden's many microclimates.

Over the years, Tasha has become a knowledgeable gardener who knows

what cultural conditions her plants require, and she gives it to them. Even so, I was surprised to see some of the plants that thrived in her garden, because Vermont winters are

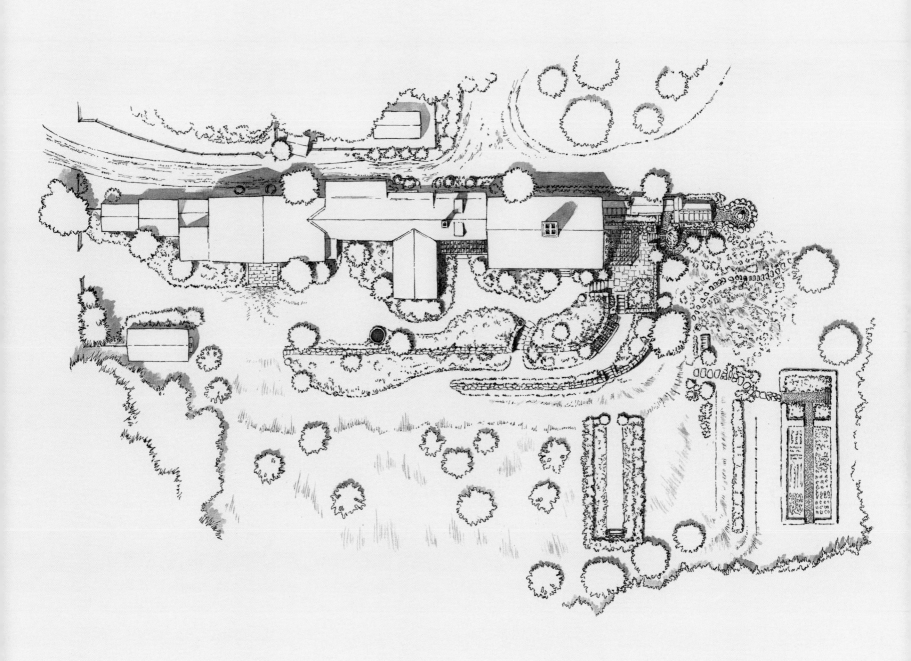

CORGI COTTAGE

CHAPTER 10

SPONTANEITY, COMBINATIONS, AND MAGIC IN MY GARDEN

(Opposite) In June, over a dozen named varieties of Siberian iris (Iris sibirica) *are the main feature of my garden. To the foreground, the white flowers of snow-in-summer* (Cerastium tomentosum) *cover a small slope. Below, a narrow sweep of common violets* (Viola odorata), *the pale, magenta-pink flowers of* Geranium macrorrhizum, *and to the left, the blue flowers of mountain bluet* (Centaurea montana).

(Right) In early June, the flowers of Iris sibirica *'Super Ego' are a bold accent. After it is through blooming, its deep green foliage remains an attractive feature right into autumn.*

ON WARM JUNE EVENINGS, when the fireflies gather in the soft light along the river's edge, my garden is a magical place. Clumps of pale blue and white *Iris sibirica* and the white candelabras of *Salvia argentea* are ghostly and beautiful in the dusk, and if I stand very still, just to the right of an old sage plant, I can make out the great blue heron wading in the shadows along the riverbank.

Although planted around an old, silver-sided barn, rather than a thatched cottage, my garden is a tightly planted, often spontaneous mix of plants; it is rich in pleasant associations. Bearded irises and lemon-yellow daylilies bring back memories of the garden where I grew up, and primulas and cottage pinks (started from divisions and cuttings) remind me of gardening friends and

old neighbors I have not seen in years. Here, too, grow a good many of the perennials I observed in England, old-fashioned favorites such as catmint *(Nepeta mussinii)*, lady's mantle *(Alchemilla mollis)*, peach-leaved bell-flower *(Campanula persicifolia)*, lamb's ears *(Stachys byzantina*, or *S. lanata)*, and lavender *(Lavandula angustifolia)*.

The cottage gardens I saw as I drove around England were full of fresh and spontaneous plant combinations. With more imagination than money, the gardeners there made the most modest yards lovely, personal spaces. A sunny front walk became a delightful herb garden, overflowing with lavender, half a dozen different thymes, silver-leaved dianthus, a few dark blue bearded irises, and peonies underplanted with lady's mantle. Right next door, the front walk might feature pink standard roses, great sprawling clumps of lavender and lamb's ear, catmint, and dozens of 6-foot regale lilies.

In many cottage gardens, *A. mollis, N. mussinii,* and *S. byzantina* were as common as cabbages, but each gardener had his or her own way of using these favorites. One gardener might mix them with old shrub roses, herbs, and perennials; another might use the same plants to edge a terrace, a path, or a small pool.

After observing the many ways these and other favorite cottage plants were used, I was curious to see how they translated into American gardens, particularly to the rigors of New England winters, with Zone 4 and 5 temperatures. How fast and wide would these various perennials spread? Would they form clumps or sprawling mounds or remain the same throughout the growing season?

In this garden combination, the violet-purple flower panicles and rich, gray-green leaves of sage (Salvia officinalis) *are the focal point, surrounded by the delicate white flowers of coralbells and the spear-like leaves of bearded irises. The silver-green foliage and white flower panicles of* Salvia argentea *provide the background.*

What would it take to maintain these old-fashioned favorites?

As a gardener and designer, I wanted to know what the foliage of various plants looked like, from the time they emerged in the spring right up to frost. Could the leaves of *A. mollis* and various hardy geraniums, including *G. endressii* 'Wargrave Pink' (so popular in cottage gardens), be relied upon for a good show till frost? Did *N. mussinii* really bloom "all summer," as the catalogs here in the United States say, or was it necessary

to cut it back as Tom Savery did in his Cotswold cottage garden? (See Chapter 7, "Gables.") If cutting back was required, how much and when? While I was traveling and photographing these cottage gardens, I wrote down my questions and kept an ongoing list of plants I wanted to grow and combinations I was anxious to try.

One of my first "cottage combinations" developed around a lavender (*Lavandula angustifolia*) from my mother's garden and a 15-year-old sage (*Salvia officinalis*). On my sunny slope on the banks of the Housatonic River, the lavender is now almost 3 feet across. The sage next to it has grown so big that when it blooms it rivals any peony for pure spectacle. Around this venerable specimen I've planted two varieties of bearded irises, *Geranium endressii* 'Wargrave Pink', *Salvia × superba* (sometimes sold as *S. nemorosa*) and *S. argentea, Stachys byzantina,* some pink and some white *Heuchera × brizoides,* and *Veronica* 'Crater Lake'.

In June this mixture of perennials and herbs is lovely and spontaneous. During the rest of the growing season, it offers a wonderful combination of silver-leaved plants and various foliage textures. With the salvias, stachys, and veronicas, there are a good many plants with spiky flowers, but they are so different from one another it is not repetitious, and there are sufficient mounded forms, including candytuft (*Iberis sempervirens*), cushion spurge (*Euphorbia epithymoides*), coralbells (*H. × brizoides*), and *G. endressii* 'Wargrave Pink', to unify the composition.

Here, as with most successful perennial groupings, the contrasts and harmonies of the foliage and plant forms are as important as the flowers. Against the thick spears of bearded irises, the slender flower stalks of lavender and coralbells appear even more graceful, while the ever useful *Stachys byzantina* becomes an effective textural and color complement to the fuzzy, silver-green foliage of *Salvia argentea,* the rich, green leaves of *S. officinalis,* and the blue-green bearded irises.

Over the years, I have collected a number of *Heuchera × brizoides,* including white 'June Bride', rose-pink 'Chatterbox' and vermillion 'Firebird'. Their clusters of small, bell-shaped flowers (on wiry stems held well above the clumps of rounded leaves) look lovely massed with epimediums in front of *Iris sibirica* or mingled with the fringed bleeding heart (*Dicentra eximia* 'Snowdrift') and *Iberis sempervirens*. At the front of a border or along the edge of a path,

both combinations have an airy delicacy when in flower and attractive foliage that lasts right up to frost.

The trick with heucheras, one cottage gardener told me, is to plant them with their crowns a good inch or so below the surface of the soil; this prevents them from heaving in the freezing and thawing of winter and early spring. The opposite is true of bearded irises. As Jean Sinfield at Yew Tree Cottage has pointed out,

bearded irises like their rhizomes in the sun.

Bearded irises and heucheras make a great pair for the front of the border, or along a path. After blooming in June, their contrasting foliage remains an effective combination and a foil for later-blooming perennials and foliage plants such as *Alchemilla mollis* and the silvery foliage of *Stachys byzantina*.

With low mats of silvery, soft,

With their rounded, scalloped leaves, coralbells remain an attractive edging plant long after their delicate sprays of tiny, bell-shaped flowers are past.

In the foreground, the silver flower stalks of lamb's ears (Stachys byzantina) *are surrounded by the dark purple flower spikes of* Salvia × superba. *In the background is a line of* Geranium himalayense *and behind that a wonderful, round mound of magenta* Geranium sanguineum.

tongue-shaped leaves, *S. byzantina* produces foot-high spikes of rather innocuous magenta blooms in late May and June. For about the first month, as they elongate, and for about two weeks after they first flower, the bloom stalks are an excellent ornamental and much needed vertical accent in my garden. After that, their freshness gone, they look disreputable, and if they are left till the end of the season, one has asked too much of an otherwise very useful plant. Sometime about midsummer, therefore, depending upon the weather, I cut the plants right back to the low leaves—a procedure that also seems to revitalize the plants, causing the leaves to grow even more lush as the summer goes on.

Many American gardeners I've talked with say they don't like *S. byzantina,* but I think this is a kind of plant snobbishness. I, along with many cottage gardeners, have found it to be a most useful plant along the edges of sunny paths and planted in masses. Combined with snow-in-summer *(Cerastium tomentosum), S. byzantina* is a wonderful filler for the spaces between the stones of steps, walls, and terraces. In perennial borders, its soft, silver foliage is a distinctive accent grouped at a corner or massed at the front edge.

The spacing and placement of plants in my garden has little to do with commonly accepted practices. The bearded iris rhizomes and heuchera crowns, for example, are practically touching one another, and the lavender is no more than 8 inches from the nearest heuchera. I like the effect of plants mingling, their foliage and flowers intertwined, and I often plant tall, bold plants at the edge of the border, counter to a good deal of popular advice.

Spacing and placement really varies, according to the effect I want to create. If I want to emphasize the form of something such as sage, it goes right up against the edge, where its bold form provides contrast in an edging of *Alchemilla mollis, Nepeta mussinii,* and clumps of tunic flower (*Petrorhagia saxifraga* or *Tunica saxifraga*). To the left and rear of the sage, the lavender is a bit cramped, but it is not meant to be a star; its flower spikes are simply a complement to the heucheras and a contrast to the green spears of iris foliage. Several *Salvia argentea* are planted about 10–12 inches apart, with scarcely enough room for their leaves, and even though I have to pinch off the leaves that have rotted from lying on top of one another, I like the silver foliage in a clump and the white-flowered can-

delabras like a huge bouquet.

If plants appear to be suffering or getting smothered by a neighbor, I move them. Much of the shifting around of plants is done in early spring, before the leaves have filled out, so invariably some things get lost and I rediscover them about midsummer. Once they are moved to where they have room to breathe, they recover nicely.

Another way I get a tight succession of bloom in this small space is to feature, wherever I can, a strong foliage plant, using it as a background for a succession of seasonal bloom. In one corner, for example, about a dozen *Iris sibirica* 'Caesar's Brother' and the shorter 'Sky Wings' form a background for a succession beginning with primroses (*Primula* species) and the hardy geraniums 'Hazel Gallagher' and 'Johnson's Blue', followed by oriental poppies (*Papaver orientale*), in bloom with the irises, *Campanula persicifolia* 'Telham Beauty', pyrethrums (*Chrysanthemum coccineum*), then Japanese anemones (*Anemone × hybrida*) in August and September.

Dark, purple-blue Iris sibirica *'Caesar's Brother' and the scarlet oriental poppy* (Papaver orientale) *are combined near the edge of the garden. To the right is a mass of the chartreuse flowers of the smaller-leaved lady's mantle* (Alchemilla glaucescens) *backed by a sweep of* Geranium macrorrhizum *and a scramble of* Geranium *'Johnson's Blue'.*

Epimediums, with delicate, orchid-like flowers held on wiry stems, are plants I also use for a long season of foliage interest. At one corner, half a dozen large clumps of *Epimedium × versicolor* 'Sulphureum' and an equal number of white-flowered *E. × youngianum* 'Niveum' are combined with forget-me-nots *(Myosotis alpestris)* and pale yellow primroses *(Primula vulgaris)* in front of a broad sweep of dark green *Iris sibirica*. After this early spring show and the deep purple irises are past, the mounds of heart-shaped epimedium leaves (in combination with the irises) remain an attractive edging right through the summer. In autumn, the epimedium foliage turns a rich reddish-bronze.

In another area of the garden, narrow drifts of about a dozen *Epimedium × versicolor* 'Sulphureum' and an equal number of *Dicentra eximia* 'Snowdrift' (with ferny, gray-green foliage) create an interesting contrast of textures and forms against the dark green sweeps of later-blooming astilbes and a large clump of July-blooming Japanese iris *(I. ensata)*.

One thing I don't do in this garden is to plant everything in groups of threes, contrary to advice in many gardening books and catalogs I've read. Sometimes I will use a single plant as an accent, or place a dozen plants in a

long, narrow drift. The number of perennials in a group depends upon the effect I want to achieve, a plant's ultimate height and width, and its character. I have found that the generally accepted Rule of Three is more of a hindrance than a help—three of any plant quickly become as arbitrary and dull as one of something, or five, or two.

One of the most popular plants in English cottage and country gardens is lady's mantle *(Alchemilla mollis)*. A handsome foliage plant 12–18 inches tall, with roundish, almost kidney-

The white flowers of Geranium sanguineum *'Album' create a delicate complement for the lilac and lavender flowers of* Iris sibirica *'Summer Sky' and the dark, purple-blue* I. sibirica *'Caesar's Brother'.*

shaped leaves 2–6 inches across, it flowers in July in England and New England, with chartreuse flowers held in panicles above the leaves. As odd as chartreuse may seem, in *A. mollis* it looks good and seems to combine well with virtually any flowering plant, in just about any style garden. Having seen it massed in front of simple cottages, thick along formal paths, practically burying teakwood benches, and combined with everything from herbs and roses to hostas and ferns, I wanted to grow it myself, observe its growth habits, and try propagating it. (See Chapter 3, "Cottage Plants.")

The soil in areas of my garden is not particularly fertile, but it is quite friable. Soil condition seems to make little difference to *A. mollis,* which I've seen growing with equal enthusiasm in gardens composed primarily of clay and subsoil. Some American catalogs suggest that *A. mollis* blooms pretty much all summer, but my experience has shown that it blooms heavily once, in late June and July. For about three weeks the flowers look good; after that, or earlier if it rains heavily, the plants look like matted straw, or worse.

The trick, I have found (if one is needed with such an obliging plant), is to cut off the flowers and a portion of the leaves after it blooms. Like the flowers, the leaves sprawl, and by midsummer the plant is no longer a tidy clump. If sheared after it blooms, however, the new leaves nestled in the crown will unfold in about three weeks, and the plants look full and fresh again. Sometimes plants will produce a second, smaller show of bloom.

In England, with its usually ample rainfall, if the flowers of *Alchemilla mollis* are not cut back at the appropriate time, the plants tend to self-seed with wild abandon. One summer a stone walk might have a dozen well-placed plants and the next year be almost solid with them. With its good looks and its ability to self-seed without becoming invasive, *A. mollis* is an exceedingly useful plant for gardeners beginning or expanding a garden. Self-sown seedlings are easily dug up and transplanted. It is also readily propagated from divisions and does an admirable job of covering bare ground and keeping down weeds.

Though hardy in Zones 3–9, *A. mollis* is not yet a mainstay in American gardens, so my first plants came from a nursery rather than from a gardening friend. The first thing I did when I got them home was knock them out of their pots. Each pot was filled with a nice, thick ball of roots, ready to be divided.

The chartreuse flowers of Alchemilla mollis *mingle with a sprawling mound of white-flowered* Geranium sanguineum 'Album'. *In the background the flowers of* G. sanguineum 'Album' *and* G. sanguineum *var.* striatum *combine to form a dense mound of attractive, dark green foliage covered with pink and white flowers.*

Holding the plants submerged in a bucket of water, I worked my fingers into the root balls, loosening the soil. Once the soil washed away, I could see the individual crowns, central nubs from which the leaves grew. Gripping a handful of foliage in either hand, right close to the crown, I gently pulled the plants apart. About 15 minutes later, I counted three

dozen new plants, many with a dozen or more leaves, and a few pretty scrawny things with only one or two small roots.

Nestled in the crown of even the tiniest plant were new leaves all curled up waiting to unfold. To reduce transplanting shock, I took a pair of clippers and removed about half, or more, of the mature leaves. I then planted all the divisions about 6 inches apart in a shallow trench dug along the edge of the garden, covered them with soil, and watered them.

By late May of the following spring, all but the tiniest divisions had filled out to 4–6 inches across. In autumn I repeated the procedure. After two years I had over a hundred plants, a good many of which went into a larger holding garden.

Division is a wonderful—and wonderfully inexpensive—way to increase a plant collection. However, plants such as peonies, false indigo (*Baptisia australis*), and my 15-year-old sage (*Salvia officinalis*) can and should be left undisturbed. Others, such as *Iris sibirica*, require periodic division. If left undisturbed, the plants will eventually die out in the center, leaving a dense ring of foliage. This ring may continue to bloom, but the number of flowers decreases each year.

How often a plant—*I. sibirica*, for example—needs division depends upon many factors, beginning with how large it was when planted, growth rate, amount of rainfall, and, of course, the soil. If the soil is a well-drained, fertile loam rich in humus, as opposed to poor soil such as clay that dries solid in the heat of summer, *I. sibirica* may need to be divided every three or four years, whereas in a poorer soil less frequent division will be adequate.

Dividing plants is not some esoteric practice; it is mostly common sense. Once a plant is dug out of the ground or removed from its pot and some of the soil knocked off its roots, a careful inspection will usually reveal how it grows and the best way to divide it. *I. sibirica*, for example, grows from a single crown, and a five-year-old clump may contain up to several dozen plants.

Red valerian (*Centranthus ruber*, or *Valeriana rubra*), catmint (*Nepeta mussinii*), and lady's mantle (*Alchemilla mollis*) are cottage garden staples, but it was their uses at Crabb Cottage in Somerset and Gables in Gloucestershire—where they were planted as edgings along paths, borders, and stone walls—that convinced me to try growing them myself. (See Chapter 3, "Cottage Plants," and Chapter 7, "Gables.")

I have seen *Centranthus ruber* listed as hardy from Zone 6 in some catalogs, but it has wintered well for several years in my Zone 5 garden on a sunny, well-drained, not very fertile slope. I have also discovered that it requires the absolute minimum of care. The most I do for it is to cut the flower stalks after they have finished blooming, usually sometime in August, and trim the plant down to the ground in late October or November.

Nepeta mussinii, on the other hand, has required a bit of experimentation to maintain it as an attractive gray-green foliage accent throughout the growing season. Again, as with many herbaceous perennials, maintenance plays a vital part in sustaining a garden's design through the growing season.

In my garden, *N. mussinii* blooms with violet-blue spikes from late May into July. The first year I grew it, it was in full bloom when a heavy rain absolutely flattened the already sprawling flower stalks. I spent about two hours untangling and propping up this pile of matted stems. Then I realized it didn't look much better than when I began, so I took a pair of hedge shears and reduced the entire edging to ugly, stubby stems about 8 inches high. Three weeks to a month later, the plants had filled out and looked respectable and, true to what I'd read, flowered heavily again in September.

The following year I tried to anticipate the inevitable: before the plant came into bloom I poked in green bamboo stakes (as inconspicuously as possible) along the entire edging. To avoid cutting back the plants while still in flower, leaving another edge of stubble. I trimmed back portions of each plant, leaving stems about 8–10 inches tall. For the most part, this selective pruning wasn't even noticeable, and by the time the remaining flowers had faded and were ready to be cut back the clipped sections had leafed out and were coming into bloom. Although this approach didn't allow for such a big repeat show in September, the edging did look better for a longer period.

There are a number of nepetas offered for sale here in the United States. In many catalogs, *N. mussinii* and *N.* × *faassenii* are offered interchangeably. I have grown them both (or at least have ordered both) and am hard put to tell the difference. *N.* × *faassenii* is sterile, but *N. mussinii*, frequently raised from seed, has produced hybrids and varieties of various heights and shades of blue. 'Blue Wonder' is compact; 'Six Hills Giant' is a lighter blue and grows to about 2 feet. Both have larger leaves than *N. mussinii* or *N.* × *faassenii*.

In my garden, *N. mussinii* and *N.* × *faassenii* grow 12–18 inches tall and have remained compact mounds, about 18 inches across. Although they haven't needed dividing, a few springs ago I did want more plants so I lifted

about half a dozen clumps with a pitchfork and shook off some soil so I could see which roots were attached where. (Unlike *Heuchera* × *brizoides* and *Geranium endressii* 'Wargrave Pink', which grow from a central crown, a good-sized clump of *N. mussinii* is made up of stems, each with its own roots.) Next, I held half of each plant just above the roots and pulled. Sometimes the whole mass gave way in the middle; at other times I ended

In several areas of my garden, Nepeta *'Six Hills Giant' is planted in masses by itself. 'Six Hills Giant' is also combined with various flowering ground covers around large specimens of oriental poppies and peonies.*

up with only a tiny piece in one hand and had to dig into the clump with the pitchfork to pry apart the mass of roots. By the time I was finished, I had two dozen divisions of various sizes. In a few months they had become well-established plants—ready to be divided the next spring if I needed more *N. mussinii* for another area of the garden.

A year ago, I added *N.* 'Six Hills Giant' to my garden. Not readily available in nurseries here in the United States, my plant was a gift from a friend in Vermont, who said it did, in fact, bloom most of the summer, didn't flop, and didn't have to be cut back. If it is all it is reported to be, there is a good chance the existing nepetas in my garden are headed for the compost pile. I have read, however, that once established, 'Six Hills Giant' does tend to be invasive. We'll see.

Probably the most important plants in my garden are the hardy geraniums. Like alchemillas and nepetas, hardy geraniums are easily grown, easily divided, and versatile staples in English cottage gardens. At East End Farm, Margaret Wray planted *Geranium endressii* 'Wargrave Pink' underneath old-fashioned shrub roses. Combined with a wide selection of perennials, including Italian bug-

(*Above*) *A mound of* Geranium sanguineum *var.* striatum *and* G. sanguineum *creates an interesting contrast of foliage and growth habit for* Iris sibirica *'Super Ego' and the dark green leaves of* G. himalayense.

(*Left*) *One of the earliest hardy geraniums to flower is* Geranium *'Johnson's Blue'. Beginning about the middle of May, it creates a lovely sprawl of blue with clumps of early and mid-blooming* Iris sibirica.

loss (*Anchusa azurea*), mountain bluet (*Centaurea montana*), and fernleaf yarrow (*Achillea filipendulina*), *G. endressii* helped provide flowers and foliage interest once the extravaganza of June roses was past. In the borders at Yew Tree Cottage, Jean Sinfield created a totally different effect by combining *G. endressii* and *G. endressii* 'Wargrave Pink' with peonies, bearded irises, and nepetas. (See Chapter 6, "Roses Cottage Style," and Chapter 8, "Yew Tree Cottage.")

Most of the hardy geraniums in my garden bloom in late May or late May and June, beginning with the sprawling, white-flowered 'Hazel Gallagher'. Some, including the 18-inch, dark purple *G. platypetalum,* bloom once. Others, such as the 12-inch pink-flowered *G. sanguineum* var. *striatum (G. sanguineum lancastriense),* bloom in June, then lightly through the summer into autumn. Also in June, *G. psilostemon (G. armenum)* produces magenta-carmine flowers with a black center; it grows 3–3 1/2 feet tall, producing a scattering of bloom right through the summer.

Of all the geraniums, *G. sanguineum* var. *striatum* is probably my favorite. A more pleasing pink than the shocking magenta of *G. sanguineum, G. sanguineum* var. *striatum* grows densely, with small, beautifully formed, long-lasting leaves, and makes an excellent ground cover in the well-drained soil beside the barn.

According to a good many catalogs, *G. sanguineum* var. *striatum* blooms all summer. From my experience, it flowers heavily in June, a 2-by-3-foot clump covered with hundreds of small flowers. In August, September, and October, there might be only a few dozen flowers, but the foliage is so good from mid-April to November, when the leaves become a handsome red-bronze, that this geranium remains a feature right at the front of the garden.

Maintenance for *G. sanguineum* var. *striatum* is low. After its heavy June bloom, the plants will literally be covered with tiny seed pods resembling crane's bills. Rather than deadheading each flower (a tedious process that would take hours), I take handfuls of the faded stems and cut part of each plant back about 5–6 inches. This creates some variation in the height of the mound, so it doesn't look as if it had a crew cut. If gardening time is short, or I have more important tasks, I wait till the seed pods are dry and brown, then run the tops of the plants through my clenched hands to remove the seeds.

Planted on 1-foot centers (12 inches between plants), this geranium will increase by thick underground roots; by the second year the clump is so dense that weeds have a hard time getting started. Although it fills in quickly, *G. sanguineum* var. *striatum* is by no means invasive, nor does it have to be separated and divided every few years. In my garden, four- and five-year-old clumps are still healthy and continue to flower heavily each June.

Rather than dividing *G. sanguineum* var. *striatum,* I take a shovel and cut into the edge of a clump to sever the underground stems. Sometimes I'll lift out a separate plant, soil intact on its roots, but more often the roots (about the thickness of a pencil) will come away bare. These I then plant about 3 inches deep and water thoroughly, so the soil settles in around them. If it is in the heat of summer, I cut off most of the plant's top growth and shade the plants for a few days with newspapers to help the plants adjust.

Geranium endressii and its larger-flowered cultivar, 'Wargrave Pink', are popular geraniums in English cottage gardens. Combined with bearded irises and thymes beside stone walks, beneath old-fashioned shrub roses, along grassy woodland paths, and as a ground cover with hostas, they are most versatile perennials. In my garden 'Wargrave Pink' plays a small but significant role, its salmon-pink flowers combining well with a variety of June perennials, including *Veronica* 'Crater Lake', both pink and white *Heuchera* × *brizoides, Stachys byzantina,* and, of course, bearded irises. In the sunny, well-drained site of my garden, 'Wargrave Pink' has one fault, but it is a major one. By July, even good-size plants are reduced to brown nubs of burnt leaves. Only in autumn, when the weather cools and the rains come, does the foliage become green again. In areas of the United States with consistently cool, moist climates, such as the Pacific Northwest, the foliage of *G. endressii* and *G. endressii* 'Wargrave Pink' remains attractive throughout the growing season.

In some places in the garden, where I want more permanent ground covers, through summer into autumn, I have planted *Geranium macrorrhizum* and *G. macrorrhizum* 'Ingwersen's Variety' (with a clearer pink flower), *G. sanguineum,* and *G. sanguineum* var. *striatum.*

Yet another hardy geranium discovered in England is 'Johnson's Blue'. As with so many cottage plants, each gardener had his or her own way of combining it. At Cobblers in Sussex, for example, I found it combined with *Spiraea* 'Gold Flame'. At Gables in Gloucestershire it was planted along a woodland path with foliage plants, including *Brunnera macrophylla* and *Iris sibirica.* (See Chapter 5, "Cottage Style," and Chapter 7, "Gables.")

In my own garden, I planted *G.* 'Johnson's Blue' as part of a combination featuring *Alchemilla mollis, Veronica* 'Crater Lake', drifts of snowdrop anemone *(Anemone sylvestris),* a ground cover with white flowers about an inch across, *Iris sibirica* 'Sky Wings', and *Anemone × hybrida.* Although planned primarily for its

June bloom, the long-lasting foliage of this little grouping provides an interesting textural complement for the July bloom of *Alchemilla mollis* and *Astrantia major* 'Margery Fish', and the August and September show of *A. × hybrida.* A few years ago I added Japanese iris *(I. ensata)* to give July a bit more impact.

Like so many gardeners, I came completely under the spell of the June garden early on in my gardening career. With all the wonderful June plant choices, July, August, and certainly September were afterthoughts.

So about a year ago I took a more objective look at my garden, with all its old favorites, and added a few plants for mid- and late summer bloom.

Some of the plants, including pink-flowered *Malva alcea* 'Fastigiata', *M. moschata* 'Alba', *M. moschata* 'Rosea', and *Anemone × hybrida,* were not necessarily traditional cottage plants, but they contribute their own unique style. *Malva alcea* 'Fastigiata' became a feature by a fortuitous mix of accident and neglect. Originally a single plant, it self-seeded. The seedlings were

The fresh, fuzzy, silvery flower stalks of Stachys byzantina *are a highlight in a combination including deep blue* Veronica *'Crater Lake', dark purple* Salvia × superba, *and* Geranium endressii *'Wargrave Pink'.*

never weeded or thinned, and the following year several dozen plants (in an area approximately 3 by 4 feet) had grown into a large bush. Almost 5 feet tall and covered with hundreds of translucent, pale pink flowers resembling small hollyhocks, this stand of malva is truly spectacular. By another accident, I also discovered that it makes an excellent cut flower and, if cut every few days, will continue blooming right through the summer.

Coreopsis verticillata 'Moonbeam', with creamy yellow, daisy-like flowers, blooms from June right into September and is one of my garden's most prolific and longest-blooming perennials. About 2 1/2 feet tall, it grows in dense clumps with dark green, feathery foliage, does not require deadheading to maintain its continuous bloom or attractive appearance, and rarely needs staking. I have discovered, however, that when it is grown in gardens with very rich soil more frequent division is necessary to prevent the plants from getting too dense and flopping over.

Like *Alchemilla mollis*, *C. verticillata* 'Moonbeam' combines well with a wide range of perennials, so I use it in several places in the garden for very different effects. Combined with the dark purple-blue pincushion flower (*Scabiosa caucasica* 'Fama'), dark violet

Throughout my garden, Campanula persicifolia *are planted as fillers; combined with everything from heuchera to lavender.*

Campanula glomerata 'Superba', and dark blue *Delphinium* 'Connecticut Yankee', its creamy yellow flowers create contrast. But planted next to the silver barn, in combination with silver-leaved *Artemisia* 'Powis Castle', *Malva moschata* 'Alba', and *M. moschata* 'Rosea', *C. verticillata* 'Moonbeam' takes on a much softer character.

Other choices for midsummer bloom include old cottage favorites such as various yarrows, including *Achillea* 'Coronation Gold', *A.* 'Moonshine', *A. millefolium* 'Red Beauty', a dark blue flax (*Linum narbonense* 'Heavenly Blue'), pink or white summer phlox (*Phlox paniculata*), pink or blue balloon flower (*Platycodon gran-*

diflorum), and tall and dwarf varieties of Michaelmas daisies (*Aster novae-angliae* hybrids and *A. novi-belgii* hybrids), which bloom from August to mid-October.

Another cottage favorite, peach-leaved bellflower (*Campanula persicifolia*), begins blooming in June with blue or white bell-shaped flowers and is altogether lovely with shrub or pillar roses or mixed with hostas, epimediums, and *Brunnera macrophylla*. Most good gardening catalogs here in the United States offer *C. persicifolia*, *C. persicifolia* 'Alba', and *C. persicifolia* 'Telham Beauty', but knowing that this campanula blooms in June, grows 2–2 1/2 feet tall, and looks well next to a shrub rose is only a beginning.

After almost a decade of growing *C. persicifolia* and its varieties, I know something, although certainly not all, about their maintenance and how that affects their use in a design.

When I first planted these campanulas, I followed the recommendations of several books and used them as mid-border plants. This was fine when they were in bloom, but for the majority of the season their rather flat mats of green leaves left a big gap where I wanted height. Since then, I have combined them with July- and August-blooming perennials, or with plants whose foliage becomes a mid-summer feature. I also plant these campanulas along the edge of a walk or border, often with *Stachys byzantina* or pink-flowered tunic flower (*Petrorhagia saxifraga,* or *Tunica saxifraga*) and various silver-leaved dianthus. In this situation, their shiny, green leaves become part of a subtle complement of leaf forms and textures.

To extend the bloom of *C. persicifolia,* I have tried several approaches. One year, after the major flush of bloom was past, I cut back the stalks to about half. The plants then bloomed again from the secondary buds. The flowers were smaller and fewer, but the effect was still worthwhile. Another year, when the campanulas were still in full bloom, I wanted them as cut flowers for a party, so I cut them all to the basal leaves. Thinking that was the last I'd see of them for the year, I was surprised and delighted when they put up entirely new flower stalks and bloomed again in August.

Still another method I tried was picking off the faded flowers along the entire length of the flower stalk, rather than cutting the plants back. This worked to a certain degree, with some secondary bloom. But the secret, if you can bear to do it, seems to be to cut them when they are in full bloom, to prevent the plants from even beginning to set seed. Once the flowers are faded, some alarm seems to go off in the plants and they know their function for the year is complete. You can try to trick them into blooming again by removing the seed heads, but the signal has been given, and the blooms simply aren't as large or as numerous.

Periodic division of *Campanula persicifolia* is also essential for a good show of bloom. After three years, those planted as good-sized nursery plants had grown so well that their crowns were packed together like tiny sardines. Divided in the autumn, a single clump produced about four dozen new plants, most about the size of a thumbnail. After the plant was lifted and most of the soil shaken off, the largest of these baby campanulas were gently pulled apart from the mat of leaves and replanted in groups of about five, 4–6 inches apart. These divisions then took about a growing season to become decent blooming size. To avoid this gap in the bloom cycle, I began starting a new crop each year in a separate holding area. Now, when it comes time to divide the campanulas, I can replace them with nice-sized clumps.

I have found the strategy to maintaining perennials is knowing what to do, what not to do, and what to put off. A good many garden books give optimal times for pinching back this or pruning that, but many of my garden chores get done when I have the time. One year, for example, it was October before I got around to deadheading the *Iris sibirica,* and the seed pods were mature. These pods were so attractive and the plants no worse for my neglect, however, so I did the same thing the next year, painted the pods silver, and stuck them in our Christmas wreath.

For most of us, gardening is trial and error; no book written can tell us everything we need to know. No matter how much we read, no author will be there to hold our hand the first time we take up a hacksaw to divide an established clump of false indigo or set out to move a favorite peony in the heat of summer because the septic tank has backed up into the perennial border.

For the most part, I like surprises in a garden, and each fall I add plants I've never before grown. Usually I forget about them over the winter, or at least forget exactly where I put them, and the next year they come as a complete surprise. I guess that's one reason my garden doesn't have a fixed color scheme and, despite my profession and initial intentions, no fixed plan.

All this results, of course, in a certain amount of disorder. I can't begin to tell you, for example, the names of the three dozen different daylilies I planted six years ago. I also confess that my garden occasionally has its share of weeds. That's okay. I enjoy weeding, but there are other aspects to gardening I also enjoy. If everything in the garden were to be kept perfect, there would be less time to wander around and gather bouquets for summer picnics, or simply to sit and appreciate how beautiful it all looks silhouetted against mountains glowing golden in the summer twilight.

In late June, the single, pink peony 'Sea Shell', underplanted with sprawls of nepeta and hardy geraniums, is a fabulous focal point in one area of my garden.

(Top) The pink and dark pink flowers of Dianthus × allwoodii *'Alpinus' are wonderful massed in drifts along the edge of the garden. In several spots of the garden, they are particularly lovely used as an underplanting for lavender.*

(Left) Pink-flowered Malva alcea *'Fastigiata' and* Geranium himalayense *have self-seeded right next to the barn. If used as a cut flower, M. alcea 'Fastigiata' will continue flowering right into September.*

CONCLUSION

(Opposite) At Crabb Cottage in Somerset, a white picket gate opens onto a path edged with red valerian (Centranthus ruber). *To the left a climbing rose is trained against the house and underplanted with pink, red, and white annual tobacco* (Nicotiana *hybrids*) *in the narrow border between the cement walk and foundation.*

(Right) Johnny-jump-ups (Viola tricolor) *self-seeded amid a bed of lilies. In bloom from early April well into October,* Viola tricolor *look wonderful with everything from tulips to hardy geraniums and can usually be relied upon for a few flowers during warm spells in December and January.*

THROUGHOUT THIS BOOK I have talked about plants, design, and the horticultural skills required to create these lovely cottage gardens. But all this is only part of the story of cottage gardening. Even more important, cottage gardening is about the power of our imaginations to transform the world immediately around us, and our lives.

There is something miraculous about taking a forlorn bit of land and making it bloom. Cottage gardening is the stuff that fairy tales are made of. But perhaps even more miraculous than the blossoming of even the most humble plots of land is the transformation in the hearts and spirits of the gardeners who create the gardens.

For some gardeners, such as Margaret Wray at East End Farm, the garden is the years, the richness of life, a place where the blooming of a favorite rose is like the return of a dear and constant friend. For others, Jean Sinfield at Yew Tree Cottage, for example, the creation of a garden becomes an opportunity to set the imagination free so the wildest dreams come true. For many, a garden is a solace, a place of healing, and of inspiration and renewal.

Peter Parker-Smith lives in Crabb Cottage, a tiny stone house overlooking a lovely valley in the heart of Somerset. A retired schoolteacher, Peter began his garden shortly after the death of his wife. Working alone, he gathered stones, built walls, and slowly terraced the steep hillside in front of his cottage. Over a period of years he built arbors and benches, dug a tiny pond, and grew hundreds of plants from seeds and cuttings given to him by friends.

The result is a charming and fanciful creation full of humor, with rose-covered arbors, exotic-looking urns, and terraces edged with the most lavish lavender hedges. In this narrow hillside garden there are vistas and focal points and intimate little places to sit with views down to the river winding through the trees and meadows. It is an idyllic spot on summer evenings. Even in winter, the view down through the garden to the gentle folds of the surrounding hills is lovely and embracing.

Each year when the lavender is in bloom and its purple spikes are bright with yellow butterflies, Peter opens his garden to benefit a local charity. On these days the white picket gate is left open and a steady stream of people fills the grassy terraces, laughing together as they climb up and down the narrow stone steps spilling over with centranthus and roses. It is a festive occasion, and people from nearby towns bring picnics to eat while sitting beside the river. At the end of the

(Right) Planted between the stones along the edge of the path, Centranthus ruber *glows in the late afternoon sun. With fern-like foliage and delicate yellow flowers from May into September,* Corydalis lutea *has self-seeded in between the stones of the steps and walls.*

(Below) Annuals, including pink cosmos, fill the borders of the lower terrace.

(Opposite) At Crabb Cottage the garden is built on the steep hillside below the house and divided into terraces of various widths by stone retaining walls. Here, a terrace paved with concrete blocks and edged with lavender 'Hidcote' leads to a homemade arbor covered with climbing roses.

day, after much horticultural banter, Peter waves the last of his visitors goodbye and closes the gate with a smile.

I am fond of many of the gardens in this book because they are old-fashioned and picturesque. But more than combinations of plants or the placement of paths and arbors, it is the deep affection their owners have for their gardens and the ways in which these creations express the rich fabric of their lives that make them so beautiful.

One cottage garden that is a particular favorite of mine is that of American poet and writer Paul Smyth. Like many gardeners in this book, Paul

began with a most unpromising set of circumstances—in this case, an eighteenth-century house almost fallen into its cellar hole and a garden run wild to maple saplings and bittersweet. The garden he carved from this wilderness of scrub growth is a simple one, but it has everything a garden needs: a stone path to the front door, ancient gnarled lilacs at the corner of the house, and honeysuckle around the windows to perfume the kitchen on warm summer afternoons. And of course, there are old-fashioned shrub roses. Throughout the garden the most whimsical stone walls, held together by the merest weight and angle of a stone, define borders, create

With deep, plum-purple flowers, Clematis × jackmanii *blooms from June to September on 12-foot vines.*

Planted in the quick-draining soil between the stones of the path, Oenothera missourensis, *with trailing stems and bright yellow, translucent flowers almost 5 inches across, provides a brilliant contrast for the magenta flowers of* Geranium sanguineum.

planting beds, and provide violas and veronicas with edges to sprawl and spill over.

In spring this garden is bright with tulips, daffodils, and yellow and purple Johnny-jump-ups. In summer hardy geraniums and old-fashioned cottage pinks line a stone path to a tiny dining area with rumpled wicker chairs and a table covered with a checkered cloth. Surrounded by shrub roses, spectacular 7-foot delphiniums, and a white wooden trellis with violet-blue clematis, it is an enchanting spot for eating breakfast and watching hummingbirds.

This tiny garden is a magical place. It is a poet's garden, a place where the hours and moments of the day become the metaphors of life. A peony bent low with voluptuous pink blooms becomes an opportunity to leave a bouquet beside a neighbor's kitchen door, an armful of delphiniums takes its place in a love poem, while the musky fragrance of phlox on a sultry summer evening evokes memories of friends and laughter, a platter of cold salmon, French bread, and bowls of raspberries in thick cream from a farm up the mountain. A yellow dianthus is a reminder of a long, snowy winter, a pot on the windowsill, and the merest, thinnest stalks of green waiting for spring.

A fieldstone wall provides a contrasting background for yellow tulips.

Much more than plants and paths, each garden in this book is a metaphor for the life and spirit of the gardener who created it. Each is as different from the others as its owner, and as rich and wonderful as each gardener's imagining, weeding, and manuring could make it.

It is my hope that readers of this book will feel moved, perhaps even inspired, to imagine what magical things might happen in their own front and back yards. Very few of us have vacant lots cluttered with refrigerators and baby carriages, or old gardens that need rescuing from maple saplings and bittersweet. The suburban and urban lots where so many of us garden are less dramatic but no less challenging. It takes courage, as well as imagination, to tear out overgrown foundation yews and replace them with lilacs and roses. It is perhaps an even bolder step to tear up a section of lawn and plant sprawling, exuberant masses of peonies, poppies, and pinks. But imagine some night, after a long day, pushing open your own gate and walking into a garden that is intimate and welcoming, a place that is truly your own, where each plant has a place in your heart.

Japanese iris (Iris ensata) *and daylilies* (Hemerocalis *hybrids*) *are combined with annual baby's breath at the edge of a path.*

With bell-shaped flowers on willowy stalks 2 feet tall, Campanula persicifolia begins blooming in June and continues into July. Plants will self-sow and naturalize if let go to seed but if cut back after flowering they will often bloom again. Division of established plants every second or third year is usually necessary to keep them vigorous.

PLANTS FOR COTTAGE GARDENERS: PERENNIALS, ROSES, AND SPRING BULBS

ROSES

Throughout this book, I have discussed the selection of roses and their placement in the cottage garden, as well as how the gardeners who grow them do it. This only begins the subject of roses. There are many more old-fashioned shrubs and climbers that are excellent choices for cottage gardens—in fact, entire books have been written on the subject. A number of these have been included in the Selected Bibliography and will provide expert advice on culture, as well as on selecting roses for specific sites and growing conditions. In *Classic Roses,* Peter Beals has noted, along with a description of the flowers and foliage, flowering period, growth habit, height and width, whether a rose will thrive in shade, grow against a north wall, or tolerate poor soil—information that is particularly helpful for cottage gardeners with difficult sites.

For many American cottage gardeners, cold hardiness is one of the first criteria for selecting roses. As a general guideline, the hardiest and best-performing "old" roses for areas of the country with extreme winter condi-

tions are (in order of priority) the gallicas, albas, damasks, centifolias, and mosses. Selected rugosas and rugosa hybrids, eglanteria hybrids, and *Rosa moyessi* are also valuable for colder climates. The least hardy roses are the chinas and noisettes. These are suitable only for mild or very mild climatic conditions.

According to rosarian Suzy Verrier, "There is a very, very simple rule. Excluding the chinensis and chinensis hybrids, the simpler the pedigree of a rose, the more tolerant it is of adverse growing conditions. In shade and dampness, for example, plant a gallica or a species. A very large percentage of the species are hardy."

Determining the cold hardiness of roses is, as with perennials, sometimes a matter of trial and error. Hardiness zones are certainly useful guidelines when selecting roses, but because roses (unlike perennials) do not die back to the ground, other factors, such as the drying effects of sun and wind and severe fluctuations in temperature, are also major considerations. In more northerly areas of the country, a constant snow cover is invaluable in helping roses survive the winter, because it

helps maintain a consistent temperature around the plants and protects them from drying winds. As is the case with most plants, roses will have a better chance of surviving if they are well grown. (Refer to books in the Selected Bibliography for further advice on rose culture.)

An excellent source of information concerning the cold hardiness or heat tolerance of particular roses for your climate is often the nurseries that grow and sell them. Some nurseries include zone ratings in their catalogs, and most nurseries, especially the smaller, owner-run establishments, are glad to answer questions. Often these nurseries sell roses to people all over the country and can advise you about which ones have been successful in climatic conditions similar to your own.

Some excellent roses for northern climates are the hardy Canadian roses in the Explorer Series, including the cane hardy climber 'William Baffin'. The Buck roses, developed by Dr. Griffith Buck, a professor of horticulture at Iowa State University, are tough, beautiful, and in many cases recurrent bloomers and include strongly scented, rose-pink 'Carefree Beauty',

(Opposite) In Paul Smyth's garden, Johnny-jump-ups (Viola tricolor), *basket-of-gold* (Aurinia saxatilis), *and evergreen thyme* (Thymus serpyllum) *are planted between the stones of a path leading to the woods. Tulips and daffodils provide bright focal points.*

pink to blush 'Hawkeye Belle', and cardinal red 'Prairie Flower'.

Locating sources for old-fashioned shrubs and climbers, as well as species roses, is like a treasure hunt. An invaluable aid is a booklet compiled each year by Beverly Dobson, *The Combined Rose List,* which provides the names and sources of all the roses grown commercially in the United States and various foreign countries. Because the list is updated yearly, it can also help you keep track of the changing lists of the smaller nurseries (see Selected Bibliography for address).

Pickering Nursery offers an extensive listing of old-fashioned and species roses and has an excellent reputation for beautifully grown plants that are true to name. You get what you actually order, rather than some surprise. Their list includes a great many of the roses featured in this book, including 'Golden Showers' (Chapter 2), 'Blanc Double de Coubert', *R. filipes* 'Kiftsgate', 'Tour de Malakoff' (Chapter 6), 'Charles de Mills' (Chapters 5 and 6), and 'Mme Hardy' (Chapters 6 and 9), as well as *Rosa hugonis,* and 'Reine des Violettes' (Chapter 9).

The Antique Rose Emporium is another nursery that grows its own roses and has an excellent reputation. They put out a wonderful catalog with many color photographs and provide each rose listed with a hardiness zone rating. Their list includes several featured in this book, including 'New Dawn', 'Ispahan', 'Louise Odier', 'Kazanlik', 'Souvenir de la Malmaison', and 'Nathalie Nypels' (all Chapter 6).

Since the first edition of *English Cottage Gardening for American Gardeners,* a lot has changed in the rose nursery business. Some nurseries are no longer in business, some have changed their name and/or place of business, while others have added extensively to their listing. There are also a few new faces on the block. Rosarian Suzy Verrier, the former owner of Forevergreen Farm in Maine, has assisted with the updating of this listing. Author of the books *Rosa Rugosa* and *Rosa Gallica,* reprinted by Firefly Books Ltd., Suzy was an early champion of old and species roses and is a knowledgeable, outspoken, and enthusiastic rose grower.

For additional information and sources, you might want to refer to the most recent edition of *Gardening by Mail* by Barbara J. Barton, published by Houghton Mifflin.

Some of these rose nurseries charge for their catalogs, the prices of which may change, so call or write for information. A number of the nurseries have Web sites, while others are planning to go on-line. So when you call and place an order, ask for their Web site address.

Rose Nurseries

Antique Rose Emporium
9300 Lueckemeyer Road
Route 5
Box 143
Brenham, TX 77833
Mike Shoup
(800) 441-0002 or (409) 836-9051
FAX (409) 836-0928
www.antiqueroseemporium.com
Excellent catalog; a rose reference guide with photographs, illustrations, and instructions with a listing of 300–400 varieties of roses.

Arena Rose Company
P. O. Box 3096
Paso Robles, CA 93447
Sylvester and Amy Arena
(805) 227-4094 FAX (805) 227-4095

Corn Hill Nursery
R.R. 5 Route 890
Petitcodiac, NB, Canada EOA 2HO
Kathleen and Robert Osborne
(506) 756-3635 FAX (506) 756-1087
Specialize in own-root old roses and modern shrub roses and feature the Explorer Series. They ship worldwide.

Forestfarm
990 Tetherow Road
Williams, OR 97544-9599
Peg and Ray Prag
(541) 846-7269 FAX (541) 846-6963
www.forestfarm.com
E-mail: forestfarm@rvi.net
Exciting selection of species roses with a large selection of David Austen roses.

Fox Hill Nursery
347 Lunt Road
Freeport, ME 04032
Jennifer and Eric Welzel
(207) 729-1511 FAX (207) 729-6108
www.lilacs.com
E-mail: catalog@lilacs.com
A small but really good nursery. They grow their own plants from rooted cuttings and do a very nice job. Specialize in roses and lilacs.

Heirloom Old Garden Roses
24062 NE Riverside Drive
St. Paul, OR 97137
Louise and John Clements
(503) 538-1576 FAX (503) 538-5902
www.heirloomroses.com
A wonderful nursery with one of the biggest selections in the United States.

They grow all their roses on their own roots. An informative catalog with good descriptions and some color photographs.

High Country Roses
P. O. Box 148
9122 East Highway 40
Jensen, UT 84035
Heather Campbell and
Day DeLaHunt
(800) 552-2082 FAX (801) 789-5517
www.highcountryroses.com
E-mail: roses@easilink.com
This very good nursery offers a good selection of shrub species and old roses, all grown on their own roots. They specialize in cold hardy and cane hardy roses and feature the hardy Canadian roses of the Explorer Series.

Hortico, Inc.
723 Robson Road, RR1
Waterdown, ON, Canada L0R 2H1
William Vanderkruk
(905) 689-6984 FAX (905) 689-6566
www.hortico.com
E-mail: hortico@bigwave.ca
A large grower of roses, with a color catalog featuring over 700 varieties.

North Creek Farm
24 Sebasco Road
Phippsburg, ME 04562
Suzy Verrier and Kai Jacob
Tele and FAX (207) 389-1341
The nursery is a delightful place to visit in June and early summer when the roses are in bloom and the Maine coast is at its most beautiful. Rose list and newsletter.

Pickering Nurseries Inc.
670 Kingston Road
Highway 2
Pickering, ON, Canada L1V 1A6

Joseph and Joel Schraven
(905) 839-2111 FAX (905) 839-4807
A large and interesting list of roses, lots of color photographs and information including which roses are fragrant.
(Note: When ordering from Pickering, no import permit is required for shipments of roses from Canada.)

Regan Nursery
4628 Decoto Road
Fremont, CA 94555
Larry Thompson and
Marsha Hildebrand
(510) 797-3222 FAX (510) 793-5408
www.regannursery.com
Excellent listing of roses with over 1,500 offered, including David Austin's English Roses.

The Roseraie at Bayfields
P. O. Box R
670 Bremen Road (Route 32)
Waldoboro, ME 04572-0919
Lloyd Brace
(207) 832-6330 FAX (800) 933-4508
www.roseraie.com
E-mail: zapus@roseraie.com

Tate Rose Nursery
10306 FM Road 2767
Tyler, TX 75708-9239
Otis, Trent, and Bobbie Tate
(903) 593-1020 FAX (903) 593-2250
A small family nursery started in the 1940s. Now in its third generation, the nursery offers a good selection of hybrid teas and grandifloras.

Vintage Gardens
2833 Old Gravenstein Highway S.
Sebastopol, CA 95472
G. Lowery, D. Fried, L. Eisen, and
G. Phy
(707) 829-2035 FAX (707) 829-9516

www.vintagegardens.com
A tremendous selection; over 2,000 rose varieties available, all grown on their own roots. This nursery is a very good source for rare, antique, and good older roses that are simply not available elsewhere. The catalog is informative with lovely drawings and paintings of roses.

Wayside Gardens
P. O. Box 1
Hodges, SC 29695-0001
(800) 845-1124 FAX (800) 457-9712
www.waysidegardens.com

White Flower Farm
P. O. Box 50
Litchfield, CT 06759
(800) 411-6159 (800) 503-9624
FAX (800) 496-1418
www.whiteflowerfarm.com

PERENNIALS

While visiting cottage gardens throughout England, I often found that the same perennials were used again and again. Certain plants, including lady's mantle (*Alchemilla mollis*) and catmint (*Nepeta mussinii*) were vital in helping to create the effusive look so characteristic of cottage gardens. Particularly intriguing was the way various cottage gardeners used the same plants to create different effects.

I remember one village in the Cotswolds where each front yard was delightfully and totally different, yet certain plants ran like a theme throughout the various gardens. In one tiny dooryard in front of an equally diminutive thatched cottage, *N. mussinii* and lavender cotton (*Santolina chamaecyparissus*) were planted as a low hedge along either side of the front walk to create an elegant yet inviting entry. Right next door the front walk was lined with shrub roses underplanted with exuberant masses of *A. mollis* and sprawling clumps of shasta daisies *(Chrysanthemum maximum)*. In front of yet another cottage the plantings were very informal, the edges of the path to the door softened with *A. mollis, N. mussinii,* and red valerian *(Centranthus ruber)*.

These and other selected perennials also run like a theme throughout this book and are featured in the Cultural Chart at the end. The majority of the plants are common and easy to grow and many will grow in a wide range of cultural conditions. Most are commonly available from mail-order nurseries here in the United States. A few of the more unusual plants may require a bit of searching, but that can be part of the fun as you discover new sources.

The following is a selected list of mail-order nurseries specializing in perennials. Since the first edition of this book, a lot of exciting things have been happening in the nursery trade across America, so I have found it necessary and appropriate to update this list; some nurseries are no longer in business or are so well known they have been taken off, while some nurseries have been added. This list is not meant to exclude other quality nurseries, but simply includes those that I have personally dealt with and found highly satisfactory (or come highly recommended by gardening friends). This selection will give you a good start as you gather your cottage garden perennials.

Some of these nurseries offer unusual varieties of perennials, while others specialize, offering wide selections of peonies or bearded irises. Along with perennials, a few nurseries also sell trees and shrubs, important in creating the framework for your cottage garden. Forestfarm and Gossler Farms Nursery in Oregon are favorites of Gary Koller, Senior Horticulturist at The Arnold Arboretum and principal of Koller Associates, who helped put together the Cultural Chart for the first edition.

All these nurseries have interesting and informative catalogs, some in full color. Some charge for their catalogs, the prices of which may change, so call or write for information. A good many of the nurseries have Web sites, while others are planning to go on-line, so when you call to ask for a catalog or to place an order, ask if they have a Web site address. Some nurseries, like Gossler Farms, don't have Web sites and, they tell me, don't want them, because they love talking to their customers in person and getting to know them.

For additional sources you might want to refer to the latest edition of *Gardening by Mail* by Barbara Barton, published by Houghton Mifflin. This provides an extensive listing of perennial nurseries in the United States, Canada, and England and is regularly updated to keep track of nurseries that move, change names, or go out of business.

If you are after a certain plant, a particularly useful book is the most recent edition of *Anderson Horticultural Library's Source List of Seeds and Plants;* available for $39.95 from Anderson Horticultural Library, Minnesota Landscape Arboretum, 3675 Arboretum Drive, Box 39, Chanhassen, Minnesota, 55317. Their phone number is (612) 443-2440.

The library also offers the same information by subscription on their Web site, which is updated regularly, at plantinfo.umn.edu

Perennial Nurseries

A & D Nursery
6808 180th S.E.
Snohomish, WA 98296
Don Smetana and Keith Abel
(360) 668-9690 FAX (360) 668-6031
E-mail: bbbloom@usa.net
Their catalog offers a wide variety of peonies, daylilies, and hosta. The plant descriptions are helpful.

Blue Meadow Farm
184 Meadow Road
Montague Center, MA 01351
Alice and Brian McGowan
(413) 367-2394 FAX (413) 367-0116
An outstanding selection of unique and unusual perennials and annuals.

Kurt Bluemel, Inc.
2740 Greene Lane
Baldwin, MD 21013-9523
(410) 557-7229 FAX (410) 557-9785
www.bluemel.com
An extensive listing of ornamental grasses, perennials, bamboos, and ferns. The descriptions are brief and include hardiness ratings.

Bluestone Perennials
7211 Middle Ridge Road
Madison, OH 44057
(800) 852-5243 FAX (216) 428-7198
www.bluestoneperennials.com
E-mail: bluestone@bluestoneperennials.com
A good selection of hardy perennials, with lots of chrysanthemums. Useful plant descriptions and cultural infor-

mation. They offer small plants at modest prices, along with larger sizes.

Busse Gardens
5873 Oliver Avenue SW
Cokato, MN 55321-4229
Ainie Busse
(800) 544-3192 FAX (320) 286-6601
A large listing of herbaceous perennials, including dozens of different *Iris sibirica*, hardy geraniums, heuchera, hosta, and many early, mid, and late-blooming astilbes and unusual verbascum.

Canyon Creek Nursery
3527 Dry Creek Road
Oroville, CA 95965
John and Susan Whittlesey
(530) 533-2166
An interesting and tempting listing of perennials, including campanulas, hardy fuschias, salvias, and violas. The plant descriptions and cultural information are detailed and useful.

Carroll Gardens
444 East Main Street
Westminster, MD 21157
(800) 638-6334 FAX (410) 857-4112
www.carrollgardens.com
An extensive selection of perennials, herbs, roses, vines, and rare or unusual plants. They have also brought back into production lots of old-fashioned perennials that were not commonly available.

Caprice Farm Nursery
15425 S. W. Pleasant Hill Road
Sherwood, OR 97140
Cyndi and Charlie Turnbow and Robin Blue
(503) 625-7241 FAX (503) 625-5588
Offer Japanese and Siberian iris and herbaceous and tree peonies. The cata-

log has some color photographs and plant descriptions are excellent.

Cordon Bleu Daylilies
P. O. Box 2033
418 Buena Creek Road
San Marcos, CA 92079-2033
Steve Brigham
(760) 744-8367 FAX (760) 744-0510
A good selection of different types of daylilies, including spider flowered, doubles, and miniatures; well described with some color illustrations.

Cricklewood Nursery
11907 Nevers Road
Snohomish, WA 98290
Evie Douglas
(360) 568-2829
Cricklewood specializes in old-fashioned cottage-style perennials, including hellebores, hardy geraniums, and primula, plus own-root old roses.

Forestfarm
990 Tetherow Road
Williams, OR 97544-9599
Ray and Peg Prag
(541) 846-7269 FAX (541) 846-6963
www.forestfarm.com
E-mail: forestfarm@aonepro.net
An excellent selection of perennials, trees, and shrubs, some quite unusual.

Geraniaceae
122 Hillcrest Ave.
Kentfield, CA 94904
Robin Parer
(415) 461-4168 Fax (415) 461-7209
www.freeyellow.com/members/geraniaceae
E-mail: geraniac@pacbell.net
A wonderful source of hardy geraniums, erodiums, and scented geraniums galore, as well as numerous cultivars of

pansy-faced pelargoniums. Robin travels around the world collecting plants and seeds. The result is an extensive and exciting list.

Gilbert Wild and Son
P. O. Box 338
Sarcoxie, MO 64862
(888) 449-4537 Fax (888) 548-6831
Their catalog offers an excellent selection of peonies, iris, and hosta, with hundreds of different daylilies. A good number of daylilies are featured in color photographs, with excellent plant descriptions, including color, bloom shape and size, height, season of bloom, and which varieties are fragrant and/or open evenings.

Gossler Farms Nursery
1200 Weaver Road
Springfield, OR 97478-9691
Marj, Eric, and Roger Gossler
(541) 746-3922 FAX (541) 744-7924
Some perennials, but Gossler is primarily known for its fantastic selection of magnolias, stewartias, franklinia, viburnum, and other unusual trees and shrubs. A collector's delight.

Heronswood Nursery
7530 NE 288th Street
Kingston, WA 98346-9502
Daniel Hinkley and Robert Jones
(360) 297-4172 FAX (360) 297-8321
www.heronswood.com
E-mail: heronswood@silverlink.net
Offers a large selection of rare, unusual, and choice perennials, with an interesting selection of woody plants—over 2,500 plants in all. The catalog has no photographs; all plants are in botanical Latin and well described.

Niche Gardens
1111 Dawson Road

Chapel Hill, NC 27516
Kim Hawks
(919) 967-0078 FAX (919) 967-4026
www.nichegdn.com
E-mail: mail@nichegdn.com
A small and delightfully idiosyncratic nursery specializing in southeastern native plants and wildflowers, perennials, and herbs. All plants are nursery propagated.

Plant Delights Nursery
9241 Sauls Road
Raleigh, NC 27603
Tony and Michelle Avent
(919) 772-4794 FAX (919) 662-0370
www.plantdel.com
E-mail: office@plantdel.com
An interesting and tempting selection of perennials, with lots of hosta, ornamental grasses, heuchera, and pulmonaria.

Reath's Nursery
N-195 County Road 577
Vulcan, MI 49892
(906) 563-9777 FAX (906) 563-9777
www.reathsnursery.com
E-mail: reathnur@up.net
A well-chosen selection of herbaceous and tree peonies. Along with some of their own hybrids, Reath's offers plants hybridized by Saunders and Daphnis and named Japanese tree peonies. The catalog has color photographs and helpful plant descriptions.

Sandy Mush Herb Nursery
316 Surrett Cove Road
Leicester, North Carolina 28748-5517
Fairman and Kate Jayne
(828) 683-2014
A superb selection of artemesias, dianthus, hardy geraniums, lavenders, monardas and salvias, and thymes,

along with numerous scented geraniums—over 1,500 plants offered.

Schreiner's Iris Gardens
3625 Quinaby Road N.E.
Salem, OR 97303-9720
(800) 525-2367 FAX (503) 393-5590
www.schreinersiris.com
In business since 1925, Schreiner's has an exciting and extensive list that includes hundreds of dwarf and tall hybrid iris, many of which they have bred themselves. The plant quality is excellent.

Song Sparrow Perennial Farm
13101 East Rye Road
Avalon, WI 53505
Roy Klehm
(800) 872-5459 FAX (608) 883-2221
Offers a very good selection of perennials, including hybrid and miniature daylilies, iris, and hosta. Peonies are a speciality and many were hybridized by various members of the Klehm family.

Sunlight Gardens
174 Golden Lane
Andersonville, TN 37705
Andrea (Andy) Sessions and
Marty Zenni
(423) 494-7086 FAX (423) 494-7086
A small, family partnership committed to and specializing in native wildflowers and perennials.

Surry Gardens
P. O. Box 145
Surry, ME 04684
James Dickinson
(207) 667-4493 FAX (207) 667-5532
A large selection of perennials, including lots of different campanulas, dianthus, veronica, and primula, along with an extensive listing of hosta and

native and non-native wildflowers and ferns. Helpful cultural information.

Andre Viette Farm and Nursery
P. O. Box 1109
Fisherville, VA 22939
Andre Viette
(800) 575-5538 FAX (540) 943-0782
www.viette.com
E-mail: viette@viette.com
A wide range of garden perennials, including lots of different astilbes, epimediums, daylilies, hosta, and peonies.

We-Du Nurseries
Route 5, Box 724
Marion, NC 28752
Dennis Niemeyer and Joani Lawarre
(828) 738-8300 FAX (704) 738-8131
A very personal catalog with many plants to delight the plant lover and collector. Among their specialities are epimediums and species iris.

SPRING BULBS

Spring bulbs are practically a must for even the smallest cottage garden. While perennials play a vital role in creating the exuberant look and feel of a cottage garden, in many areas of the United States and Canada they don't begin blooming until May. Planted between the crowns of perennials or in drifts beneath shrub roses and flowering fruit trees, early-blooming spring bulbs such as scilla, galanthus, species and hybrid crocuses, and muscari can cover a lot of bare ground long before most perennials have even begun to poke through the soil.

Many of the cottage gardeners I talked with while researching this book created the most delightful spring-bulb combinations. Many of the same bulbs were used again and again, but each gardener had his or her own way of combining them. One cottage gardener might plant dark blue scilla (*Scilla siberica*) and snowdrops (*Galanthus nivalis*) between the stones of a path to the kitchen door, while another gardener might use the same combination and throw in dozens of the early-flowering *Crocus chrysanthus* 'Cream Beauty' and yellow-flowered *Tulipa tarda*.

At Waystrode Manor in Kent (see Chapter 5, Cottage Style), Jill Wright's perennial border begins blooming in April with masses of scilla and snow-drops, followed by sweeps of narcissus selected to bloom with blue forget-me-nots and various colored primula. In her white garden, which features potentilla and silver-leaved dianthus in June and July, Jill planted white-flowered narcissus around clumps of lung-wort (*Pulmonaria angustifolia*) and small-flowered bleeding heart (*Dicentra eximia* 'Alba') for early spring bloom.

In Tasha Tudor's Vermont cottage garden, spring bulbs have been planted in the most lavish displays. Along the edges of stone paths, various miniature narcissus and violas are tucked between clumps of later-blooming violets and forget-me-nots. In the meadow dozens of different narcissus are naturalized in the grass beneath the apple trees. One of Tasha's favorite narcissus, the late-blooming 'Thalia', with clusters of fragrant white flowers, is used throughout her garden. In her foundation borders, Tasha has combined 'Thalia' with bright blue pansies. Just about the time 'Thalia' is finished, the border's next show begins, featuring apricot-colored tulips, old-fashioned bleeding heart (*Dicentra spectabilis*) and masses of blue forget-me-nots.

The majority of the bulbs mentioned in this book are hardy from Zones 3 to 8 or 9 and are commonly available from any good bulb supplier. The following is a list of suppliers, updated since the first edition. Many have full-color catalogs; some charge for them. Some of these suppliers offer unusual varieties and a good many offer (or will be glad to provide) zone information to make it easier to select bulbs that are appropriate for your particular geographic and climatic conditions.

A number of these bulb suppliers have Web sites and/or E-mail allowing you to order on-line. For computer aficionados, these Web sites have lots of color photographs and cultural information and are often updated regularly. Other suppliers are planning to go on-line. So when you call and place your order or request a catalog, ask if they have a Web site address.

Bulb Suppliers

Brent and Becky's Bulbs
7463 Heath Trail
Gloucester, VA 23061
Brent and Becky Heath
(877) 661-2852 FAX (804) 693-9436
www.brentandbeckysbulbs.com
The founders of the Daffodil Mart, Brent and Becky are enthusiastic, knowledgeable bulb hybridizers. Their catalog offers an interesting selection of spring and summer bulbs. Their book *Daffodils for American Gardens,* with 300 color photographs, is an excellent handbook.

Cascade Daffodils
P. O. Box 10626
White Bear Lake, MN 55110-0626

Linda and David Karnstedt
(651) 426-9616
E-mail: davekarn@aol.com
Offers hundreds of daffodil cultivars with many old favorites, as well as novelty daffodils.

Colorblends/Schipper and Co.
P. O. Box 7584
Greenwich, CT 06836-7584
Timothy Schipper
(888) 847-8637 FAX (203) 862-8909
www.colorblends.com
Features "color-blends"—bulbs selected to color-complement or create striking contrasts when planted together. Offers larger quantities.

Daffodil Mart
30 Irene Street
Torrington, CT 06790-6668
(800) 255-2852 FAX (860) 496-1418
www.800ALLBULB.com

Dutch Gardens
P. O. Box 200
Adelphia, NJ 07710-0200
John and Nick Langeveld
(800) 818-3861 FAX (908) 780-7720
www.dutchgardens.nl
E-mail cs@dutchgardens.nl
Offers a color catalog of spring-flowering bulbs and a summer-flowering-bulb catalog featuring lilies, dahlias, and more.

French's Bulb Importer
P. O. Box 565
Pittsfield, VT 05762-0565
Howard French
(800) 286-8198 FAX (802) 746-7940

Grant Mitsch Novelty Daffodils
P. O. Box 218
Hubbard, OR 97032
Richard and Elise Havens

(503) 651-2742 FAX (503) 651-2792
www.web-ster.com/havensr/mitsch
E-mail: havensr@web-ster.com
An interesting and informative catalog
with color photographs and good
descriptions. This small, family-run
business offers hundreds of daffodil
cultivars, with many of their own
introductions, including rarer daffodils
and some enchanting miniatures.

Mad River Imports
P. O. Box 1685
Fayston, VT 05660
Jeffrey M. Rice
(802) 496-3004 FAX (802) 496-3004

McClure & Zimmerman
P. O. Box 368
108 W. Winnebago St.
Friesland, WI 53935
(800) 883-6998 FAX (800) 374-6120
www.mzbulb.com
E-mail: info@mzbulb.com
A wide range of spring- and summer-
blooming bulbs, along with more difficult to locate species, including
muscari, camassia, fritillaria, and alliums. Good descriptions.

Old House Gardens—Heirloom Bulbs
536 Third Street
Ann Arbor, MI 48103-4957
Scott Kunst
(734) 995-1486 FAX (734) 995-1486
www.oldhousegardens.com
A source for historic bulbs, many from
the nineteenth and twentieth centuries,
with some from as far back as the thir-
teenth century. A consultant on historic garden restoration, Scott has
researched the dates of introduction
for the bulbs he offers, which include
tulips, hyacinths, and narcissus. This is
a wonderful catalog of old-fashioned
and historic bulbs (many of which are

more fragrant than modern introductions), with lots of information and
personal anecdotes.

Oregon Trail Daffodils
41905 S.E. Louden Road
Corbett, OR 97019
Diane and Bill Tribe
(503) 695-5513 FAX (503) 695-5573
E-mail: daffodil@europa.com
The fourth generation of the Evans
family in the daffodil business, this
nursery offers a good choice of speciality and show daffodils.

John Scheepers, Inc.
23 Tulip Drive
Bantam, CT 06750
Jan Ohms
(860) 567-0838 FAX (860) 567-5323
www.johnscheepers.com
E-mail: catalog@johnscheepers.com
Color catalog with spring- and summer-flowering bulbs. Lots of color
photographs and good descriptions.
Same ownership as Van Engelen
(below) but offers smaller quantities.
Very helpful to their customers with
practical advice.

Van Bourgondien Bros.
P. O. Box 1000
245 Farmingdale Road, Route 109
Babylon, NY 11702-0598
(800) 622-9997 FAX (516) 669-1228
www.dutchbulbs.com
E-mail: blooms@dutchbulbs.com
Spring and fall color catalogs with
brief descriptions.

Van Engelen, Inc.
23 Tulip Drive
Bantam, CT 06750
Jan Ohms
(860) 567-8734 FAX (860) 567-5323
www.vanengelen.com

An excellent selection of spring bulbs,
including numerous varieties of muscari, fritillaria, and species tulips.
Offers bulbs in large quantities; from
50 to 500 or 1,000, also bulb collections.

CULTURAL CHART

Compiled with the help of Gary Koller, Assistant Director of Horticulture of The Arnold Arboretum

This chart is designed as a quick reference and general guide to the cultural requirements of selected cottage garden plants. It is not a definitive list of cottage garden plants—I don't believe there is such a thing. Each cottage gardener has his or her own list, and you will, no doubt, have your own favorites to add. The plants listed are either featured in the text or play an important role in creating the exuberant look and feel of cottage gardens. With a few exceptions, they are available from local or North American commercial mail order nurseries, and most are easy to grow if provided with cultural conditions to their liking.

Plants are arranged alphabetically, by genus. The botanical name of the genus is in italics beginning with a capital letter, followed by the species in lower case, also in italics (for example, *Geranium sanguineum*), sometimes followed by a subspecies or variety name *(Geranium sanguineum* var. *striatum)*. Cultivar names are capitalized and enclosed by single quotation marks (*Geranium* 'Johnson's Blue'). Hybrids, plants that are a result of crossing two species within a genus, are denoted by "×" *(Geranium × cantabrigense)*.

We have also included in the chart (as well as the text) commonly used synonyms for some plants. These synonyms were at one time correct botanical names but have been revised. Basket-of-gold *(Aurinia saxatilis)*, for example,

used to be called *Alyssum saxatile.* The world of botanical nomenclature is an ever-changing one due to reclassification of plants and changing views on how they should be organized, and it is often difficult for professionals, never mind amateur gardeners, to keep up with the "latest" and "newest" names of plants. As a result, some plants are still listed in catalogs or sold under these "synonyms." So with some plants we have included a synonym.

In the interest of clarity, we have made each plant heading as simple as possible. In some cases, where it might be useful for reference (or to avoid confusion), the name of a plant is followed by "species" or "species and hybrids"—primarily to indicate that a number of plants are covered in the material under that heading. Throughout the chart we have often used "hybrid" as a collective term referring to plants of hybrid parentage, as well as varieties of a species which are distinctive.

Throughout the text, I have emphasized the botanical names of plants. To help make cross-referencing easier, all of the plants included in this chart also appear in two lists: one alphabetized according to common names, the other according to botanical, Latinized names. Once you get used to it, botanical nomenclature is not all that difficult, and it makes talking about plants with other gardeners, as well as ordering plants from mail order nurseries, a lot

easier. Knowing the correct botanical name of a plant also makes it more likely that you'll get the plant you intended.

LIGHT

Full sun means that a plant receives a minimum of six hours of sun each day. *Light shade* refers to sun filtered through a lightly branched tree such as a birch or locust. *Partial shade* refers to sun for part of the day. *Full shade* means that a plant receives no direct sunlight, as in areas beneath densely branched evergreens.

Shade won't prevent you from creating a lovely cottage garden. While you won't be able to grow plants such as sun-loving delphiniums, a wide range of plants that prefer full sun will also grow in light or partial shade. Even in an area that receives no direct sunlight (such as the north side of a house), many plants will thrive as long as there is abundant light and the plants are carefully chosen to fit their environment. A lot of plants that might be perfectly happy in full sun in New England *need* light or partial shade in areas of the country with glaring sunlight and high summer temperatures.

Though many plants are flexible about their cultural requirements, there are limits, and you are not going to have success with delphiniums if your garden is in full or partial shade all day. But even with full shade, you can create rich and varied effects with plants having colored or variegated foliage.

As Gary Koller, who has created some wonderful shade gardens, says, "Shade should not set you back because it gives you so many opportunities; it is simply a matter of how you look at it. Many people who are partial to full shade still want to grow lots of flowers. They think if they look at a plant hard enough or wish it hard enough the plant will do what they want it to. That just doesn't work. Instead consider substituting foliage form and color for flowers. Select plants with leaves of various sizes, shapes, and textures in different shades of green or shade-loving plants that have variegated or colored foliage. Many plants with colored foliage can be used to brighten dark areas."

SOIL

This category provides a range of soil conditions in which each perennial will thrive. Each garden site offers its own unique combination of soil types and drainage. You may well discover that some plants thrive in very different conditions than those listed. I have found, for example, that *Crambe cordifolia* thrives and grows with almost astounding vigor in the heavy soil of my perennial nursery garden. Now this is contrary to a number of sources I have read on growing *C. cordifolia* that say it prefers or requires *well-drained* soil. But tell that to my six-year-old plants. (I have since read in yet another book that *C. cordifolia* will grow in any soil.)

ZONES AND HARDINESS

The zone ratings for this chart are based upon the new U.S. Department of Agriculture Plant Hardiness Map, which should, in the next few years, become the standard reference for zone information throughout the United States and parts of Canada. (See map page 236 for temperatures. *Note that the temperatures given for each zone are an average.*)

The term "plant hardiness" refers to a plant's ability to survive in various climatic and environmental conditions. Beginning gardeners, as well as more experienced gardeners, often think of hardiness as a plant's ability to thrive in a combination of cold winter temperatures and frozen soil for extended periods. But a good many plants (including perennials, of course) will not tolerate excessive heat, particularly if combined with high humidity and continued high temperatures at night. Many factors influence a plant's hardiness, including type of soil, wind, degree of sun or shade, amount of water, and drainage. In Zone 8, for example, where winters are relatively mild, the rapid and often extreme changes of temperatures from day to day also influence a plant's ability to survive. In colder areas of North America, severe or rapid fluctuations of winter temperatures and the amount (or lack) of snow are also critical factors.

For a number of years I took zone ratings as a kind of gospel, using them to determine which plants I did and didn't grow, but as I became more confident as a gardener I began buying plants that, according to books or catalogs, I had no business growing in Zone 5. Some have been abject failures, but many more have been the most

wonderful successes. One summer in England, for instance, I saw *Crambe cordifolia* in a cottage garden and was totally taken with it. Back in the states, I found *C. cordifolia* listed in catalogs as hardy only from Zones 6 or 7. Ignoring the zone ratings, I located a source and ordered some plants. For years now, these crambes have been absolutely spectacular—5 feet tall and almost as wide—grown in heavy soil, with no cover, in the most exposed site imaginable.

I have also observed that a good many plants often listed as Zone 6 (and occasionally Zone 7) have proven hardy in some of my clients' Zone 4 or 5 gardens. Often a garden may contain as many as three or four distinct microclimates, areas that may, in fact, have very much the same temperature range as Zones 6 or 7. I have also found the opposite to be true—that plants listed as hardy from Zone 4 or 5 are not hardy in those zones. Here, again, soil conditions, drainage, rainfall, snow cover, and the site itself all undoubtedly play a part.

One of the best ways to determine whether a plant is hardy in your area (north or south) is to ask the horticulturist at your local public garden or nursery (preferably the person who actually grows the plants) and refer to the gardens of friends and neighbors and ask whether they have found it grows well. But if you can't find out anything conclusive either way and want to try growing a plant—do it. Perennials are relatively inexpensive, so why not?

As I have said, this chart is not meant as a definitive reference, but combined with good old common sense and careful observation of your own and various gardens around your neighborhood, as

SIZE AND HABIT

The height of most of the perennials in this chart is when the plants are in flower. Fernleaf yarrow (Achillea filipendulina), for example, is listed as 3½ to 4 feet tall. But if the flower stalks are cut back when plants are through blooming, the plants are reduced to thick clumps of gray-green, fernlike leaves about 6 to 8 inches tall. On the other hand, Japanese anemone (Anemone × hybrida) is listed as growing 1 to 3½ feet tall, but because it blooms relatively late in the season (in August or September to October) it can provide your garden with an attractive mass of foliage for most of the growing season. This chart is designed to help give you a sense of what these plants look like at various stages of their season's growth.

The height and width of the perennials included in this chart will vary depending upon their cultural conditions and care. Astilbes, for example, that would grow to 2½ feet across (and more) in light shade and moist soil may only reach 1½ or 2 feet across if grown in full sun with soil that is allowed to dry out. All sizes are meant only as a general guide to help you plan the spacing in your garden.

The *habit* of the perennials attempts to give you an idea of what each plant looks like in its various stages of growth throughout the growing season—information that is particularly useful when combining plants or placing them in borders. One example I have used in the text (see Chapter 10) is peach-leaved bellflower (Campanula persicifolia). When in bloom it is 2 to 2½ feet tall, but before and after it blooms it is a compact clump of leaves about 3–4 inches tall. Years ago I saw C. *persicifolia* listed in several books and catalogs as a plant for the middle of the border. I tried planting groupings of a dozen plants and was most disappointed to find that after they were through flowering they left a gap. I have since experimented and found that C. *persicifolia* is indeed wonderful in the middle of a border when planted in quantity around oldfashioned shrub roses or planted as fillers between clumps of perennials such as *Iris sibirica* with a tall, bold habit and foliage that remains attractive throughout the growing season.

BLOOM PERIOD AND FLOWERS

The flowering time specified in this chart is for the Northeast section of the United States—simply because that is the area I know best because that is where I live and garden. Gardeners in more southerly and temperate areas where spring comes earlier, or where the growing season is continuous, will usually find that bloom times for many perennials tend to be both earlier in the spring and possibly later into the fall. For example, in Zone 5 the flowering time for *Centranthus ruber* begins about mid-June, whereas in Zone 8 it might begin blooming as early as mid- to late April, or as late as mid-May, depending upon the idiosyncrasies of a particular growing year. Bloom time in various areas of North America can vary anywhere from two to six weeks, depending upon climate and cultural conditions. So in order to coordinate the bloom periods of the various perennials, roses, and vines featured in this book, you will want to talk with local gardeners and consult local nurseries and public gardens.

During the growing season Gary and I will frequently walk through our own gardens and those of friends observing which plants are in bloom. Very often we will discover plants that may not be growing side by side but that we can easily imagine would look great together and thrive in similar conditions. Some of Gary's best plant combinations were serendipitous discoveries made walking through nurseries—plant combinations he would never have considered.

FOLIAGE

This category is meant to serve as a quick reference, a glance at each plant's foliage, to help gardeners think of cottage plants as more than just flowers. An abundance of flowers helps create the effusive, bountiful look of a cottage garden. But because most perennials bloom for two to three weeks (with some repeat bloom), it is the foliage (and varied growth habits) of these plants that helps maintain a garden's interest for much of the growing season. In gardens with little or no sun, varied foliage becomes even more important in creating the look and feel of a cottage garden.

CULTURAL NOTES

In a good many areas of the United States, gardeners have been experiencing drought or are limited as to the amount of water they can use in their gardens. With this in mind, I have noted plants that are most tolerant of drought or dry soil with the symbol *.

While specific plants may be drought tolerant once they are established, it is important to keep in mind that newly planted or transplanted plants require water. There is no point in planting daylilies (as forgiving as they are) in mid-summer, in the blazing hot sun, in soil that is dry as dust, then expecting them to root, never mind thrive. Where water is limited, I have found it is helpful to enrich the soil with plenty of organic matter such as compost, shredded leaves, or well-rotted cow manure—whatever is readily available and inexpensive. The addition of organic matter and mulching is important for most soils but is particularly useful for retaining water in dry areas and will help prevent soil from becoming compacted, thus leaving it more permeable to water or rain.

In areas where water is in limited supply, I have also found it is often helpful to plant a section of a garden, let the plants become stabilized, then plant the next area. This way, with the water that is available (even if you have to use bath water) the plants can be soaked thoroughly, mulched, and shaded to help them get established. This will go a long way to help give perennials, even tough plants such as *Achillea filipendulina* and *Centranthus ruber,* the start they will need to put up with dry growing conditions. It is also very helpful to group plants with similar water requirements together so that any irrigation or watering will be most efficient.

In this section I have included the highlights of each plant's cultural requirements. Here, and in the sections on light and soil requirements, I have also emphasized optimal growing conditions. But many plants will often put up with less than the ideal, though their growth, size, and number of flowers may be reduced. Peonies, for example, bloom best in full sun but will also do well with partial or dappled shade. You may have your heart set on growing peonies, Siberian irises, and oriental poppies but have only garden areas in light shade or in sun part of the day. Don't let that stop you. The irises will, of course, be fine. Oriental poppies are listed in this chart as requiring full sun, but Tom Savery (see Chapter 7, "Gables") grows them in the dappled shade beneath apple trees. They will probably never reach the voluminous girth and abundant flowering of poppies in full sun, but these poppies are a wonderful accent surrounded by masses of nepeta, hardy geraniums, and drifts of epimediums and provide a most surprising splash of color in a partially shaded garden.

DESIGN USES

The plant combinations and design uses for the plants in this chart are those I've seen in American and English cottage gardens that Gary or I have grown ourselves or imagined for future plantings in our own and clients' gardens. I have also included some ideas for plant combinations that are particularly well suited to hot areas with limited rainfall. By selecting and mixing some of the plants for dry or drought conditions listed in the chart with perennials and shrubs that do well in the specific conditions of your area, you can come up with some distinctive cottage combinations. For example, a combination to accent an arbor in light, dry soil in Zones 7–10 might include the beautiful (but sometimes invasive) California native *Romneya coulteri,* with diaphanous white flowers 5–9 inches across, surrounded by *Nepeta* 'Six Hills Giant', *Achillea filipendulina,* and *Oenothera missourensis.*

The design ideas in this section suggest only a few of the many ways in which these plants can be used. I hope that, as the cottage gardeners in this book have done, you too will take your own favorite perennials and combine them with some of the old-fashioned plants featured in this chart to create lovely, informal dooryards and cottage gardens.

INDEX OF COTTAGE PERENNIALS · LATIN TO COMMON

Latin Name	Common Name	Latin Name	Common Name
Achillea filipendulina	Fernleaf yarrow	*Coreopsis grandiflora*	Tickseed
Aconitum napellus	Monkshood	*Coreopsis verticillata*	Threadleaf coreopsis
Alcea rosea (Althaea rosea)	Hollyhock	*Crambe cordifolia*	Heartleaf crambe
Alchemilla mollis	Lady's mantle	*Delphinium* hybrids	Delphinium *or* Larkspur
Anchusa azurea (A. italica)	Italian bugloss *or* Alkanet	*Dianthus plumarius* hybrid	Cottage *or* Garden pink
Anemone species and hybrids	Japanese anemone	*Dianthus* × *allwoodii*	Cottage *or* Garden pink
Anemone pulsatilla	Pasqueflower *or* Wind-flower	*Dicentra eximia*	Fringed bleeding heart
		Dicentra spectabilis	Bleeding heart
Angelica archangelica	Wild parsnip	*Dictamnus albus (D. Fraxinella)*	Gas plant *or* Burning bush
Aquilegia × *hybrida*	Columbine hybrids		
Artemisia schmidtiana 'Silver Mound'	Silver mound artemisia	*Digitalis purpurea*	Foxglove
		Echinops ritro	Globe thistle
Aster novae-angliae hybrids	Michaelmas daisy or Hardy aster	*Epimedium* species	Barrenwort *or* Bishop's hat
		Erigeron × *hybridus*	Fleabane
Aster novi-belgii hybrids	Michaelmas daisy or Hardy aster	*Euphorbia epithymoides (E. polychroma)*	Cushion spurge
Astrantia major	Masterwort	*Gaillardia* × *grandiflora*	Blanket flower
Aubrieta deltoidea	Purple rock cress	*Geranium* species and hybrids	Cranesbill *or* Hardy geranium
Aurinia saxatilis (Alyssum saxatile)	Basket-of-gold	*Gypsophila paniculata*	Baby's breath
Baptisia australis	False indigo	*Helenium autumnale*	Sneezeweed *or* Helen's flower
Bergenia cordifolia	Heartleaf bergenia		
Brunnera macrophylla (Anchusa myosotidiflora)	Siberian bugloss	*Helianthemum nummularium*	Rock rose
		Heliopsis helianthoides	False sunflower
Campanula persicifolia	Peach-leaved bellflower	*Heuchera* × *brizoides*	Coralbells
Centaurea montana	Mountain bluet	*Iberis sempervirens*	Candytuft
Centranthus ruber (Valeriana rubra)	Red valerian	*Iris ensata (I. kaempferi)*	Japanese iris
		Iris hybrids	Bearded iris
Cephalaria gigantea (C. tatarica)	Giant scabies	*Iris sibirica*	Siberian iris
		Lamium maculatum	Spotted dead-nettle
Cerastium tomentosum	Snow-in-summer	*Lavandula angustifolia*	Lavender
Chrysanthemum coccineum	Pyrethrum *or* Painted daisy	*Lupinus* Russell hybrids	Lupine
Chrysanthemum × *superbum (C.* × *maximum)*	Shasta daisy	*Lychnis chalcedonica*	Maltese cross

Latin Name	Common Name	Latin Name	Common Name
Lychnis coronaria	Rose campion *or* Mullein pink	*Primula* species	Primrose
Lysimachia punctata	Circle flower *or* Yellow loosestrife	*Pulmonaria* species and hybrids	Lungwort
Lythrum salicaria	Purple loosestrife	*Salvia* species and hybrids	Sage *or* Salvia
Malva alcea	Hollyhock mallow	*Stachys byzantina (S. lanata)*	Lamb's ears
Monarda didyma	Bee balm	*Thalictrum* species and hybrids	Meadow rue
Myosotis species	Forget-me-not		
Nepeta species and hybrids	Catmint	*Tiarella* species	Foamflower *or* False miterwort
Paeonia hybrids	Peony		
Papaver orientale	Oriental poppy	*Trollius* species and hybrids	Globeflower
Petrorhagia saxifraga (Tunica saxifraga)	Tunic flower	*Valeriana officinalis*	Common valerian *or* Garden heliotrope
Phlox paniculata	Summer phlox	*Veronica* species and hybrids	Speedwell
Platycodon grandiflorus	Balloon flower	*Viola cornuta*	Horned violet *or* Tufted pansy

INDEX OF COTTAGE PERENNIALS · COMMON TO LATIN

Common Name	Latin Name	Common Name	Latin Name
Alkanet	*Anchusa azurea (A. italica)*	Coralbells	*Heuchera × brizoides*
Baby's breath	*Gypsophila paniculata*	Cottage pink	*Dianthus plumarius* hybrid or *D. × allwoodii*
Balloon flower	*Platycodon grandiflorus*		
Barrenwort *or* bishop's hat	*Epimedium* species	Cranesbill	*Geranium* species
Basket-of-gold	*Aurinia saxatilis (Alyssum saxatile)*	Cushion spurge	*Euphorbia epithymoides (E. polychroma)*
Bee balm	*Monarda didyma*	Delphinium *or* Larkspur	*Delphinium* hybrids
Bishop's hat	*Epimedium* species	False indigo	*Baptisia australis*
Blanket flower	*Gaillardia × grandiflora*	False miterwort	*Tiarella* species
Bleeding heart	*Dicentra spectabilis*	False sunflower	*Heliopsis helianthoides*
Burning bush	*Dictamnus albus (D. fraxinella)*	Fernleaf yarrow	*Achillea filipendulina*
		Fleabane	*Erigeron × hybridus*
Candytuft	*Iberis sempervirens*	Foamflower	*Tiarella cordifolia*
Catmint	*Nepeta* species and hybrids	Forget-me-not	*Myosotis* species
Circle flower	*Lysimachia punctata*	Foxglove	*Digitalis purpurea*
Columbine	*Aquilegia × hybrida*	Fringed bleeding heart	*Dicentra eximia*
Common valerian	*Valeriana officinalis*	Garden heliotrope	*Valeriana officinalis*

Common Name	Latin Name	Common Name	Latin Name
Garden pink	*Dianthus plumarius* hybrid or *D. × allwoodii*	Mullein pink	*Lychnis coronaria*
		Oriental poppy	*Papaver orientale*
Gas plant	*Dictamnus albus* (*D. fraxinella*)	Painted daisy	*Chrysanthemum coccineum*
		Pasqueflower	*Anemone pulsatilla*
Giant scabies	*Cephalaria gigantea* (*C. tatarica*)	Peach-leaved bellflower	*Campanula persicifolia*
		Peony	*Paeonia* hybrids
Globe flower	*Trollius* species and hybrids	Primrose	*Primula* species
Globe thistle	*Echinops ritro*	Purple loosestrife	*Lythrum salicaria*
Hardy aster	*Aster novae-angliae* hybrids and *A. novi-bellgii* hybrids	Purple rock cress	*Aubrieta deltoidea*
		Pyrethrum	*Chrysanthemum coccineum*
Hardy geranium	*Geranium* species and hybrids	Red valerian	*Centranthus ruber* (*Valeriana rubra*)
Heartleaf bergenia	*Bergenia cordifolia*		
Heartleaf crambe	*Crambe cordifolia*	Rock rose	*Helianthemum nummularium*
Helen's flower	*Helenium autumnale*	Rose campion	*Lychnis coronaria*
Hollyhock	*Alcea rosea* (*Althaea rosea*)	Sage	*Salvia* species and hybrids
Hollyhock mallow	*Malva alcea*	Salvia	*Salvia* species and hybrids
Horned violet	*Viola cornuta*	Shasta daisy	*Chrysanthemum × superbum* (*C. × maximum*)
Italian bugloss *or* Alkanet	*Anchusa azurea* (*A. italica*)		
Japanese anemone	*Anemone* species and hybrids	Siberian bugloss	*Brunnera macrophylla* (*Anchusa myosotidiflora*)
Japanese iris	*Iris ensata*	Siberian iris	*Iris sibirica*
Lady's mantle	*Alchemilla mollis*	Silver mound artemisia	*Artemisia schmidtiana* 'Silver Mound'
Lamb's ears	*Stachys byzantina* (*S. lanata*)		
Larkspur or Delphinium	*Delphinium* hybrids	Sneezeweed	*Helenium autumnale*
Lavender	*Lavandula angustifolia*	Snow-in-summer	*Cerastium tomentosum*
Lungwort	*Pulmonaria* species and hybrids	Speedwell	*Veronica* species and hybrids
		Spotted dead-nettle	*Lamium maculatum*
Lupine	*Lupinus* Russell hybrids	Summer phlox	*Phlox paniculata*
Maltese cross	*Lychnis chalcedonica*	Threadleaf coreopsis	*Coreopsis verticillata*
Masterwort	*Astrantia major*	Tickseed	*Coreopsis grandiflora*
Meadow rue	*Thalictrum* species and hybrids	Tufted pansy	*Viola cornuta*
		Tunic flower	*Petrorhagia saxifraga* (*Tunica saxifraga*)
Michaelmas daisy	*Aster novae-angliae* and *A. novi-belgii* hybrids		
		Wild parsnip	*Angelica archangelica*
Monkshood	*Aconitum napellus*	Windflower	*Anemone pulsatilla*
Mountain bluet	*Centaurea montana*	Yellow loosestrife	*Lysimachia punctata*

*ACHILLEA FILIPENDULINA—FERNLEAF YARROW

Light: full sun but will tolerate light shade
Soil: well-drained to dry, average to poor fertility
Zones of Hardiness: 3 to 9

Size: 3½–4 feet tall; 2–3 feet wide
Habit: plants erect and multistemmed

Bloom Period: late June into July or August
Flowers: dense, flat, yellow heads 4–6 inches across

Foliage (D): gray-green, slightly hairy, fernlike leaves; crushed foliage has a pungent odor

Cultural Notes

A. filipendulina is low-maintenance, tough, drought resistant, and especially useful for dry, inhospitable landscapes and gardens. To prevent overcrowding and maintain vigorous growth (or to propagate), divide *A. filipendulina* every third or fourth year. Where space isn't a problem and the soil isn't particularly fertile, it can be left longer without division.

Design Uses

Excellent feature plant for the summer border—as specimens toward the middle or rear of the border. Create a bold combination by planting *A. filipendulina* with *Echinacea purpurea* and *Echinops ritro*, or combine *A. filipendulina* with *E. ritro* and *Malva alcea* 'Fastigiata' to anchor a border for mid- and late summer bloom.

Achillea filipendulina 'Gold Plate', with bright yellow flowers almost 6 inches across, grows up to 4 or 5 feet tall and is one of the most popular hybrids.

The hybrid *A.* 'Coronation Gold', with mustard yellow flowers, grows from 2½ to 3 feet tall, is less likely to require staking, and will bloom well into summer if faded flowers are removed to prevent the formation of seeds.

ACONITUM NAPELLUS—MONKSHOOD

Light: partial shade to full sun, provided the soil is moist
Soil: fairly rich, with liberal amounts of compost
Zones of Hardiness: 3 to 8

Size: 2½–6 feet tall; 1–2 feet wide
Habit: erect stalks

Bloom Period: July, August, September

*Indicates drought tolerance

Flowers: helmet-shaped blue, dark violet, and white on dense racemes

Foliage (D): dark green, deeply cut, glossy foliage that remains attractive throughout the growing season

Cultural Notes

Plants are slow to increase and can be left for many years before division (for rejuvenation or to relieve crowding) is required. Watering during dry periods of the growing season is helpful and, in fact, often necessary. Taller varieties may require staking.

Design Uses: *Aconitum napellus* 'Bressingham Spire', with deep violet-blue flowers in July and August, and *A. napellus* var. 'Bicolor', with bright blue flowers fading to white in the center, create dramatic features in the middle or toward the rear of the border. In a partially shady garden, try combining bold groupings of aconitums with drifts of *Alchemilla mollis*, ferns, late-blooming astilbes, and various cimicifugas.

N.B. Because all parts of aconitums are poisonous, avoid planting them near vegetable gardens or in areas used by children.

ALCEA ROSEA (ALTHAEA ROSEA)—HOLLYHOCK

Light: full sun
Soil: well-drained soil of average fertility
Zones of Hardiness: 3 to 10

Size: 2–9 feet tall; 10–12 inches wide
Habit: tall, thick, upright stalks

Bloom Period: July to September
Flowers: single and double funnel-shaped flowers from 3 to 5 inches across in a wide range of colors, including deep maroon, crimson, scarlet, pink, yellow, and white

Foliage (D): basal; large, rough, and hairy

Cultural Notes: Taller cultivars will need to be staked, particularly in windy sites. Hollyhocks are short-lived perennials and are at their best when grown as biennials, but if left to self-seed they will often perpetuate themselves. Plants are extremely prone to rust (a fungus disease that produces orange spore cases on stems and leaves that later turn brown and unsightly), and flowers are often attacked by Japanese beetles. Water during dry weather and mulch with well-rotted manure or compost.

Design Uses: Hollyhocks make wonderful accents among foundation plantings featuring old-fashioned shrub roses and are particularly charming against a background of brightly colored climbing roses, a weathered old barn, or the side of a garage. Try planting half a dozen hollyhocks next to a clump of plume poppies *(Macleaya cordata)* to highlight the corner of a garage or toolshed. In borders or informal plantings, hollyhocks are dramatic as specimens or massed at the rear of the border with *Achillea filipendulina, Phlox paniculata,* tall asters, and long-blooming *Boltonia asteroides* 'Snowbank'. Drifts or large clumps of long-blooming *Astrantia major* or *A.* 'Margery Fish' can be planted in front of hollyhocks to hide the bottom half of their stalks and any ratty foliage.

ALCHEMILLA MOLLIS—LADY'S MANTLE

Light: partial shade to full sun
Soil: average to rich, well-drained to moist
Zones of Hardiness: 3 to 9

Size: 12–18 inches tall; 18–30 inches wide
Habit: low, sprawling mounds

Bloom Period: June and July
Flowers: sprays of tiny chartreuse blossoms

Foliage (D): medium to gray green, fan-shaped, slightly hairy with serrated edges, noted for the way they capture and hold beads of dew and rain

Cultural Notes
Alchemilla mollis prefers light or partial shade and rich, moisture-retentive soil in hot or dry areas of the country. In cooler areas, such as the Pacific Northwest and areas of the Northeast where summers are cooler, I have seen it growing and self-seeding with abandon in everything from clay to ordinary garden soil—all in full sun.

Alchemilla mollis is easily propagated by division or self-sown seedlings. To prevent it from self-seeding, shear off spent flowers. After flowering, plants have a tendency to flop and look sloppy. To tidy up, shear plants back to the crown and in a few weeks they will be covered with fresh, new leaves.

Alchemilla vulgaris may be slightly different, its foliage less tomentose, and is often sold as *A. mollis,* and vice versa.

Design Uses
Alchemilla mollis is a mainstay in cottage gardens—as an edg-

ing or accent along brick and stone paths or grouped at the front of informal borders. Planted in masses beneath shrub roses, *A. mollis* is an excellent ground cover and is particularly striking when planted in drifts between bold clumps of hardy geraniums, *Iris sibirica,* and plants having purple or maroon foliage such as *Heuchera* 'Palace Purple'.

Planted as a unifying element throughout the garden, *A. mollis* can tie together everything from shrub and rose borders to perennial borders of delphinium and hollyhocks, to partially shady woodland paths with epimediums, ferns, and various forms of *Dicentra eximia.*

Lady's mantle can also be underplanted with drifts of early-season bulbs such as *Galanthus nivalis, Chionodoxa gigantea,* and *Scilla siberica.* Later-blooming daffodils and tulips, including the pink, semidouble 'Angelique', look lovely combined with *A. mollis,* particularly after a spring shower, when lady's mantle's young green leaves are covered with beads of water.

ANCHUSA AZUREA (ANCHUSA ITALICA)— ITALIAN BUGLOSS OR ALKANET

Light: prefers full sun, but will also grow in light shade
Soil: well-drained, average fertility
Zones of Hardiness: 3 to 9

Size: 1½–5 feet tall, depending upon cultivar; 1–3 feet wide
Habit: erect and multibranched, with rough, dark green leaves; entire plant has a coarse but not unattractive appearance

Bloom Period: early June into July
Flowers: multiple clusters of small, azure-blue flowers held on branching spikes

Foliage (D): large, coarse, dark green, tongue-shaped basal leaves

Cultural Notes
Usually short-lived, plants often need to be replenished every few years, either by division, root cuttings, or seeds sown in spring or early summer. If the crown appears dead in early spring, wait a bit and look for new growth on roots before discarding. Plants will often self-sow with enthusiasm, a problem or an asset depending upon how you look at it. If leaves and stalks are cut back to the ground, plants will often bloom again later in the summer or early fall. Water well during dry periods but avoid planting in areas that remain soggy or wet in winter.

Design Uses

Several cultivars are available, including 'Little John' (1½ feet), 'Loddon Royalist' (3 feet), and 'Dropmore' (4–5 feet). The shorter cultivars are stunning in combination with lemon-yellow daylilies and/or gray-leaved, magenta-flowered *Lychnis coronaria*. Taller varieties are very dramatic as single specimens or grouped toward the back of the border with yellow and white June-blooming Asiatic lilies and are particularly effective when mixed with lupine and bearded irises. Tall and short anchusas are fabulous interplanted with shrub roses of any color.

ANEMONE SPECIES AND HYBRIDS— JAPANESE ANEMONE

Light: light or partial shade to full sun
Soil: moisture retentive but well-drained
Zones of Hardiness: 5 to 9

Size: 1–3½ feet tall, depending on cultivar; 2–2½ feet wide
Habit: erect, multibranched flowering stems with loose floral sprays

Bloom Period: August or September to October
Flowers: single to double; from clear white through shades of pink and rose
Foliage (D): dark green, deeply lobed

Cultural Notes

Japanese anemones are not drought tolerant, so plants require a moisture-retentive soil rich in humus and thorough watering during dry periods. In hot areas of the country, plants can benefit from some shade, particularly during the hottest times of the day.

Plant out potted plants in the spring so they have time to become fully established before winter. Avoid planting in an area where soil remains wet during winter because plants dislike soggy soil in winter. In more northern areas of the country a mulch of oak leaves, straw, or evergreen boughs placed over the plants after the ground has frozen will help them through the winter. Various cultivars exhibit varying degrees of winter hardiness.

Anemone japonica may spread via underground stolons, but plants are not invasive. Once established, plants can be left undivided indefinitely and, in fact, don't like being disturbed. Taller cultivars may need staking.

Anemone vitifolia 'Robustissima', with silvery pink flowers in July and August, is more tolerant of less than ideal conditions and may be a good choice for gardeners in more northern areas of the country who have trouble wintering over cultivars of *A. japonica* and *A. hupehensis*. But be forewarned, *A. vitifolia* 'Robustissima' can be highly invasive. So plant it between shrubs where it can naturalize or with perennials that can compete successfully.

Design Uses

Cultivars of *A. japonica,* including semidouble rosy pink 'Queen Charlotte' and single white 'Honorine Jobert', and those of *A. hupehensis,* including single silvery pink 'September Charm', are excellent as specimens or planted in drifts in the middle or toward the rear of the border. Because their foliage is so attractive and long lasting, they make a handsome dark green background for earlier-blooming perennials, including campanulas, veronicas, and Siberian irises.

Combine *A. japonica* and *A. hupehensis* with *Boltonia asteroides,* asters, and *Physostegia virginiana* for striking combinations in late summer and autumn perennial borders. The cultivar 'September Sprite', with single rose-pink flowers on 15-inch stems, is lovely at the edge of the border, or massed with drifts of ferns and clumps of *Brunnera macrophylla* along a partially shaded woodland path. Anemone hybrids can also be planted in drifts amid shade-tolerant groundcovers such as *Vinca minor* and *V. minor* 'Bowles Variety' to give foundation borders added foliage interest and flowers later in the season.

ANEMONE PULSATILLA—PASQUEFLOWER OR WINDFLOWER

Light: prefers light shade, but will also grow in full sun
Soil: well-drained to gravelly
Zones of Hardiness: 5 to 8

Size: 8–12 inches tall; 10–12 inches wide
Habit: erect mound

Bloom Period: mid-April to mid-May
Flowers: single, cup-shaped, violet-purple; also available are a white form and hybrids in various shades, from magenta to red; by early summer seed heads are attractive, feathery white globes

Foliage (D): finely divided, fernlike, gray-green leaves remain attractive all summer; tiny foliage hairs create a glistening effect on new foliage, stems, and flower buds

Cultural Notes

In cooler climates, plants will grow in sunny, dry conditions, but in hotter areas of the country, some shade is recommended for stronger growth.

Anemone pulsatilla is easily propagated from seed and will also self-sow.

Design Uses

Anemone pulsatilla makes an excellent border edging when planted in drifts or in clumps as accents. Combined with lower-growing astilbes, *A. pulsatilla*, with its feathery leaves and pretty, ball-shaped seed heads resembling those of clematis, will provide the edge of a border with interesting foliage contrasts for the entire growing season. Try massing *A. pulsatilla* in sweeps beneath trees such as white birch, or combine with ferns and Virginia bluebells *(Mertensia virginica)*, primulas, and narcissus for a spring or partially shady woodland garden.

ANGELICA ARCHANGELICA—WILD PARSNIP

Light: full sun to partial shade
Soil: moist, rich in humus but well-drained
Zones of Hardiness: 3 to 9

Size: 5–8 feet tall; 2½–3 feet wide
Habit: thick upright stalks with big, bold leaves

Bloom Period: July and August
Flowers: small greenish white or yellow-green flowers in clusters of rounded umbels

Foliage (D): thrice compound, aromatic, light green

Cultural Notes

Angelica archangelica is a short-lived perennial or biennial. Classified as a garden herb, it is used for cooking fish, in confections, and as a cooked vegetable. The plants usually die after flowering and producing seed, so if you cut them back before seeds form (or cut back flowers before they open, if you are only interested in foliage and form), the plants will often live longer. If allowed to set seed, plants will readily self-sow.

Design Uses

More statuesque than beautiful, wild parsnip can be a bold feature at the back of a midsummer border or become a dramatic focal point when grouped with heliopsis or decorative grasses beside a large wooden arbor in an herb garden.

AQUILEGIA × *HYBRIDA*—COLUMBINE

Light: full sun to light or partial shade
Soil: moist but well-drained, to hot, dry conditions
Zones of Hardiness: 4 to 10

Size: 1–3 feet tall; 6–8 inches wide
Habit: stiff upright stalks with wiry, gracefully branching stems; clumps of basal foliage

Bloom Period: late May and June
Flowers: graceful nodding yellow, pink, red, white, blue, and lavender, 1½–4 inches across, depending upon variety; sepals (surrounding the petals) may be the same or contrasting color as the petals, with "spurs" of varying lengths attached to the back of each petal

Foliage (D): smooth, green or gray-green, fernlike

Cultural Notes

Plants are often fairly short-lived but will often maintain and increase their numbers through self-seeding. Leaf miners, insects that tunnel through the leaves, are often a nuisance. They don't kill the plants but can leave foliage tattered and bedraggled. You can remove the affected leaves of plants in conspicuous positions—along paths or in front of the border—to control but not solve the problem.

Many hybrid strains are available, including the vigorous 'McKana Giants' and 'Mrs. Scott Eliot'; which both grow 2½–3 feet tall in a variety of colors. Single-color strains are also available including 'Snow Queen', 'Crimson Star', and yellow 'Maxi Star'.

Design Uses

The shorter aquilegias, including the 'Biedermeier' strain, which grows only 12 inches tall with a neat, compact habit, and *A. flabellata* 'Nana Alba', with white flowers on 12- to 16-inch stems, are lovely in drifts at the very edge of a border with various campanulas, including *C. persicifolia* and *C. carpatica*, or combined with *Viola cornuta* and *Dicentra eximia* 'Snowdrift' between the stones along the edge of a path. Tall and short columbines are lovely in drifts of the same or mixed colors alongside a path or in a woodland border with forget-me-nots *(Myosotis alpestris)*, windflower *(Anemone pulsatilla)*, and foamflower *(Tiarella cordifolia)*.

ARTEMISIA SCHMIDTIANA 'SILVER MOUND'—SILVER MOUND ARTEMISIA

Light: full sun
Soil: well-drained, relatively poor
Zones of Hardiness: 4 to 9

Size: 6–12 inches tall; 1–1½ feet wide
Habit: rounded mound

Bloom Period: August
Flowers: small, drooping, white or yellow balls along the stems; of insignificant ornamental value

Foliage (D): bright silver-gray, finely cut

Cultural Notes

Artemisia schmidtiana 'Silver Mound' is an excellent plant where conditions are hot and sunny and the soil well-drained but in hot, humid climates the dense foliage may rot. Avoid planting in a spot that remains wet in winter.

Rich soil encourages lush growth that flops about mid-season, leaving a gap in the center of the plant. If plants are trimmed back sharply before they flower, however, clumps tend to remain tighter and better formed. If plants do flop, prune back sharply to encourage new growth. Plants can also be lifted, divided, and reset every few years to help maintain vigorous and compact growth.

Design Uses

Bold sweeps of 'Silver Mound' can transform a sunny dooryard garden and help create a light airy effect when surrounded with annual and perennial baby's breath and yellow and white daisies, including *Chrysanthemum × superbum* and the dwarf *C.* 'Tinkerbelle'.

Planted alternately with *Lavandula angustifolia* 'Hidcote' and surrounded by clumps of yellow-flowered *Anthemis tinctoria* 'E. C. Buxton' and *Santolina chamaecyparissus*, 'Silver Mound' can create a simple but lovely garden alongside brick paths and stone terraces.

Along the edge of a border, mounds of *A.* 'Silver Mound' offer a striking contrast for all manner of blue veronicas, including the long-blooming dark, violet-blue 'Sunny Border Blue'. In an herb garden, this artemisia's mounds of finely cut silver foliage can provide a contrast for spreading thymes, sprawling mints, and the spiky forms of various sages, including *Salvia officinalis*.

ASTER NOVAE-ANGLIAE AND *A. NOVI-BELGII* HYBRIDS—MICHAELMAS DAISY

Light: full sun
Soil: well-drained, light soil of ordinary fertility
Zones of Hardiness: 3 to 9

Size: 3–6 feet tall; 2½–3 feet wide
Habit: upright, multibranched

Bloom Period: late August to mid-October
Flowers: multipetaled, daisylike, in various shades of pink, red, violet, blue, and white

Foliage (D): light to dark green depending upon the cultivar.

Cultural Notes

Cultivars of New England aster *(A. novae-angliae)* and New York aster *(A. novi-belgii)* are fast growers and may require frequent division—sometimes yearly—to maintain health and vigorous growth.

With pure pink blossoms on 48-inch stems, *A. novae-angliae* 'Harrington's Pink' is a particularly desirable variety because it requires less frequent division and is quite frost resistant.

Taller cultivars, including *A. novi-belgii* 'Eventide' (with deep violet-blue flowers on 36-inch stems), may require staking. To provide unobtrusive support, stake with twiggy branches 2½–4 feet high (depending upon variety), placed among the plants in the spring when growth is still low; as plants grow, the twigs will be hidden by the foliage.

Both New England and New York asters may be pinched back early in the season to prevent them from growing too tall.

Design Uses

Plant Michaelmas daisies as bold features toward the rear of the border for late summer color. Try mixing 'Harrington's Pink' and 'Eventide' with *Boltonia asteroides* and cultivars of *Anemone japonica* to accent an arbor in late summer and autumn. Some cottage gardeners I met didn't bother to stake their asters. Instead, they let them sprawl through their borders and among their shrubs and late-blooming shrub roses. In a foundation border, Michaelmas daisies create a lovely complement to the powder blue flowers of *Caryopteris × clandonensis* 'Blue Mist' and the pale purple flowers of *Hydrangea villosa*.

ASTRANTIA MAJOR—MASTERWORT

Light: partial shade or sun
Soil: average, moist in summer
Zones of Hardiness: 4 to 8 or 9

Size: 2–3 feet tall; 1½–2 feet wide
Habit: dense clump with upright flower stalks

Bloom Period: late May and June, then through the summer if plants are watered
Flowers: clusters of small white, pink, or greenish-white flower heads surrounded by "collars" of silvery or pink bracts; faded flowers remain attractive through the summer

Foliage (D): large, mid-green, deeply lobed

Cultural Notes
Easily grown plants not usually bothered by pests and diseases, astrantias are best in moist soil that isn't allowed to dry out, especially if in a sunny location. Plants spread and self-seed but their roots are not invasive and unwanted plants are easily dug up. Astrantias are also easily propagated by division.

Design Uses
Astrantia major, with starlike greenish pink flowers and bracts, is excellent planted in drifts in a shady foundation border or as a ground cover with *Alchemilla mollis* and ferns beneath birch trees. One of my favorite uses for *A. major* 'Margery Fish', with pink and white bracts on stalks 24–30 inches tall, or *A. major* 'Rosensinfonie', with rose pink flower bracts, is as an accent along a walk planted with *Rosa rugosa* hybrids 'Blanc Double de Coubert' and 'Roseraie de l'Hay'. 'Margery Fish' is also lovely massed in front of summer-blooming *Clethra alnifolia* 'Rosea' and interplanted between masses of the long-blooming rose 'The Fairy'.

*AUBRIETA DELTOIDEA—PURPLE ROCK CRESS

Light: full sun to light shade
Soil: well-drained
Zones of Hardiness: 4 to 8

Size: 3–6 inches tall; 18–24 inches wide
Habit: prostrate forming a dense, sprawling mat

Bloom Period: April to June

Flowers: short terminal clusters of four-petaled flowers in shades of red to pink and purple held above the mat of leaves

Foliage (D or E): dark green

Cultural Notes
Cut back plants after bloom to encourage a neat growth habit and autumn bloom, but do not cut back plants trailing over walls. Instead, trim back old flowering stems. Rock cress is easily propagated by division or seeds in spring or by layered stems.

Design Uses
Plant *A. deltoidea* with varieties of white and pink *Arabis caucasica* and golden-yellow *Aurinia saxatilis (Alyssum saxatile)* in the cracks, between the stones or along the tops of walls. Plant 'Cascade Strain' (with colors from soft pink to deep purple) along the top edge of walls so they can cascade over the edge. Both *A. deltoidea* 'Variegata' (with white-edged leaves) and *A. deltoidea* 'Aurea' (with gold-edged leaves) have purple flowers and are charming combined with white *Arabis caucasica*, rapidly spreading *Anemone blanda* 'White Splendor', and miniature narcissus in the gravel of paths or between paving stones.

*AURINIA SAXATILIS (ALYSSUM SAXATILE)—BASKET-OF-GOLD

Light: full sun
Soil: dry to well-drained
Zones of Hardiness: 3 to 9

Size: 9–12 inches tall; 18–24 inches wide
Habit: prostrate, mat-forming

Bloom Period: April to May and June
Flowers: clusters of small yellow blossoms

Foliage (D): blue or gray-green, cloverlike, on upright branched stems; remains attractive through the growing season

Cultural Notes
Easy to grow if provided with excellent drainage and full sun, but in hot, humid areas of the country its dense foliage tends to rot. Cut back plants a third to a half immediately after flowering to encourage new growth. If grown in rich or moist soil, or partially shady conditions, plants will sprawl and become weedy looking.

Design Uses

Massed as a ground cover, *A. saxatilis* is spectacular under-planted with early-season hybrid and species tulips. Plant *A. saxatilis* in the gaps of a stone wall or alternate with *Alchemilla mollis* between the stones of a terrace or a walk. Various cultivars are available ranging in color from soft lemon-yellow 'Citrina' and bright golden-yellow 'Compactum' (with a more compact growth habit) to apricot-tinted 'Sunnyborder Apricot'. All look lovely cascading from a dry stone wall.

BAPTISIA AUSTRALIS—FALSE INDIGO

Light: full sun to light shade
Soil: tolerant of a wide range of soil, including dry, infertile conditions
Zones of Hardiness: 3 to 10

Size: 3–5 feet tall; 3 feet wide
Habit: thick, multistemmed clump

Bloom Period: mid-spring to early summer
Flowers: violet-blue racemes of lupinelike flowers

Foliage (D): blue or gray-green, cloverlike, on upright branched stems; remains attractive through the growing season

Cultural Notes

Baptisia australis is very easy to grow, does not require staking, has no serious insect or disease problems, and is noninvasive. It produces a long tap root, is long-lived, and is best left undivided. Established plants *can* be lifted and divided, but plan on making it a two-person job. Plants grown from seed started in spring or fall will blossom when two or three years old.

Design Uses

In combination with peonies and/or roses (in the middle or rear of a border), a clump or two of *B. australis* can anchor a June border. Although it has a short season of bloom, its handsome foliage and dark seedpods make it an attractive feature right into autumn.

For an informal foundation planting alongside a house, garage, or toolshed, plant *B. australis* and bold groupings of Asiatic lilies with deciduous shrubs having distinctive foliage such as silver-leaved Russian olive *(Elaeagnus angustifolia)* and silver-edge dogwood *(Cornus alba* 'Argenteo-marginata'), with variegated cream and green leaves.

BERGENIA CORDIFOLIA—HEARTLEAF BERGENIA

Light: full sun to light shade
Soil: tolerant of a wide range of conditions but will grow best in soil rich in humus
Zones of Hardiness: 3 to 9

Size: 1–2 feet tall; 1–2½ feet wide
Habit: clump of bold leaves

Bloom Period: late June to July
Flowers: erect terminal heads of waxy, bell-shaped flowers ranging from white to rose-pink, depending on cultivar

Foliage (E): large, leathery, thick, oval leaves; dark green and glossy in early summer, duller green by midsummer and purplish bronze in the winter

Cultural Notes

Bergenia cordifolia will grow in almost any soil in full sun or light shade but prefers light shade in hot areas of the country. Bergenias are also tolerant of a wide range of conditions ranging from dry to moist but will grow more rapidly if planted in moist areas. If grown in an area of low moisture and/or fertility, *B. cordifolia* can remain for years before division is necessary, but where soil is fertile (or overly so), division may be necessary after the fourth year. In colder zones (3–5) bergenia foliage is usually pretty battered by the end of the winter, and pruning back to new leaves is frequently necessary in the spring.

Design Uses

Bergenia cordifolia can be most effective in a cottage garden if used as an accent. Placed at strategic points along a path, it can give a path rhythm, emphasize a turn, or provide contrast with sprawling cottage plants such as *Nepeta mussinii* and *Alchemilla mollis*. Several bergenias grouped at the front of a border of perennials and shrubs can create a dramatic focal point. Bergenias are also great as an edging next to ponds or water features, particularly when combined with the distinctive foliage of astilbes and Siberian irises. Various bergenia hybrids are available with flowers ranging from the white of 'Bressingham White' and the pinkish-white flowers of 'Silver Light' to the carmine-red of 'Morning Red'.

BRUNNERA MACROPHYLLA (ANCHUSA MYOSOTIDIFLORA)—SIBERIAN BUGLOSS

Light: light or partial shade to full sun (if soil is moist)
Soil: prefers moist conditions, but if shaded will grow in dry areas
Zones of Hardiness: 3 to 9

Size: 12–18 inches tall; 12–16 inches wide
Habit: large, bold clumps

Bloom Period: April to early June
Flowers: branched clusters of small, blue flowers resembling forget-me-nots, held above the foliage

Foliage (D): in early spring, the dark green (or variegated), heart-shaped leaves are roughly textured, deeply veined, and about 2 inches across; by midsummer the leaves have increased to 6 and 8 inches across and remain a striking feature till hard frost

Cultural Notes

Brunneras are very easy to grow, providing their cultural requirements are met; division is necessary only after many years, when clumps have separated in the middle.

The cultivar 'Variegata' has attractive cream variegation but is a bit more particular about growing conditions. To avoid having the sun and wind scorch and burn the leaves, plant 'Variegata' in a sheltered, lightly shaded spot.

Design Uses

Brunnera macrophylla is an excellent ground cover among shrubs in a foundation border or beneath ornamental trees such as birch and magnolia; particularly when combined with flowering evergreen ground covers such as *Vinca minor* 'Bowles' Variety' or *V. minor* 'Alba' and underplanted with a succession of spring bulbs, including narcissus, which bloom at the same time.

In perennial and shrub rose borders, the large, heart-shaped leaves of *B. macrophylla* can help create an interesting contrast of scale when combined with perennials having distinctive forms and foliage, including heucheras, hardy geraniums, astilbes, and hostas. Brunneras are equally effective with epimediums and planted in masses or drifts (15–24 inches on center) alongside garden or woodland paths.

CAMPANULA PERSICIFOLIA—PEACH-LEAVED BELLFLOWER

Light: full sun to light or partial shade
Soil: well-drained, average fertility
Zones of Hardiness: 4 to 9

Size: 24–28 inches tall; 8–12 inches wide
Habit: neat basal rosettes

Bloom Period: late June to July
Flowers: white or shades of blue, single or semidouble, cup-shaped, along thin stalks arising from basal rosettes of lance-shaped leaves

Foliage (E or D): low mats or mounds of narrow leaves that are evergreen in milder areas

Cultural Notes

Depending upon soil and cultural conditions, plants often benefit from division every second or third year to maintain vigor, as well as the size and number of flowers. Long blooming, particularly if faded flowers are removed before they have a chance to go to seed, even the taller varieties of *C. persicifolia* do not usually require staking. Allowed to self-sow, *C. persicifolia* can naturalize in open woodlands or alongside roads.

Numerous forms are available, including *C. persicifolia* 'Telham Beauty', with large, single, 3-inch lavender-blue flowers, and *C. persicifolia* 'Blue Gardenia', with deep silvery-blue, double flowers.

Design Uses

Campanula persicifolia is lovely and delicate in small drifts at the very edge of the border or scattered between clumps of silver-leaved dianthus, including salmon-colored 'Helen' and light salmon-pink 'Doris'. Or plant *C. persicifolia* amid *Aquilegia* hybrids and clumps of long-blooming *Petrorhagia saxifraga* (with small, double pink flowers resembling baby's breath) as an edging for a border or to create a picturesque walk through an herb garden full of silver-leaved plants.

Mix 'Telham Beauty' and white-flowered 'Grandiflora Alba' with hardy geraniums, including magenta-flowered *G. sanguineum* and soft-pink *G. s.* var. *striatum* beneath old shrub roses or between the stones of paths.

CENTAUREA MONTANA—MOUNTAIN BLUET

Light: prefers full sun but will grow in light shade
Soil: average fertility, well-drained especially in winter, but can put up with a wide range of soil conditions
Zones of Hardiness: 3 to 10

Size: 2–3 feet tall; 2–2½ feet wide
Habit: loose, upright

Bloom Period: May to June, then sporadically throughout the summer into September
Flowers: deep, cornflower blue; 2–3 inches wide

Foliage (D): narrow, silvery-gray, green foliage, young foliage silvery white

Cultural Notes

Centaurea montana is particularly useful in new garden areas where quick, cheap, or easily propagated cover is wanted. Unless deadheaded, *C. montana* will self-sow with a certain abandon, but seedlings are easily removed or transplanted to another area. Regular deadheading will keep plants from self-seeding and often encourage secondary bloom. If plants flop over and look disreputable, cut them to the ground to induce new growth.

Depending upon the conditions where it is grown and the style of garden, this centaurea *may* require division every few years to keep it from spreading and flopping. In low-maintenance situations, where clumps can be allowed to sprawl, I have left it for five years without division.

Design Uses

Centaurea montana does not produce an extravagant display of flowers and can be a bit weedy-looking in the more formal perennial border, but in the informal setting of a cottage garden it makes an excellent filler around long-lived plants such as shrub roses, peonies, and dictamnus while they are becoming established. It is also effective when combined with white and pale blue *Iris sibirica* and the bold foliage of *Brunnera macrophylla* along the edge of a sunny or partially shady path or mixed with foxgloves and Asiatic lilies at the edge of a woodland.

CENTRANTHUS RUBER (VALERIANA RUBRA)—RED VALERIAN

Light: sun but will also grow in light or partial shade
Soil: prefers well-drained soil of modest fertility but will grow in most well-drained conditions
Zones of Hardiness: 4 to 10

Size: 1½–3 feet tall; 1–1½ feet wide
Habit: loose stems sprawling 2½–3 feet

Bloom Period: June, with sporadic flowering through the summer
Flowers: large terminal clusters of tiny salmon, light or rosy pink, red or white, depending upon variety

Foliage (D): smooth, gray-green, glaucous, spear-shaped, placed opposite along the length of stems

Cultural Notes

Not usually bothered by pests or diseases, *C. ruber* is easy to grow in most conditions, except damp and deep shade, and is particularly valuable for dry or infertile areas and areas of limestone. Though it is frequently short-lived, it is easily propagated by seed or spring division. It self-sows with enthusiastic abandon, but seedlings are easily removed. In areas of the country where it blooms early, cutting back can induce repeat bloom.

Design Uses

Centranthus ruber is picturesque planted along the tops of stone or brick walls and beside steps where its flowers can cascade. Plant *C. ruber* and *C. ruber* 'Albus' (the white form) along the edge of gravel paths or driveways where the plants can spill over and soften the edges. Combine *C. ruber* with various shades of pink and cream-colored bearded irises and masses of *Alchemilla mollis* along either side of a walk to the front door. For hot, dry dooryard gardens and paths, try mixing *C. ruber* 'Albus' with blue cupid's dart (*Catananche caerulea*), blue flax (*Linum perenne*), deep violet-blue *Lavandula angustifolia* 'Hidcote', and ivory, pink, and pale yellow *Achillea* 'Debutante'.

CEPHALARIA GIGANTEA (C. TATARICA)—GIANT SCABIES

Light: sun
Soil: average garden soil
Zones of Hardiness: 3 to 9

Size: 5–8 feet tall; up to 3 feet wide
Habit: well-branched and bushy

Bloom Period: June and July
Flowers: primrose yellow (similar to scabiosa), about 1½–2 inches wide, held high above the foliage on slender, upright, branching stems

Foliage (D): deeply toothed, dark green

Cultural Notes
Propagate *Cephalaria gigantea* by dividing plants in spring or sowing seeds. Plants are easy to grow and low maintenance, though they may need staking and a sheltered spot out of the wind.

Design Notes
For the back of a large border, alternate *C. gigantea* with large clumps of *Echinops ritro* and *Crambe cordifolia* to provide rhythm, height, color, and contrasting forms. Giant scabies is also attractive to butterflies, so you might want to plant it as an extravagant feature beside a large arbor or combine it with buddleia as a background for a garden bench.

CERASTIUM TOMENTOSUM—SNOW-IN-SUMMER

Light: sun to light shade
Soil: well-drained to dry, low fertility
Zones of Hardiness: 3 to 9

Size: 6–10 inches tall when in flower; 24 inches wide and more
Habit: low mats

Bloom Period: late May and June
Flowers: small, single, white; on short stalks

Foliage (D or E): silvery-gray, all summer

Cultural Notes
I have seen *C. tomentosum* growing in everything from gravel to sand. By late summer foliage often becomes flat and somewhat ratty, so to help keep plants tidy, shear back after blooming.

A rampant grower when planted in soils with good moisture or high fertility, *C. tomentosum* may be difficult to get rid of once it is established. Because it can easily overwhelm less vigorous plants (given the conditions it likes), plan on thin-ning it out at regular intervals or combining it with plants that can compete.

Design Uses
Plant *C. tomentosum* on the top of walls (so it drapes over the edge), in pockets of dry walls, or in spaces between stone steps. In May and June, it can cover stone steps with a delicate sprawl of white flowers and looks lovely planted between the stones of terraces, particularly with other gray and blue foliage plants, including rock roses *Helianthemum nummularium* 'Wisley Pink', with gray foliage and pale pink flowers, and *H. nummularium* 'Wisley Primrose', with single lemon-yellow flowers, and various silver-leaved dianthus.

CHRYSANTHEMUM COCCINEUM—PYRETHRUM OR PAINTED DAISY

Light: full sun
Soil: well-drained, on the light side, fairly rich
Zones of Hardiness: 5 to 9

Size: 1–3 feet tall; about 1 foot wide
Habit: clumps with many upright stems each holding a single flower

Bloom Period: June and July
Flowers: single, semidouble, and double, daisylike; 2–4 inches across; in white, brilliant shades of pink, and red

Foliage (D): dark green, finely divided

Cultural Notes
Chrysanthemum coccineum doesn't require staking, is not usually bothered by pests, and makes an excellent cut flower. If faded flowers are cut back to the crown, a second flowering may result. Excellent drainage in summer and winter is important. To avoid winter-kill, do not plant in heavy clay or soils that remain wet during winter. Buy plants locally because they don't ship well. Plants will need division the third or fourth year. This is best done in the spring in colder climates.

Design Uses
Plant vivid pink *C. coccineum* 'Robinson's Rose' toward the front of the border interplanted with various campanulas including dark violet *C. glomerata*. Try combining *C. coccineum* 'Robinson's Crimson' with sprawls of *Centranthus ruber* and *C. ruber* 'Albus' along the edge of sunny paths for a simple contrast of foliage and plant forms.

CHRYSANTHEMUM × SUPERBUM (C. MAXIMUM)—SHASTA DAISY

Light: full sun to light shade (particularly in hot climates)
Soil: rich, moist, and well-drained
Zones of Hardiness: 5 to 9

Size: 1–3 feet tall; about 1 foot wide
Habit: clumps with strong upright stems

Bloom Period: June through August
Flowers: single, semidouble, and double, white, daisylike; 2–5 inches across

Foliage (D): dark green, lanceolate, and toothed

Cultural Notes
Chrysanthemum × superbum requires division every second or third year to maintain vigor. To help plants become established before winter, divide and reset the clumps in spring. Avoid soggy soil in winter. The winter hardiness of shasta daisies will vary. Two of the hardiest for Zone 5 are single-flowered 'Alaska' and frilly, double 'Aglaya'. Shastas grow best in areas of the country with cool summers and benefit from some shade in hot areas. In hotter areas of the country, plants may tend to be short-lived. Taller varieties can be kept more compact by pinching or cutting back the entire plant in spring. To prolong bloom, remove flowers as soon as faded.

Design Uses
Taller varieties of shasta daisies are excellent features when planted in bold groupings toward the middle of the border. Or plant smaller clumps of shastas and scatter them among various perennials having contrasting flowers and growth habits, including blue and white bellflowers (*Campanula persicifolia*), deep blue alkanet (*Anchusa azurea*), pink and blue delphiniums, and pink astilbes. Combine dwarf varieties of shasta daisies such as semidouble *C. × superbum* 'Little Miss Muffet' and single-flowered *C. × superbum* 'Snow Lady' with *Nepeta mussinii* or groupings of *Jasione perennis* (with light blue balls on 8- to 12-inch stems over tufts of dark green foliage) and *Santolina ericoides* for edgings of perennial borders and for herb and vegetable gardens.

COREOPSIS GRANDIFLORA—TICKSEED

Light: full sun
Soil: prefers light, sandy, well-drained soil, but will thrive in a variety of conditions
Zones of Hardiness: 5 to 10

Size: 2–3 feet tall; 2–2½ feet wide
Habit: dense clumps

Bloom Period: June, through the summer, depending upon climate
Flowers: bright yellow, daisylike; about 2 inches across

Foliage (D): dark green, slender

Cultural Notes
Coreopsis grandiflora is easy to grow and not only is tolerant of dry soil but seems to prefer it. Plants tend to sprawl, particularly if grown in soil that is moist and rich. Remove spent flowers to maintain a continuous show of bloom. Plants grow rapidly and benefit from regular (sometimes annual) division. Many cultivars are available and there is some question as to whether they should be listed under *C. grandiflora* or *C. lanceolata*.

Design Uses
Coreopsis grandiflora 'Double Sunburst', with gold semidouble flowers, grows about 2 feet tall, and if planted in clumps toward the middle of the border, but near enough to the edge so it can be deadheaded, it will provide bright color most of the summer.

The cultivar 'Early Sunrise' grows 18–24 inches with bright gold double flowers, and 'Sunray' grows 16–18 inches with semidouble gold flowers. Both bloom for most of the summer and, if planted in drifts between clumps of pink and blue *Erigeron* hybrids and *Nepeta mussinii*, create a quick-growing, picturesque, sprawling border edging.

COREOPSIS VERTICILLATA—THREADLEAF COREOPSIS

Light: full sun or light shade
Soil: prefers light, sandy, well-drained soil, but will thrive in a variety of conditions
Zones of Hardiness: 3 to 9

Size: 1–3 feet tall; 2–3 feet wide
Habit: dense clumps

Bloom Period: June, through the summer, depending upon climate

Flowers: various shades of yellow, daisylike; about 1½ inches across

Foliage (D): dark green, finely textured, threadlike

Cultural Notes
Coreopsis verticillata is easy to grow and tolerant of dry soil conditions. In fertile soil, plants can increase dramatically in size in a year or two. To maintain the health of the plants and control their spread, division (spring or fall) will frequently be necessary after the fourth year. Apparently not bothered by diseases and pests, *C. verticillata* is easily propagated by division spring or fall. I have found that deadheading the cultivar 'Moonbeam' is not necessary to maintain continuous flowering, but if you find that flowering has stopped, try shearing the plants back to induce new growth.

Design Uses
The long season of bloom and attractive foliage of various *C. verticillata* cultivars make them excellent fillers for the perennial border. *Coreopsis verticillata* 'Moonbeam', with its pale yellow flowers, grows about 2 feet tall and is wonderful in bold clumps toward the middle of the border, perhaps combined with dark violet *Iris sibirica*, *Scabiosa caucasica* 'Fama', and *Chrysanthemum × superbum*. Or try planting 'Moonbeam' in drifts in front of hybrid delphiniums interplanted with Asiatic lilies. *Coreopsis verticillata* 'Zagreb', with its bright, golden-yellow flowers, grows from 12 to 18 inches tall and makes a bright, long-blooming edging for perennial borders or paths.

CRAMBE CORDIFOLIA—HEARTLEAF CRAMBE

Light: full sun
Soil: good drainage in soil that is slightly alkaline
Zones of Hardiness: 5 to 9

Size: up to 6 or 7 feet tall when in flower; basal leaves form bold clumps up to 3 feet across
Habit: widely branched stems

Bloom Period: June and early July
Flowers: loose clouds of small, white flowers in huge panicles, resembling an enormous baby's breath

Foliage (D): large, thick, crinkled, dark purple-green, heart-shaped, basal leaves

Cultural Notes
Crambe cordifolia is easy to grow in most conditions but requires lots of room and may require staking to prevent it from toppling over. It can easily be propagated by division or root cuttings and can also be grown from seed, but seedlings will take three years to flower. After flowering, cut back flowering stalks to the cabbagelike leaves unless you want to collect the seeds or let the plants self-sow.

Design Uses
A single *C. cordifolia* makes a most dramatic focal point at the end of a path or in a large border in June and early July. But keep in mind that once crambe's three- or four-week flowering season is over the plant is reduced to a large clump of leaves about a foot high.

For an exuberant display in a large cottage garden (that won't leave any gaps when it is through blooming), combine *C. cordifolia* with *Cynara cardunculus* (see Chilcombe, Chapter 6), billowing shrub roses such as hybrids and forms of *Rosa rugosa*, including crimson-purple 'Roseraie de l'Hay' and salmon-burnished bronze 'Vanguard'. 'Roseraie de l'Hay' will continue flowering almost continually throughout the summer; 'Vanguard' will provide repeat or recurrent bloom. Or pair *C. cordifolia* with pink or white baby's breath (*Gypsophila paniculata*), which flowers at the same time.

DELPHINIUM HYBRIDS—LARKSPUR

Light: full sun
Soil: deep, rich, moist, slightly alkaline soil enriched with compost or well-rotted manure
Zones of Hardiness: 3 or 4 to 8 (depending upon variety) and selected areas along the West Coast where nights are cool

Size: 2–8 feet tall; 2–2½ feet wide
Habit: clumps of stiff, upright stalks

Bloom Period: June and early July and often again in late August and September if plants are cut back
Flowers: loose or dense racemes or spikes ranging from white, through pink and purple, to shades of blue

Foliage (D): dark green, lobed, deeply cut

Cultural Notes
Numerous delphinium hybrids are available; among the best are Blackmore and Langdon hybrids and Pacific Coast

hybrids. The Blackmores and Langdons may not be as hardy, and the Pacific Coast hybrids are more heat resistant. Both hybrids grow up to 8 feet tall and come in a variety of colors, including lavender-pink, white, shades of blue, and violet—both require staking. Belladonna hybrids grow up to 5 feet tall, with branched stems and flowers in various shades of blue, and white.

'Connecticut Yankee' hybrids are bushier and grow from 2½ to 3 feet tall. One of the hardiest hybrids, they are available in shades of lavender, white, blue, and purple. In warmer areas of the country, delphiniums are often treated as annuals and grown from seeds started early the previous autumn.

To prevent overcrowding, reduce the chance of mildew, and produce more spectacular flower spikes, thin out established plants (when 4–6 inches tall) to five or six of the strongest shoots and stake the stalks so they don't break under the weight of the flowers. For repeat bloom in late summer or early fall, cut the faded flowers just below the spike, leaving the old foliage. When new shoots (from the crown) reach 4 or 5 inches tall, cut the old flower stalks right to the ground. The resulting blooms will be smaller than the June display but will remain a feature right up to hard frost. Water deeply during dry periods. Hybrid delphiniums are demanding and if their cultural requirements are not met, or the environmental conditions not to their liking, they are poor performers.

Design Uses
One or two well-grown clumps of delphiniums can make a cottage garden. Plant between clumps of lavender-pink *Delphinium* 'Astolat', with white Martigon lilies, *Digitalis purpurea* 'Alba' and *Gypsophila paniculata* 'Perfecta', or plant between white *Delphinium* 'Galahad' with sprawls of *Nepeta mussinii* and *Chrysanthemum × superbum* to create an exuberant planting beside a sunny kitchen doorway.

Dark, royal-blue *Delphinium* 'King Arthur', scarlet *Lychnis chalcedonica*, yellow *Lysimachia punctata,* and bright orange hemerocallis create a dramatic highlight either side of an apple-green garden gate or arbor. 'Connecticut Yankee' hybrids (in various shades of blue) make an excellent choice for the middle of the perennial border, particularly when combined with July- and August-blooming lilies that then fill the gaps when the delphiniums are cut back.

DIANTHUS PLUMARIUS HYBRIDS— COTTAGE OR GARDEN PINKS (INCLUDING *D. × ALLWOODII*)

Light: full sun
Soil: well-drained, light sandy soil, to average garden soil with some lime
Zones of Hardiness: 3 to 9, or 5 to 8, depending upon variety

Size: 12–14 inches tall in bloom; 6–8 inches wide
Habit: dense, grasslike tufts or compact hummocks

Bloom Period: June or July until frost for selected modern hybrids
Flowers: fragrant, single or double, 1–1½ inches across, with smooth or fringed petals in solid or bicolors ranging from white to pale pink, salmon, rose, red, or purplish

Foliage (E): blue-gray or gray-green, lance-shaped

Cultural Notes
Cut back untidy plants after flowering to prevent them from becoming scraggly later in the season; cutting back will also induce repeat bloom through the summer.

Design Uses
Dianthus plumarius 'Spring Beauty', with fully double, fringed flowers in rose, salmon, and white, *D. plumarius* 'Excelsior' (or 'Pink Mrs. Sinkins'), with carmine flowers having a darker eye, *D. plumarius* 'Mrs. Sinkins White', which is very fragrant if a bit untidy, and *D. plumarius* 'Inchmerry', a pale, silvery pink, create a lovely cottage display when combined with clumps of lavender 'Hidcote' and massed under roses for June and July bloom.

Combine the neat clumps of *D. × allwoodii* 'Doris' (with double light salmon-pink flowers having a darker eye) and *D. × allwoodii* 'Ian' (with velvety red flowers) in groupings along the edge of perennial borders or in narrow drifts sprawling over the edges of brick or stone garden paths. Various dianthus combined with *Santolina ericoides* and *Jasione perennis* make an excellent edging for herb gardens. Dianthus planted in the cracks of dry walls can create a lovely, cascading effect when in bloom.

DICENTRA EXIMIA—FRINGED BLEEDING HEART

Light: light shade but will grow in full sun
Soil: moist but well-drained
Zones of Hardiness: 3 to 9

Size: 1 foot tall; 1–2 feet wide
Habit: informal mound

Bloom Period: heavily in May–June; various cultivars may continue blooming through the summer, particularly in cooler climates
Flowers: small, pink, heart-shaped flowers in loose clusters at the end of graceful stems held above the foliage

Foliage (D): deeply dissected, bluish-green

Cultural Notes
Dicentra eximia won't need dividing for a number of years, but when plants begin to deteriorate, divide them in early spring just as new growth appears, being careful not to break the tender, brittle stems.

Various cultivars of *D. eximia* are available, with flowers ranging from the crimson-red of 'Adrian Bloom' to the deep rose of 'Zestful' and 'Summer Beauty'. *Dicentra eximia* 'Luxuriant', with cherry-red flowers from late April until October, has withstood temperatures to −35°F., and at the same time, it is more tolerant of sun and summer heat than most varieties.

The commonly available white form *D. eximia* 'Snowdrift' has a long season of bloom, beginning in late April and continuing into October. In New England, I have grown both 'Snowdrift' and 'Zestful' in full sun with excellent results. In hot areas of the country, plant *D. eximia* and its various cultivars and forms in shade.

Design Uses
Distinctive, fernlike foliage all summer makes this a valued foliage plant for color and texture in the garden or border. Plant small groupings of *D. eximia* 'Snowdrift' and *Digitalis ambigua* (the pale yellow perennial foxglove) with clumps of maidenhair ferns to accent a bench beneath a vine-covered arbor. *Dicentra eximia* 'Snowdrift' and *D. eximia* 'Zestful' are excellent as edging plants for partially shaded woodland gardens and paths or massed in shaded courtyards, especially in combination with *Pulmonaria saccharata* 'Sissinghurst White', with clear white flowers over silver-spotted, lance-shaped leaves and European ginger (*Asarum europaeum*).

DICENTRA SPECTABILIS—BLEEDING HEART

Light: light shade but will grow in full sun
Soil: prefers a deep, rich, well-drained soil rich in organic material
Zones of Hardiness: 3 to 9

Size: 2½–3 feet tall; 2½–3 feet wide
Habit: large clump with arching branches

Bloom Period: May and June
Flowers: pink, heart-shaped flowers along graceful arching stems held above the foliage

Foliage (D): deeply divided, dark blue-green

Cultural Notes
Dicentra spectabilis is long-lived in Zones 3–7 but tends to be shorter-lived in areas with long, hot summers. If grown in full sun, foliage has a tendency to yellow or die down completely in the heat of the summer; when this happens, cut plants back to the ground. Place *D. spectabilis* in a spot where it can remain undisturbed for years, and if it is in a dry or sunny spot, plant a sprawling perennial nearby, or one with large foliage to cover the gap left when its foliage disappears. It is propagated by division or root cuttings in early spring.

Design Uses
Try combining *D. spectabilis* with white-flowered *D. spectabilis* 'Alba', late-blooming narcissus and tulips, violets, forget-me-nots, and yellow-flowered *Doronicum caucasicum,* and add a few ferns and hostas to fill in any gaps left by the bleeding heart's fading foliage. Old-fashioned bleeding heart will make a beautiful specimen in a partially shaded corner or foundation planting—against the evergreen foliage of box (*Buxus microphylla* or *B. microphylla* var. *japonica*) or in combination with deciduous azaleas. *D. spectabilis* 'Alba' is lovely when planted amid drifts of the ground cover sweet woodruff (*Galium odoratum*) and wake robin (*Trillium grandiflorum*) and creates a charming spring effect when planted around common lilacs (*Syringa vulgaris*) and various species of shrubby fothergilla.

DICTAMNUS ALBUS (D. FRAXINELLA)—GAS PLANT OR BURNING BUSH

Light: prefers sun, but will tolerate light shade
Soil: moderately rich, well-drained soil
Zones of Hardiness: 3 to 9

Size: 3 feet tall; 3 feet wide
Habit: large, multibranched clump

Bloom Period: two weeks in June
Flowers: terminal racemes of 2-inch white or pinkish flowers reminiscent of salvia

Foliage (D): glossy, pinnate, dark green; attractive through the summer

Cultural Notes

Slow to start, gas plants are rugged, long-lived, require little care, are not bothered by pests or diseases, and do not require staking. It is possible to move gas plants, but it is chancy and should be done in the spring so plants have time to become reestablished before winter. Gas plants definitely do not like being divided, so place plants where you want them and they will most likely become family heirlooms. Flowering stalks can be cut back or left on the plant to provide interest after the flowers have faded.

N.B. Some gardeners may experience a rash if the sap touches their skin.

Design Uses

Plant *D. albus* with *D. albus* 'Purpureus', the pink-flowered form, as a feature toward the rear of the border. Even though their season of bloom is brief (about two weeks), once established, the plants (with or without their winged seedpods) will remain an important foliage feature throughout the growing season. Try planting a group of sea lavender *(Limonium latifolium)* in front of a gas plant for an interesting contrast of foliage forms in a foundation border. Both plants are long-lived and thrive in similar conditions and in July and August; sea lavender's airy mass of bright lavender blooms are beautifully set off against the gas plant's dark green foliage.

Place gas plants as focal points in the herb garden, surrounded by herbs and perennials of various growth habits and foliage textures, including sprawling mounds of *Nepeta mussinii,* clumps of the lavender 'Hidcote', and rue *(Ruta graveolens)*.

DIGITALIS PURPUREA—FOXGLOVE

Light: prefers light shade, but will grow in full sun given moist, organic soil conditions
Soil: damp, well-drained (particularly in winter), rich in leaf-mold or other organic matter
Zones of Hardiness: 4 to 8

Size: 2–5 feet tall; 1–2½ feet wide
Habit: sturdy spikes of flowers arise from a basal cluster of leaves

Bloom Period: mid-June to mid-July
Flowers: bell-shaped flowers borne on one side of a tall spike appear on 2-year-old plants; colors range from white to pale yellow to pink and purplish-red

Foliage (D): the first year a flat cluster of basal leaves and the second summer a fuller basal cluster of large, wrinkled, medium-green leaves

Cultural Notes

Digitalis purpurea is biennial, but if growing conditions are right, plants will often self-seed (provided seedpods are not removed) and establish themselves. Seedlings will often appear in different positions each year, resulting in subtle changes in the landscape or garden. Self-sown seedlings can also be transplanted at the end of their first summer of growth to selected spots. *Digitalis purpurea* 'Excelsior Hybrids' (in shades of pink, red, mauve, yellow, and white) is particularly desirable because its flowers encircle the entire 4–5 foot stalk. In areas with wet or snowy winters, mulch with evergreen branches (after the ground freezes) to help avoid crown rot.

Design Uses

Naturalize foxgloves in open woodlands and wild gardens, along with ferns and goat's beard *(Aruncus dioicus)*. Foxgloves can also be used as specimen plants from the middle to the rear of an informal border, with dark pink and yellow peonies in a foundation planting, or as vertical accents among old-fashioned shrub roses. In the dappled shade of an old apple tree, try surrounding foxgloves with masses of hardy geraniums *Geranium* 'Johnson's Blue' and *G. himalayense,* aquilegias, and the biennial honesty *(Lunaria annua)*.

*ECHINOPS RITRO—GLOBE THISTLE

Light: full sun
Soil: well-drained and not overly fertile
Zones of Hardiness: 3 to 9

Size: 3–5 feet tall; up to 3 feet wide
Habit: dense clumps of stiffly upright stems

Bloom Period: July to August
Flowers: spiky blue balls

Foliage (D): coarse, thistlelike, dark green, with white undersides

Cultural Notes

Long-lived and tough, echinops is tolerant of dry and poor-quality soils, will tolerate drought, and does not require staking. Plants can remain in a garden for years before they need dividing. Should you decide to lift the plants or divide them, be prepared for some heavy work because the roots are deep and many. Plants sold as *E. ritro* are usually *E. humilis* or hybrids.

Design Uses

Echinops create a bold effect when used as features at the rear of a border. Large clumps placed at several points can give a large border the backbone it needs for mid- and late-summer bloom. *Phlox paniculata* and *Malva alcea* 'Fastigiata' will help offset echinops' coarse appearance. Combine *E. ritro* 'Taplow Blue' (with large steel-blue flowers) with named varieties of *Lythrum salicaria* and *Macleaya cordata* to create a bold and exuberant summer grouping alongside a garage, toolshed, or garden wall.

EPIMEDIUM SPECIES—BARRENWORT OR BISHOP'S HAT

Light: prefers light shade, but will grow in a variety of conditions from full shade to full sun (if kept moist during summer)
Soil: prefers soil enriched with leafmold or compost, but will also grow, albeit less vigorously, in dry shade in competition with tree roots
Zones of Hardiness: 4 or 5 to 8 (depending upon species or cultivar)

Size: 8–12 inches tall; 1½ feet wide
Habit: dense, well-shaped mound

Bloom Period: May to June
Flowers: small clusters of yellow, white, deep rose, orange, or crimson spurred flowers on wiry stems

Foliage (D and/or E): heart-shaped, 2- or 3-inch leaves that vary from reddish to light green in early spring, changing to glossy green by midsummer, then reddish-bronze in autumn and through the winter (depending upon climate)

Cultural Notes

Epimediums are very long-lived plants that can go many years (often indefinitely) without division. If planted approximately 12 inches apart, in a few years the plants will overlap and form a dense cover, shading the ground so weeds can't get started. Cut the old leaves of deciduous epimediums back to the ground in early spring so emerging foliage and flowers appear at their best. To propagate, divide plants in the spring.

Design Uses

Planted in drifts or massed in groups with forget-me-nots, various anemones, and later-blooming astilbes, epimediums such as yellow-flowered *E. × versicolor* 'Sulphureum' and *E. grandiflorum* create delicate, long-lasting foliage accents along the edge of a terrace or path or in an informal shrub border, particularly when underplanted with spring-flowering bulbs such as small-flowered narcissus, which bloom at the same time. Combined with ferns, forget-me-nots, and *Vinca minor* 'Bowles' Variety' epimediums, such as the compact white-flowered *E. × youngianum* 'Niveum', are lovely in woodland areas or massed beneath small flowering trees such as magnolias and dogwoods.

ERIGERON × HYBRIDUS—FLEABANE

Light: full sun
Soil: prefers light, well-drained or sandy soil, low or moderately fertile
Zones of Hardiness: 5 to 9

Size: 1–2 feet tall; 1½–2 feet wide
Habit: sprawling mound

Bloom Period: June and July
Flowers: single, daisylike; white, blue, pink to purple, with a yellow eye

Foliage (D): mid- to light green, lanceolate; plants form dense clumps of basal foliage

Cultural Notes

Try removing the faded flowers to prolong bloom, then cut back after flowering to induce another period of flowering. Erigerons, particularly the taller cultivars, may require stalking *if* you want the plants upright. A good plant for soil that is dry; propagate erigerons by division in the spring. Erigerons are also an excellent cut flower.

Design Uses

Erigeron's sprawling habit makes it a good filler when planted in masses close to other perennials in the front of a border.

Named varieties (selected for enriched flower color), such as 'Prosperity', with nearly double, mauve-blue flowers on plants 15–18 inches tall, and 'Foerster's Liebling', with double pink flowers on plants 18 inches tall, are useful in a border for covering bare soil around newly planted shrub roses and peonies while these long-lived plants fill out.

*EUPHORBIA EPITHYMOIDES (E. POLYCHROMA)—CUSHION SPURGE

Light: full sun to light shade
Soil: average fertility, well-drained to dry
Zones of Hardiness: 3 to 9

Size: 1–1½ feet tall; 1½–2 feet wide
Habit: neat, bushy mound

Bloom Period: late April through May
Flowers: dense clusters of small flowers surrounded by umbels of bright chartreuse-yellow bracts

Foliage (D): dark green leaves turn red in the fall

Cultural Notes

In hot areas of the country, plant *E. epithymoides* in light shade. It is not a good choice for hot, humid areas, but it does well where summers are cooler. Plants are long-lived and do not like being disturbed. They are not bothered by pests and diseases. *N.B.* The milky sap of *E. epithymoides* may cause skin irritation, so to avoid problems wear gloves and a long-sleeved shirt when working with these plants.

Design Uses

Plant *E. epithymoides* at regular intervals along the edge of a dry, sunny path and fill in between them with silver-leaved *Cerastium tomentosum*, sprawls of *Centranthus ruber* 'Albus', and *Coreopsis verticillata* 'Moonbeam'.

*GAILLARDIA × GRANDIFLORA— BLANKET FLOWER

Light: full sun
Soil: dry and very well-drained
Zones of Hardiness: 3 to 9

Size: 6–36 inches tall, depending on cultivar; 1–1½ feet wide
Habit: sprawling clump

Bloom Period: June to September
Flowers: single to semidouble; deep yellow to maroon-red, often with yellowish tips to petals; selected forms are bright solid colors

Foliage (D): thick, medium-green, in a basal clump

Cultural Notes

Gaillardia × grandiflora will not tolerate wet growing conditions, and in winter, poorly drained soils cause the crowns to rot. While easy to grow, plants are often short-lived, particularly if the soil is heavy. In spring, if crowns seem dead, check the surrounding roots for new growth and replant. An excellent plant for cutting, varieties of gaillardia have an extended period of bloom from late May or early June right through the summer. Stake plants early in the season with twigs stuck among the plants if you don't want plants to sprawl. Frequent deadheading helps keep plants from looking sloppy.

Design Uses

Massed in drifts or placed in bold clumps at key points toward the middle of the border, 'Dazzler' (2–3 feet tall with bright yellow flowers and maroon centers) or 'Yellow Queen' (1½–2 feet with golden yellow flowers) can hold a border together, even in August, when so many gardens are blah. The sprawling habit of taller cultivars can help soften the hard edges and straight lines of walls, terraces, and even driveways.

Dwarf gaillardias such as 'Baby Cole' (large, yellow-edged, red flowers on 6-inch plants) and 'Golden Goblin' (pale yellow flowers in late spring and summer on 8–12 inch plants) can assure a long season of bloom along the edge of brightly colored borders. These same dwarf plants can also provide spots of bright color when planted along the edges of well-drained paths or between the stones of sunny terraces.

GERANIUM SPECIES AND HYBRIDS—CRANESBILL OR HARDY GERANIUM

Light: full sun to light or partial shade
Soil: almost any garden soil that is well-drained
Zones of Hardiness: 4 or 5 to 9

Size: 6–36 inches tall; 12–24 inches wide
Habit: moundlike to loosely sprawling

Bloom Period: May or June to July, with some repeat bloom, depending upon the species
Flowers: five-petaled, 1–2 inches across; ranging from white to light pink and magenta, through purple, and shades of blue

Foliage (D): medium to dark green, palmate and/or deeply lobed

Cultural Notes

Hardy geraniums can be left four years or longer before division is necessary. When clumps begin to deteriorate or additional plants are needed, divide the plants in the spring.

Some species, including *G. endressii* (12–18 inches tall with a spread of about 24 inches), do best in cool, moist climates. In the Pacific Northwest, *G. endressii* will grow in full sun, but in many other areas of the country (including New England and the Midwest), it will flower in June and is then reduced to a nub by hot summers. In my own garden, the floral beauty of *G. endressii* 'Wargrave Pink' is short-lived, but it is so lovely with bearded iris and heuchera that I leave it.

Geranium sanguineum, with magenta flowers on bushy mounds, will grow in full sun, even in hot areas of the country. To encourage new growth and secondary bloom, cut back flowering stalks of hardy geraniums to the crown. Some cottage gardeners shear a few inches off *G. sanguineum, G. sanguineum* 'Album', and *G. sanguineum* var. *striatum* (sometimes sold as *G. sanguineum* var. *prostratum* or *G. sanguineum* var. *lancastrense)* to get rid of the numerous seedpods and encourage a second major flush of bloom in late summer. Cranesbills are seldom if ever bothered by pests or diseases and do not require staking, except for the tall-growing species such as *G. psilostemon (G. armenum),* which may need to be supported by twiggy sticks, especially in shady areas.

Design Uses

Hardy geraniums are a favorite of cottage gardeners as edgings and fillers for borders, as edgings along paths, as ground covers, and as underplantings for old-fashioned shrub roses.

When planted in bold clumps at the edge of a border, both *G. pratense* 'Double Violet', with blue-violet flowers on 1½- to 2½-foot stems and *G. pratense* 'Mrs. Kendall Clark', with clear blue flowers, provide an extended season of bloom from late June to September.

Geranium sanguineum will form large clumps about 12 inches tall and 18–24 inches across with a heavy flush of crimson-magenta flowers in June. By itself, *G. sanguineum* makes a striking accent at the edge of a border or in an herb garden full of blue- and silver-leaved plants. *Geranium sanguineum,* alternated with *G. sanguineum* var. *striatum,* makes a most effective edging for formal or informal borders.

With soft pink flowers veined red, *G. sanguineum* var. *striatum* forms mounds of small dark green leaves that remain attractive through the growing season and is lovely under and around shrub roses, particularly when combined with *Iris sibirica, Aquilegia* hybrids, *Campanula persicifolia,* and perhaps a clump or two of *Bergenia cordifolia* and *Alchemilla mollis* for dramatic accent.

With violet-blue flowers in June and July, *G. ibericum (G. platypetalum)* and *G. himalayense (G. grandiflorum)* are lovely combined with the loosely sprawling clumps of *G. sanguineum* 'Album', ferns, epimediums, *Iris sibirica,* and late-blooming golden-orange trollius in the partially shady border. And when the border is finished blooming, the foliage shapes and textures keep the border attractive through the summer.

From 2½ to 4 feet tall (depending upon the site and growing conditions), *Geranium psilostemon (G. armenum)* will form a dense shrub covered with vivid magenta flowers in June and July. Repeated as a focal point in a border, *G. psilostemon* is pure drama; or it can be used as an accent against a dark stone wall, combined with pale yellow and white daylilies and vivid blue *Anchusa azurea* and highlighted by masses of silver artemisias, including 'Valerie Finnis'.

GYPSOPHILA PANICULATA—BABY'S BREATH

Light: full sun or light shade for part of the day
Soil: average, well-drained neutral or alkaline soil
Zones of Hardiness: 3 to 9

Size: 3–3½ feet tall; 3–4 feet wide
Habit: loose, airy mass when in bloom

Bloom Period: June and July

Flowers: small, single, white flowers in large panicles; double-flowered cultivars are available

Foliage (D): narrow, light green

Cultural Notes

A bit slow to get started, baby's breath will not do much the first year or two, but once plants become established, they can be long-lived and their long taproots make them difficult (if not impossible) to move successfully. Plant in the spring so plants become established before winter, and apply limestone every few years (or so) to keep the soil on the alkaline side.

If you want your gypsophila to look like a big, thick ball when in bloom, it will have to be staked with a girdle of bamboo stakes placed around the plant (when the stems are 12–18 inches), then wound around with twine or enclosed within a galvanized metal contraption designed to support these and peonies. As the plant grows, it should spill over the top of its sturdy support and hide it.

But if you want relief from the aggravation of staking and would like to see baby's breath as a delicate and lacy filler, try not staking it and see what happens. You may be delighted with the results.

Design Uses

Baby's breath can be used as a feature or a filler, depending upon how it is placed and whether you chose to stake it or let it sprawl. White, doubled-flowered *G. paniculata* 'Bristol Fairy' or 'Perfecta' placed as features throughout the border can complement the spikes of delphiniums and hollyhocks. The lower-growing 'Pink Fairy' blooms for most of the summer, and its double pink flowers are lovely intertwined among the delicate stalks of blue *Campanula persicifolia,* various shades of pink and salmon *Dianthus barbatus,* and pale lemon-yellow *Anthemis tinctoria* 'E. C. Buxton'.

HELENIUM AUTUMNALE—SNEEZEWEED OR HELEN'S FLOWER

Light: full sun
Soil: moist, rich in organic material
Zones of Hardiness: 3 to 9

Size: 2–6 feet tall, depending upon cultivar; 2½–3 feet wide
Habit: coarse, multibranched

Bloom Period: August and September

Flowers: daisylike; in yellow, orange, red, and mahogany

Foliage (D): dark green, with notched edges

Cultural Notes

Heleniums don't like dry soil. Plants prefer soil that does not dry out and will tolerate soil that is constantly moist during the growing season. Divide plants in the spring. Some gardeners divide them as frequently as every year, others every three or four years to help maintain strong growth and abundant flowering. To keep taller cultivars from getting too tall, pinch out the tips of the plants in spring. Plants are not bothered by pests or diseases and make excellent cut flowers.

Design Uses

Plant *H. autumnale* 'Butterpat' (clear yellow flowers on 3-foot stalks), 'Moerheim Beauty' (mahogany-red flowers on 3-foot stalks), and 'Wyndley' (yellow and copper flowers on 2- to 2½-foot stalks) as features toward the middle of the border to give the garden color after the phlox have passed. Or, for an easy-to-care-for border along a fence or stone wall, alternate heleniums with drifts of late-blooming red daylilies, including *Hemerocallis* 'Challenger', an Altissima Strain with brick-red flowers on 5- to 6-foot stalks.

HELIANTHEMUM NUMMULARIUM—ROCK ROSE

Light: sun
Soil: dry, well-drained, neutral to alkaline
Zones of Hardiness: 5 to 9

Size: 6–18 inches tall (when in flower); 1–2½ feet wide
Habit: low, spreading, and matlike

Bloom Period: late May or early June to July
Flowers: single and double, white, yellows, oranges, and pinks of crepe-papery texture; each flower lasts only one day, but there are lots of them

Foliage (D or E): narrow, gray-green; deciduous in the north, evergreen in the south

Cultural Notes

Cut back plants hard after spring flowering to maintain a tidy shape and encourage repeat bloom in late summer. Helianthemums do not transplant well and plants tend to be short-lived, but they are seldom bothered by pests and are easily propagated from seeds or cuttings taken in summer. Mulch with evergreen branches after the ground has frozen.

Design Uses

Helianthemums, in all their shades of pink, gold, yellow, crimson, and scarlet, can be combined as edgings along gravel paths or planted in masses of single colors between the stones of terraces and patios, where the foliage will remain an attractive feature all summer. Plant helianthemums with variegated arabis and *Aurinia saxatilis (Alyssum saxatile)* in dry stone walls, or plant in irregularly shaped groupings as part of a thyme lawn—to provide height and contrasting textures.

HELIOPSIS HELIANTHOIDES—FALSE SUNFLOWER

Light: sun or partial shade
Soil: average garden soil that does not dry out during summer
Zones of Hardiness: 4 to 9

Size: 3–4 feet tall; 2–2½ feet wide
Habit: bushy and branching

Bloom Period: late June into September
Flowers: flowers in shades of yellow resemble small sunflowers

Foliage (D): coarse, dark green, with toothed edges

Cultural Notes

Plants are easy to grow, seldom need staking, and are excellent for cutting. Divide plants in spring (so their flowering is not interrupted) after they become crowded, usually after three or four years. The species are tolerant of poor, dry soil and drought but will respond well to regular watering and more fertile soil.

Design Uses

Heliopsis cultivars 'Summer Sun', with 3-inch, golden yellow flowers on plants 4 feet tall, and 'Golden Plume', with double yellow flowers on plants 3½ feet tall, flower from June to September. In combination with *Malva alcea* 'Fastigiata', they can provide a long period of bloom for a simple, informal border. 'Karat', with single deep yellow flowers, grows about 4 feet tall and looks great planted next to an arbor with clumps of daylilies.

HEUCHERA × *BRIZOIDES*—CORALBELLS

Light: full sun to light or partial shade
Soil: will put up with a wide range of growing conditions but prefers moist, well-drained soil (particularly in winter) with enough humus so they don't dry out in summer
Zones of Hardiness: 3 or 4 to 9

Size: 12–30 inches tall; 12–18 inches wide
Habit: wiry, flowering stems arise from a tight basal clump of leaves

Bloom Period: mid-June to September
Flowers: individual flowers are tiny and bell-shaped, arranged in loose, open clusters on stems held high above the foliage, in colors from white through pink to scarlet

Foliage (E): evergreen basal leaves, dark green and often veined, mottled or crinkled

Cultural Notes

Mulch heuchera in cold northern locations because crowns have a tendency to heave in winter. Plant in spring to establish plants before winter, setting crowns just below the surface; then water regularly during dry periods. Divide plants in spring every three to five years or when plants get woody and flower production becomes reduced. When this happens, dig up and discard the old woody parts and reset the younger, more vigorous, well-rooted divisions.

Design Uses

Dozens of hybrids are available, with flower stalks ranging from 10 to 28 inches tall. Many gardeners and nursery people consider *Heuchera* × *brizoides* and its hybrids an improvement over the red-flowered species *H. sanguinea* and its cultivars. Many cottage gardeners combine *H.* × *brizoides* with their existing plants of *H. sanguinea* for a charming and nostalgic mix of new and old. Group several heuchera together as specimens or plant them in narrow sweeps along the edge of borders and paths where their neat clumps of heart-shaped leaves will remain an attractive, long-lasting accent.

Combine *H.* × *brizoides* hybrids 'June Bride' (large white flowers on 15-inch stems) and 'Scarlet Sentinel' (large scarlet-red flowers on 24- to 30-inch stems) with *Stachys lanata* and blue and lavender bearded irises at the edge of a border; then mix in a few *Filipendula vulgaris (F. hexapetala)*, 'Flore Pleno', and several clumps of intense blue *Scabiosa caucasica* 'Fama' to create a cottage garden edging for a sunny front walk.

IBERIS SEMPERVIRENS—CANDYTUFT

Light: full sun, but will tolerate partial or light shade
Soil: well-drained
Zones of Hardiness: 3 to 10

Size: 6–12 inches tall; 12–36 inches wide
Habit: low mounded mats

Bloom Period: May, with some cultivars blooming again in the fall
Flowers: flat, white clusters

Foliage (E): dark green, shiny mounds in milder areas; in more northern regions leaves turn brown and require cutting back after a hard winter

Cultural Notes
Iberises are long-lived and easy to grow if their simple cultural requirements are met. To keep plants tidy and encourage vigorous new growth, shear spent flowering stems; this light shearing also encourages denser growth.

Different cultivars vary in intensity of white, number of flowers, bloom time, and habit. 'Autumn Snow' and 'October Glory' bloom in spring and again in autumn.

Design Uses
Plant *Iberis sempervirens* in drifts or in clumps at key points along the edge of a border or path to complement spring bulbs. 'Little Gem' and 'Pygmae' grow 4–6 inches tall and are excellent beneath lilacs, dogwoods, and crab apples, particularly in combination with *Trillium grandiflorum, Dicentra spectabilis,* and May-blooming Darwin tulips such as green and pink 'Greenland' and lemon-yellow 'Sweet Harmony'. After candytuft's spring bloom and after being sheared, its evergreen leaves remain a dense, dark green ground cover that is attractive into late autumn.

IRIS ENSATA (IRIS KAEMPFERI)—JAPANESE IRIS

Light: full sun
Soil: moist to wet, enriched with organic matter and free of lime
Zones of Hardiness: 5 to 9

Size: 2½–4 feet tall; 1½ feet wide
Habit: clumps of erect foliage

Bloom Period: June and July

Flowers: single, semidouble, or fully double flowers 5–12 inches across; from white to blue, rose, purple, and red-violet, often with attractive veining or speckles in contrasting colors

Foliage (D): sword-shaped, upright, and medium green

Cultural Notes
Japanese irises are easy to grow given the right cultural conditions. They will grow in shallow water (less than 2 feet deep) at the edge of a pond. These irises prefer moist soil, but I have grown them in partially shaded borders and in the light shade beneath ash trees. They do not, however, take kindly to hot, dry conditions. To maintain vigor, divide plants every third or fourth year. In more northern areas winter protection may be advisable. Spring planting is also recommended.

Design Uses
Plant Japanese irises as specimens or drifts near the edge of streams and ponds. In a border, feature several large clumps of deep violet 'Cry of Rejoice' or pale blue 'Ise' and surround them with blue and white forms of *Campanula glomerata,* drifts of dark pink or red astilbes, and later-blooming *Trollius ledebourii* 'Golden Queen'.

IRIS HYBRIDS—BEARDED IRIS

Light: sun or in light shade in the hottest areas of the country
Soil: fairly rich, slightly alkaline, well-drained soil
Zones of Hardiness: 3 or 4 to 9

Size: 1½–4 feet tall; 1–1½ feet wide
Habit: clumps of erect foliage

Bloom Period: May and June
Flowers: hundreds of varieties in a rainbow of colors; from pure white, yellow to golden, apricot to orange, red, pink and rose, and from blue to lavender, and violet, with some that are almost black; some are very fragrant

Foliage (D): sword-shaped; medium green

Cultural Notes
Irises are easy to grow and tough when provided with growing conditions to their liking. To help maintain vigor and free flowering, division is necessary every third or fourth year (usually right after the plants have flowered or in late summer). After plants have been lifted and separated, discard the

old centers, enrich the soil with well-rotted compost, and plant the healthiest rhizomes (after they have dried in the sun for a day and their foliage has been trimmed to about 6 inches) with the fans facing outward and with their top surfaces almost even with the surface of the soil. Then each spring, or in very early fall, topdress each plant with steamed bone meal or superphosphate.

The one real problem with irises is their high susceptibility to iris borers. To help prevent problems, keep the rhizomes free of leaves, grass clippings, and old iris leaves. If irises are planted in small groupings rather than in mass plantings, they apparently are less likely to have problems.

Design Uses

Plant tall white and pale yellow bearded irises between clumps of pyrethrums, salmon-pink or raspberry-colored oriental poppies, and bright coral peonies; then plant lots of blue *Campanula persicifolia* between them as a light and airy complement. As an accent at the top of stone steps or in the wide spaces between the stones of an informal terrace, try planting pink and apricot bearded irises with *Nepeta* 'Six Hills Giant' and yellow-flowered evening primrose (*Oenothera missourensis*). In a sunny dooryard garden, plant masses of rose campion (*Lychnis coronaria*) accented by clumps of dark violet bearded irises.

IRIS SIBIRICA—SIBERIAN IRIS

Light: full sun to light or partial shade
Soil: prefers rich, moist soil that is slightly acid but will grow in average conditions
Zones of Hardiness: 4 to 9

Size: 1½–3 feet tall; 2–3 feet wide
Habit: clumps of erect foliage

Bloom Period: mid-June to early July
Flowers: from white, shades of blue to purple, violet, lavender, lavender-pink, and rose

Foliage (D): narrow, lance-shaped, medium to dark green

Cultural Notes

Undemanding and long-lived, Siberian irises do not require staking, are resistant to pests and diseases, and are drought resistant once established. After a number of years (from three to six, depending upon growing conditions), when plants have formed large clumps and begun to die out in the center, they will require division and replanting. In colder areas of the country, division is best done in the spring so plants can reestablish themselves before winter. Because the clumps are thick and deeply rooted, this lifting and dividing is quite a task, so plan on a two-person operation to pry them out of the ground and two spading forks to separate the largest ones. Cut back the foliage to the crown before division and in late autumn.

Design Uses

Combine *Iris sibirica* with oriental poppies and/or peonies as features in a June border. For soft color complements try planting *I. sibirica* 'Sea Shadows' or *I. sibirica* 'Dreaming Yellow' (white with yellow falls) with the semidouble, coral-colored peony 'Ann Berry Cousins' or with single white 'Lotus Queen'. For a sharp color contrast, mix deep violet 'Caesar's Brother' with scarlet-orange *Papaver orientale* 'Oriental' or with a deep red peony such as 'Cardinal's Robe' or 'Flame' (both single, early-blooming, and about 26 inches tall). Along a path to the front door, *I. sibirica* combined with hardy geraniums, *Anthemis* 'E. C. Buxton', and July- and August-blooming hemerocallis 'Suzie Wong' and 'Little Much' can provide a succession of color and attractive foliage right through the growing season—with a minimum of care.

LAMIUM MACULATUM—SPOTTED DEAD-NETTLE

Light: light to medium shade
Soil: average garden soil
Zones of Hardiness: 3 to 10

Size: 8–12 inches tall; 12–18 inches wide
Habit: low and sprawling

Bloom Period: June to August
Flowers: white to pink and red-purple, depending upon cultivar, in axillary or terminal whorls

Foliage (D or E): small, ovate, crinkled; some cultivars have silver-gray leaves or a gray-green to white blotch in the center of the leaf; evergreen in areas of the country with mild winters

Cultural Notes

Lamiums will grow in ordinary garden soil and withstand a certain amount of drought, but prefer moist, well-drained soils. The cultivars are superior to the species and tend to be less invasive. The cultivar 'Album' has white blossoms. 'Beacon Silver' has pinkish flowers and silver leaves with a narrow green edge, 'Aureum' has pink flowers and golden leaves, and 'White Nancy' has white flowers and silver-gray foliage with green-gray edges. Propagate plants by division. Enthusiastic growers, lamiums will form dense ground covers.

Design Uses
Plant narrow drifts of lamiums along the edge of partially shady paths or under flowering trees and shrubs; then interplant with spring bulbs. Lamiums are a bit weedy-looking and certainly not the most choice ground covers, but they will grow in dry shade, and those cultivars with silver or gold leaves are useful for adding light beneath small trees and in dark corners.

*LAVANDULA ANGUSTIFOLIA— LAVENDER

Light: full sun
Soil: dry and well-drained
Zones of Hardiness: 5 to 9

Size: 1–3 feet tall; 1–3 feet wide
Habit: compact, moundlike, resembles a small shrub

Bloom Period: late June to September
Flowers: terminal spikes of fragrant, lavender or purple flowers in whorls

Foliage (E): short, blunt, fragrant, silvery to gray, needlelike; semi-evergreen to evergreen

Cultural Notes
Lavenders are long-lived and easy to care for. In more northern areas where plants are not really evergreen, each spring clip back dead and brown foliage to new growth. In my garden, lavender will sometimes die back to a few inches above the ground. So I wait to see where (and if) plants put out new growth before I cut them back or pull them out.

Design Uses
Lavender 'Hidcote', with deep purple-blue flowers on compact plants 22 inches high, makes a lovely low hedge along a path to the front door or planted in a sunny mixed border at several points along the edge and then surrounded with dianthus. Or mass 'Hidcote' beneath leggy shrub roses. Long-blooming 'Munstead', with rich lavender flowers on even more compact plants about 12 inches tall, is delightful com-

bined with various silver- and gold-leaved thymes between the stones and along the edges of a sunny path.

LUPINUS RUSSELL HYBRIDS—LUPINES

Light: full sun to light shade
Soil: prefer moderately rich, slightly acid, well-drained
Zones of Hardiness: 5 to 8, except in areas where nighttime temperatures remain high and summers are hot or dry

Size: 2–4 feet tall; 1½–2 feet wide
Habit: erect stems, bushy with compound leaves

Bloom Period: mid-June into July
Flowers: multiple, pealike flowers along the length of tall, erect stalks; colors are solid or mixed and range from white and cream, yellow, blue, purple to pink, and red

Foliage (D): attractive, palmate, medium-green

Cultural Notes
Lupines are sometimes short-lived and do not like areas of the country where summers are hot and dry. But in areas such as New England and the Pacific Northwest, where summers are relatively cool, they are easy to grow. In hot, dry weather, deep watering and mulch are helpful. Because plants do not transplant well, it is better to begin with seedlings or container-grown nursery plants. Remove faded flower stalks to prevent seed set, unless you want to try naturalizing them in sunny meadows.

Design Uses
Russell hybrid 'Chandelier', with 2- to 3-foot creamy-white and yellow spikes, and 'Chatelaine,' with 2- to 3-foot pink and white spikes, are spectacular massed as features or in small groups toward the middle or rear of the border. Or try planting 'Noble Maiden', with pure white flowers, as accents amid drifts of blue Siberian and Japanese irises. Create an informal, picturesque effect by planting drifts of lupines in a sunny meadow or lightly shaded woodland.

LYCHNIS CHALCEDONICA—MALTESE CROSS

Light: sun
Soil: moist but well-drained
Zones of Hardiness: 3 to 9

Size: 2½–3 feet tall; up to 1 foot wide
Habit: upright stalks

Bloom Period: June and July
Flowers: small, brilliant scarlet, in dense, flat heads

Foliage (D): mid-green lanceolate

Cultural Notes

Easy to grow, *L. chalcedonica* can remain for years before they need division. Plants can be propagated by division, preferably in the spring. In dry conditions, the lower leaves of flowering stems may wither and die.

Design Uses

Lychnis chalcedonica is one of the brightest-colored perennials, and there is no point in trying to tame it. Instead, make the most of it and pair it with pale yellow hemerocallis or *Lysimachia punctata* and create a bold feature combination for a brightly colored border.

To create a cheery and welcoming dooryard garden, plant *L. chalcedonica* with dark purple salvias, bold groupings of pale yellow *Anthemis* 'E. C. Buxton', and the deep blue flower spikes of *Veronica* 'Sunny Border Blue' either side of a white wooden gate opening onto a brick path lined with more 'E. C. Buxton' and varieties of tall and dwarf *Chrysanthemum × superbum* 'Little Miss Muffet' and *Coreopsis verticillata* 'Moonbeam'.

LYCHNIS CORONARIA—ROSE CAMPION OR MULLEIN PINK

Light: full sun
Soil: dry or well-drained
Zones of Hardiness: 3 to 9

Size: 1½–3 feet tall; 1½–2 feet wide
Habit: clumps with upright branching stems

Bloom Period: June and July
Flowers: magenta

Foliage (D): small, spear-shaped, silver-gray, and woolly

Cultural Notes

Lychnis coronaria is short-lived and often behaves as a biennial but will self-sow throughout the garden. Plants grown from seed sown in spring or fall will flower in one or two years.

Design Uses

For a brilliant dooryard garden, or bright border, *L. coronaria* and silver-leaved artemisias, including 'Valerie Finnis', are wonderful fillers between clumps of yellow *Achillea filipendulina*, named cultivars of *Lythrum salicaria*, and *Gaillardia* 'Yellow Queen'.

In hot, dry areas in Zones 5–9, try lining a walk to the front door with desert mallow (*Sphaeralcea munroana*), with delicate trailing stems and bright orange, red, or pink flowers, drifts of long-blooming *Gaura lindheimeri*, with wiry stems and panicles of white flowers, clumps of flaxes including *Linum flavum*, with bright yellow flowers, and *L. narbonense*, with azure-blue flowers on graceful willowy stalks, and surround them all with masses of rose campion (*Lychnis coronaria*). The white-flowered lychnis, *L. coronaria* 'Alba', grows from 2 to 5 feet tall and is enchanting when combined with a mass of *Coreopsis* 'Moonbeam'.

LYSIMACHIA PUNCTATA—CIRCLE FLOWER OR YELLOW LOOSESTRIFE

Light: sun to light shade
Soil: moist to dry
Zone of Hardiness: 4 to 9

Size: 1½–2½ feet tall; 2 feet wide
Habit: dense, spreading colony

Bloom Period: June and July
Flowers: spikes of yellow, star-shaped, clustered in whorls in leaf axils

Foliage (D): broad, lanceolate, mid-green

Cultural Notes

Reliable, persistent, and easy to cultivate, *L. punctata* can be invasive. Plants prefer moist soil and full sun but will grow in dry soil if provided with shade.

Plants are handsome in bloom but somewhat weedy-looking afterward, so cut back foliage to the crown to induce new growth. Plants are easy to propagate by division.

Design Uses

Combine *L. punctata* with hardy geraniums, *Anchusa azurea*, and *Campanula persicifolia* in the light shade beneath old-fashioned shrub roses. For an easy-to-maintain June and July border, plant clumps of *L. punctata* alternated with *Lychnis chalcedonica*, *Achillea filipendulina*, and deep purple *Campanula glomerata* 'Superba' and surround them all with masses of *Alchemilla mollis*.

LYTHRUM SALICARIA—PURPLE LOOSESTRIFE

Light: full sun to light shade
Soil: moderately fertile to average garden soil; dry to moist or wet and boggy
Zones of Hardiness: 3 to 9

Size: 1½–5 feet tall; 2–3 feet wide
Habit: erect branching stems

Bloom Period: late June and mid-July to late August and September, depending upon variety
Flowers: slender terminal spikes of small, rosy purple flowers; cultivated varieties available in shades of pink, bright carmine, and rich purple

Foliage (D): slender, lance-shaped, and medium green

Cultural Notes
The species (native to Europe) is extremely invasive and in wet meadows is so aggressive that it crowds out native plant species. Named cultivars of *Lythrum salicaria* are available, with the claims that they are sterile and therefore do not self-seed.

Design Uses
Lythrum cultivars such as 'Happy', with dark pink flowers on 15- to 18-inch stalks, 'Morden's Pink', with clear pink flowers on 3- to 4-feet stalks, and 'Dropmore Purple', with rich purple flowers on 2½- to 3-feet stalks, are very effective as single specimens, grouped as features in borders or areas with moist soil, or along the edges of streams and ponds, particularly when combined with large-leaved hostas for foliage contrast.

*MALVA ALCEA—HOLLYHOCK MALLOW

Light: full sun
Soil: average, well-drained, tolerant of dry conditions
Zones of Hardiness: 4 to 9

Size: 3–4 feet tall; crowns up to 2½ feet wide
Habit: dense clumps with many upright, branched stalks

Bloom Period: July to September or October
Flowers: rose-pink to soft pink, hollyhock-like, 2–3 inches across

Foliage (D): medium to dark green, lobed, attractive for most of the summer

Cultural Notes
Malva alcea 'Fastigiata' is superior to the species, seldom requires staking, and is easily grown from seed or self-sown seedlings. Plants readily self-seed, but seedlings are easily removed. Once established, its long roots make it difficult to move successfully. To prolong malva's bloom period, cut back faded blooms before they go to seed and use as cut flowers.

Design Uses
An excellent long-blooming plant for the middle or back of the border. Well-placed clumps of *M. alcea* 'Fastigiata', *Echinops humilis,* and *Physostegia virginiana* 'Alba' can give a border its framework for mid- and late summer.

MONARDA DIDYMA—BEE BALM

Light: full sun to light or partial shade
Soil: average to rich, moist soil
Zones of Hardiness: 4 to 8

Size: 2½–3 feet tall; 2–4 feet wide or more
Habit: clumps of upright stalks

Bloom Period: late June into August
Flowers: 2- to 3-inch, bright scarlet, tubular, forming dense, round heads; cultivars in shades of pink, white, and violet-purple

Foliage (D): mid-green, with toothed margins; leaves and stems have a mintlike fragrance

Cultural Notes
Given conditions to their liking, monardas are long-blooming and easy to grow but in areas of the country with long, hot summers, they tend to be short-lived. With optimum growing conditions monardas spread rapidly (often invasively), and division every second or third year (preferably in spring) is necessary to keep plants healthy and prevent them from taking over. Partial shade encourages this plant's invasive tendencies.

Monardas are highly susceptible to mildew, especially in dry areas or soil that has been allowed to dry out. Each year about the end of July the monardas in my dry garden become covered with mildew and all their leaves drop, leaving the plants very forlorn-looking. I am tempted to rip them all out, but the flowers are such a lure for hummingbirds, I cut the plants right back to the ground instead, and that encourages fresh, clean growth.

Design Uses

Try *M. didyma* 'Croftway Pink' as a filler between clumps of yellow hemerocallis and *Coreopsis verticillata* 'Moonbeam'. For a bolder effect for late summer borders, I plant the brilliant *M. didyma* 'Cambridge Scarlet' as a contrast to white *Phlox paniculata*, purple *Liatris scariosa*, and *Echinops ritro* 'Taplow Blue'. Bold sweeps of monardas (in single colors or mixed) create a vivid, yet serendipitous effect in a meadow or at the edge of a woodland.

MYOSOTIS SPECIES—FORGET-ME-NOT

Light: full sun to light or partial shade
Soil: average to moist soil
Zones of Hardiness: 3 to 9

Size: 3–8 inches tall; 12 inches wide
Habit: bushy or sprawling with prostrate stems

Bloom Period: April into June
Flowers: clusters of small azure-blue flowers often with a yellow eye; pink and white forms are available

Foliage (D): green, oval

Cultural Notes

Myosotis alpestris will grow in ordinary garden soil, but for best results plant it in partial shade in soil enriched with organic matter. *Myosotis scorpioides* or *M. palustris*, a hardy perennial with a long period of bloom from April to July, requires constantly moist soil and is often grown in streams or in wet soil around the edges of ponds. If left to self-seed, forget-me-nots will pop up in the most unexpected places and create the most romantic effects between stones of paths, walls, and terraces, or you can sprinkle the seeds yourself.

Design Uses

Mass *M. alpestris* in borders with tulips or in drifts along the edges of paths with bold groupings of aquilegias as accents. The rich azure-blue of forget-me-nots creates a lovely spring effect when massed around varieties of yellow and pale orange trollius in a border or in a partially shaded area at the edge of a woods with pale yellow *Primula vulgaris*. Try planting various myosotis between pink or white *Dicentra spectabilis*, *Trillium grandiflorum*, and *Doronicum cordatum* 'Madam Mason'.

NEPETA SPECIES AND HYBRIDS— CATMINT

Light: full sun to partial shade
Soil: average, well-drained or sandy
Zones of Hardiness: 3 to 8

Size: 12–36 inches tall; 12–18 inches wide
Habit: compact or sprawling mounds, depending upon variety and the specific growing conditions of a season

Bloom Period: late May or June and July and intermittently until September
Flowers: spikes with whorls of small tubular flowers in various shades of blue, including lavender-blue and blue-violet

Foliage (D): small, aromatic, gray-green or silvery-gray

Cultural Notes

Selected forms and cultivars of various heights and shades of blue are available, including the variety 'Six Hills Giant', 2½–3 feet tall with light blue flowers, 'Blue Wonder', with lavender-blue flowers on compact mounds 12–15 inches tall, and 'Dropmore', 12–15 inches tall with deep lavender flowers. *Nepeta × faassenii* (a sterile hybrid of *N. mussinii* and *N. nepetella* often confused with and sold as *N. mussinii*) is a compact grower about 12 inches tall, with lavender-blue flowers and gray-green foliage.

If stalks of nepetas are cut back sharply after first flowering, plants will produce new shoots from the crown and, frequently, another strong show of flowers in early autumn. All nepetas can be propagated by division, and *N. mussinii* can also be grown from seed.

Design Uses

Nepetas are excellent as edgings for borders or along paths and are particularly effective when combined with plants having bold or distinctive foliage such as *Alchemilla mollis*, *Brunnera macrophylla*, *Bergenia cordifolia*, and *Iris sibirica*.

Plant 'Six Hills Giant' along the top of a wall or steps, where it will cascade and soften hard edges.

PAEONIA HYBRIDS—PEONY

Light: full sun to light shade
Soil: average to rich, well-drained
Zones of Hardiness: 3 to 8, and 9 (where nights are cool)

Size: 1½–3½ feet tall; 2½–3 feet wide

Habit: shrublike

Bloom Period: May and June

Flowers: single, anemone to double-flowered, depending on cultivar, 4–8 inches across; in white, pink to red, with a very occasional pale, creamy yellow; some cultivars are fragrant

Foliage (D): medium to dark green; attractive most of the summer; the new foliage of some is a dark reddish color, gradually changing to green

Cultural Notes

Peonies are hardy, low-maintenance, and long-lived and make excellent cut flowers. Late August or early September (in the north) and October (in the south) are the preferred times for transplanting or division. Make sure when planting or transplanting that the buds (or eyes) at the top of the roots are set about an inch or two below the soil level. If peonies are planted too deeply or grown in too much shade, they will have few, if any, flowers. In spring and fall, work a handful of bone meal around each plant.

Peonies prefer full sun but in the warmer areas of the country a little shade will prolong their period of bloom. The taller and heavy-flowered double peonies will need staking to prevent them flopping at flowering time. Or let them sprawl for a wonderful, luscious cascade over the edge of walls—provided they can be seen from below. Peonies are very hardy and can put up with a lot of summer heat, but they do need a period of cold and winter dormancy and grow best in climates with cold winters.

Design Uses

Several large clumps of peonies, with their attractive dark green foliage, can anchor a border for the entire growing season. By selecting early-, mid-, and late-season cultivars, you can extend the brief period of bloom.

Peonies are wonderful combined with soft-colored oriental poppies (so they don't get blasted out of the border by too much color) and drifts of Siberian irises. Some of my favorite combinations feature the late-blooming peony 'Sarah Bernhardt' with large, fragrant, rose-pink flowers, and late-blooming *Iris sibirica* 'White Swirl'. Early-blooming 'Ann Berry Cousins', a salmon-colored semidouble, and mid-season 'Seashell', a warm pink single, are both lovely with dark violet and light blue Siberian irises.

PAPAVER ORIENTALE—ORIENTAL POPPY

Light: full sun
Soil: light or heavy soil of moderate fertility, well-drained, particularly in winter
Zones of Hardiness: 3 to 9

Size: 1–4 feet tall; 2–3 feet wide
Habit: sprawling clumps

Bloom Period: late May and early June
Flowers: the species is a brilliant orange with flowers 5–8 inches across; numerous cultivars are available with crepey, translucent, bowl-shaped flowers in a wide range of colors, including luscious shades of pink, red, orange, and white

Foliage (D): coarse, hairy, deeply cut, mid- to deep green

Cultural Notes

Oriental poppies do not like hot humid weather but do well where summers are moderate. Plants often flop under the weight of their flowers and stems tend to sprawl, so for a tidy appearance staking is frequently necessary. Some cottage gardeners leave their poppies unstaked and the effect is naturally enchanting. Their flowering season is relatively short (1–2 weeks) and plants go dormant and disappear from July to September, leaving large gaps in the border. Plants can be propagated by root cuttings or division. Divide or transplant plants in late summer and early autumn when new growth begins.

Design Uses

Dozens of cultivars of *P. orientale* are available. 'Beauty of Livermore', with deep red flowers with black spots at the base of the petals, 'Warlord', with deep crimson-red flowers, and 'Raspberry Queen', a brilliant, deep salmon, provide bold accents in late spring and early summer planted toward the middle of the border.

To create a dramatic but much softer effect in a border, plant 'Mrs. Perry', a large salmon-pink with a tint of apricot, and 'Helen Elizabeth', a clear, soft pink, and surround them with pale blue and white Siberian irises, perennial fillers such as *Nepeta mussinii* and *Centaurea montana*. Later-blooming asters planted to the rear and left unstaked will spill over and cover the bare spots left when the poppy foliage dies back.

PETRORHAGIA SAXIFRAGA (TUNICA SAXIFRAGA)—TUNIC FLOWER

Light: full sun to light shade
Soil: average, well-drained
Zones of Hardiness: 4 to 8

Size: 6–10 inches tall; 12–18 inches wide
Habit: tufted mounds with thin, wiry, sprawling stems

Bloom Period: July into September and October
Flowers: small, double, pink; very similar to baby's breath

Foliage (D): small, delicate, linear

Cultural Notes
Easy to grow, tunic flowers can be propagated by division in the spring. Plants will also self-seed and are easily transplanted. These plants prefer full sun, but I have also grown them in partial shade with success.

Design Uses
Plant small drifts of *P. saxifraga* 'Pleniflora Rosea' between lavender cotton *(Santolina chamaecyparissus)* and clumps of lavender 'Hidcote' along the path of an herb garden or the edge of a border for a long season of flowers and foliage interest. Or plant self-sown seedlings of *P. saxifraga* 'Pleniflora Alba' between the cracks of walls and the stones of terraces, and with bright blue *Viola cornuta* 'Jersey Gem' along the edge of borders and in between dianthus.

PHLOX PANICULATA—SUMMER PHLOX

Light: full sun to light shade
Soil: heavily enriched with organic matter and moist but well-drained
Zones of Hardiness: 3 to 9

Size: 3–4 feet tall; 2½–3 feet wide

Habit: clumps of stiffly upright stalks with terminal panicles

Bloom Period: late June to September, depending on cultivar
Flowers: terminal clusters of 1-inch-wide, disc-shaped florets in white, blue, pink to red; many with "eyes" of contrasting colors; some varieties such as Symons-Jeune are extremely fragrant

Foliage (D): lance-shaped, 6 inches long, medium dull green.

Cultural Notes
Most cultivars are extremely susceptible to *powdery mildew,* which covers the leaves with a whitish powder. To help avoid this problem, place plants far enough apart, thin established clumps in early spring to four or five stalks to allow good air circulation, and avoid overhead watering. Water plants thoroughly during dry periods.

To encourage a second flowering, deadhead plants immediately after flowering. Deadheading also prevents the plants from self-seeding and producing seedlings that are often inferior in color to parent plants. Phlox are heavy feeders, so fertilize them regularly.

Design Uses
Use large clumps of phlox selected to create a succession of bloom as features in the border for July and August and combine with bold drifts of lilies for an extravagant display. A selection of several Symons-Jeune phlox will keep a border in bloom from July right into September. Plant a succession of rich pink phlox between bold clumps of globe thistle *(Echinops ritro)* and silver-blue Russian sage *(Perovskia atriplicifolia)*.

PLATYCODON GRANDIFLORUS—BALLOON FLOWER

Light: full sun to light shade
Soil: moderately fertile, light, well-drained
Zones of Hardiness: 3 to 9

Size: 1–3 feet tall; 1–2 feet wide
Habit: erect and densely branched in larger forms; more rounded in compact cultivars

Bloom Period: late June to August
Flowers: inflated terminal buds followed by large, open star-shaped single or double flowers in white, blue, and pink

Foliage (D): glossy, dark green, glabrous

Cultural Notes
Platycodons are slow to get going, but once established, the large clumps are long-lived, are not bothered by pests or diseases, and can thrive for decades. Because plants emerge late in the spring, be careful not to damage their fragile shoots as you work in the garden. It helps to mark their location. To extend their period of bloom, deadhead spent flowers. If left to their own devices, plants will self-sow and flower the sec-

ond year. The growth habit of platycodons can be a bit lax and floppy, so if you want them upright, some staking may be required. *P. grandiflorus* 'Shell Pink' retains its color better in partial shade.

Design Uses
Compact-growing *P. grandiflorus* 'Mariesii', with single blue flowers, and *P. grandiflorus* 'Album', with single white flowers, are lovely planted in groups toward the middle of the border, fronted by several plants of *Limonium latifolium,* with airy sprays of lavender-blue flowers. Both plants bloom at about the same time, are long-lived, and don't like being disturbed. Plant clumps of *P. grandiflorus* 'Shell Pink' in a partially shady border for a color accent amid lady's mantle, hostas, and epimediums.

PRIMULA SPECIES—PRIMROSE

Light: light shade to sun
Soil: fertile, high in organic matter, and moist, particularly in summer
Zones of Hardiness: 5 to 8 or 9

Size: ½–2½ feet tall in bloom; 8–12 inches wide
Habit: thick clumps or rosettes of leaves with upright flower stalks

Bloom Period: April and May or May and June, depending upon species
Flowers: bell-shaped or tubular, in shades of pink, red, yellow, blue, lavender, purple, and white

Foliage (D or E): pale or bright to mid-green, oblong, corrugated

Cultural Notes
In my sunny garden, clumps of English primrose (*P. vulgaris,* or *P. acaulis),* with clusters of pale yellow flowers above rosettes of green, wrinkled leaves, bloom in April and May, then go dormant during the heat of the summer. After the fall rains, they look fresh and green again. (Cultivars of *P. vulgaris* are available in white and shades of yellow, orange, red, blue, and purple.)

I have not grown the 'Barnhaven' strain of English primroses, but they are reputed to be more tolerant of dry conditions and very hardy and are available in shades of white, cream, yellow, blue, orange, and pink. *Primula japonica,* with tiers of pink, red, lavender, and purple flowers on stalks up to

2½ feet tall, flowers in late spring and early summer and is among the easiest primroses to grow. Because *P. japonica* requires lots of moisture, plants are best grown along the banks of streams or ponds, where they will self-sow abundantly.

Lift, divide, and reset your primulas every two or three years—or every year if you want more plants.

Design Uses
Plant blue and white *P. vulgaris* and miniature yellow narcissus along the edges or between the stones of a partially shady path; or surround a bench in the shade of an arbor with clumps of *P. vulgaris, Asarum europaeum,* and *Dicentra eximia* 'Snowdrift'. *Primula japonica* 'Millar's Crimson' is dramatic when planted as a filler around clumps of dark violet *Iris sibirica* 'Caesar's Brother'; or combine *P. japonica* 'Potsford White' with the light blue flowers of *I. s.* 'Sky Wings' and *I. s.* 'White Swirl'.

PULMONARIA SPECIES AND HYBRIDS—LUNGWORT

Light: partial to full shade
Soil: moist, ordinary to rich
Zones of Hardiness: 3 to 8

Size: 12 inches tall; 12 inches wide
Habit: loose mounds

Bloom Period: late April and May
Flowers: drooping clusters of small, blue, pink, and white, bell-shaped flowers, depending upon the cultivar

Foliage (D or E): clumps of broad, lance-shaped leaves; often spotted white or silver-gray

Cultural Notes
Pulmonarias prefer shade but will grow in full sun in soil enriched with humus, although they will often wilt in the heat of the summer even if the soil is moist. Plant pulmonarias approximately 10–12 inches apart when used as a ground cover and divide them when they become overcrowded. Because lungworts bloom so early in the spring, divide them in the early fall.

Design Uses
Pulmonaria officinalis and *P. saccharata* have similarly shaped leaves with silver-gray spots. *P. saccharata* 'Mrs. Moon', with pink flowers that turn blue as they age, and *P. saccharata* 'Sis-

singhurst White', with clear white flowers, are lovely combined with ferns and forms of *Dicentra eximia* surrounding a bench in the partial shade of an arbor or pergola. To lighten up shady areas beneath flowering trees and shrubs and along partially shady paths, combine bold clumps of pulmonaria with *Lamium maculatum* 'White Nancy', with silver-gray leaves and white flowers, and evergreen ground covers such as *Vinca minor* 'Bowles Variety', and underplant them all with yellow and white narcissus and masses of species tulips—*T. tarda*, *T. turkestanica*, and *T. saxatilis*.

SALVIA SPECIES AND HYBRIDS—SAGE OR SALVIA

Light: prefer full sun
Soil: average, well-drained to dry
Zones of Hardiness: 4 or 5 to 9

Size: 1–3 feet tall, depending upon species and cultivars; 12–36 inches wide
Habit: clumps or basal rosettes of gray-green or dark green leaves

Bloom Period: June and/or July
Flowers: spikes or panicles; from white to lavender, blue, and violet

Foliage (D): usually dark green with toothed or deeply cut margins; *S. argentea* has large, hairy, silvery, woolly leaves

Cultural Notes
Most salvias are tolerant of dry conditions or drought. Propagate plants by division. Deadhead *S.* × *superba* (sometimes sold as *S. nemorosa*) and its cultivars to prolong the blooming period from mid-June into August.

   Salvia argentea is a short-lived perennial and is often treated as a biennial, but the first season its silvery leaves are so beautiful and the second year its spikes of white flowers flushed with mauve so striking, I replace it if it disappears. Unlike some salvias, which can tolerate partial shade, *S. argentea* requires full sun.

Design Uses
Salvia haematodes, a short-lived perennial with large panicles of lavender-blue flowers about 3 feet high, is considered by some to be a superior form of *S. pratensis*. Whatever its proper botanical standing, it is a cottage garden favorite, especially when mixed with herbs and perennials in borders and when planted among old-fashioned shrub roses. The

common culinary sage *S. officinalis* is spectacular in June, with whorls of purplish and white flowers on 3-foot spikes; combine it with bearded irises, *Stachys byzantina*, and other salvias, including *S. argentea*, with 3-foot spikes of white flowers, *S.* × *superba* 'May Night', with dark violet-blue flowers on spikes 18–24 inches high, and *S. haematodes*. *Salvia officinalis* and the variegated and purple-leaved salvias are worth planting in herb or perennial borders solely for their foliage.

STACHYS BYZANTINA (S. LANATA)—LAMB'S EARS

Light: full sun
Soil: average, well-drained to sandy and gravelly
Zones of Hardiness: 4 to 9

Size: 18 inches tall; 12–24 inches wide
Habit: low and spreading

Bloom Period: late June and July
Flowers: spikes of soft, gray leaves accented with small magenta flowers

Foliage (D): silver-gray, tongue-shaped, and woolly

Cultural Notes
Stachys byzantina will not tolerate heavy or poorly drained soils. In hot and humid climates, its thick foliage tends to rot.

   When the flower stalks of *S. byzantina* begin to look faded and tired, cut them back; the fuzzy, gray leaves will then remain an attractive foliage accent right through the growing season. When stems of stachys get woody, lift the plants and divide. In a border with rich soil, plants may require division or thinning every year or two to keep them from crowding less enthusiastic growers.

   The cultivar 'Silver Carpet' remains low and does not flower.

Design Uses
Planted in clumps at regular intervals along the front of a border, stachys can make a most effective edging and is especially attractive at twilight, when its leaves seem almost luminescent.

   Combine lamb's ears with other plants of silver-gray foliage having different forms and growth habits, such as mound-forming dianthus, tall and spiky *Eryngium alpinum,* and sprawls of *Lychnis coronaria,* with brilliant pink or reddish-purple flowers.

The foliage of *S. byzantina* is especially handsome when contrasted with the rich blues of various veronicas and the saturated pinks of peonies and oriental poppies.

THALICTRUM SPECIES AND HYBRIDS— MEADOW RUE

Light: partial shade to full sun
Soil: moist soil enriched with organic matter
Zones of Hardiness: 5 to 8 or 9

Size: 2–6 feet tall; 1–2 feet wide
Habit: large clumps with many upright stems

Bloom Period: May and June or August, depending upon species
Flowers: single or double lacy "flowers" composed of sepals in yellow, white, pink, lavender and various shades of purple with yellow stamens

Foliage (D): mid-green to gray-green and gray-blue compound leaves resembling those of columbine

Cultural Notes

Propagate thalictrum species from seed (sown or self-sown), the varieties from division. Plants that are divided are slow to reestablish. If not planted in close quarters with other plants to hold them up, the taller varieties of thalictrum may require staking. Usually not bothered by pests or diseases.

Design Uses

Combine *T. aquilegifolium,* with tiny, fluffy, mauve flowers on 2–3-foot stems in late May and June, *T. aquilegifolium* 'Roseum', and *T. aquilegifolium* 'Album' with *Valeriana officinalis* and old-fashioned shrub roses in a foundation border.

In June and July, the bright yellow flowers of *T. speciosissimum (T. glaucum)* on stalks 5–6 feet tall are lovely mixed with delphinium hybrids and foxgloves at the back of the border. From mid-July through August, *T. rochebrunianum,* with lavender flowers and yellow stamens on 5-foot stems, is a lovely airy filler toward the back of a border or combined with *Cimicifuga racemosa* as a dramatic but delicate feature.

In August, *T. dipterocarpum,* with sprays of delicate mauve or lavender flowers and yellow stamens on upright stalks 4–6 feet tall, and *T. dipterocarpum* 'Hewitt's Double' (a double form) are lovely in bold sweeps or interplanted with deep blue *Lobelia siphilitica.*

TIARELLA SPECIES—FOAMFLOWER OR FALSE MITERWORT

Light: partial shade
Soil: moist soil, slightly acid, enriched with organic matter
Zones of Hardiness: 3 to 9

Size: 6–24 inches tall; 1–2 feet wide
Habit: neat basal clumps

Bloom Period: April to June with occasional or heavy flowering through summer, depending upon species
Flowers: erect wiry stems with feathery, cream-white or pure white racemes or panicles

Foliage (D or E): ivy- or maple-shaped, evergreen in mild climates

Cultural Notes

Moist, enriched soil is important, as is partial shade. Given these conditions, tiarellas are easy to grow. If planted about 12 inches on center, *Tiarella cordifolia,* with pale to mid-green maplelike leaves and cream-white flowers from April to June, will spread by surface runners to form a dense ground cover.

Design Uses

Combine *T. cordifolia* and *T. trifoliata,* with ivy-shaped green leaves and pure white flower panicles 12–18 inches tall from June through the summer, with *Phlox divaricata,* ferns, and epimediums in a shady foundation border featuring small-leaved rhododendrons and deciduous azaleas. Plant *T. wherryi,* a neat tuft of pale green, ivy-shaped leaves with spikes of cream-white flowers in May and June, then sporadically through the summer, amidst early-blooming hellebores, hostas, and hardy geraniums along the edge of a partially shady path or foundation border. Tiarellas are wonderful woodland plants and lovely with trilliums, ferns, and astilbes.

TROLLIUS SPECIES AND HYBRIDS— GLOBE FLOWER

Light: light shade to full sun, if soil is moist
Soil: moist soil enriched with organic matter
Zones of Hardiness: 3 to 8

Size: 1–3 feet tall; 1–1½ feet wide
Habit: large clumps with many upright stems

Bloom Period: late May and June
Flowers: 2- to 3-inch, single or double, globelike, from light yellow to deep orange-gold

Foliage (D): deeply lobed, dark green

Cultural Notes

Globe flowers are low-maintenance and free of pests and diseases and will grow in a range of conditions from the edge of ponds to borders with moisture-retentive soil. Moist soil is important, particularly during summer months. Division is infrequent and probably won't be needed till after the fifth or sixth year. Then divide plants in late summer or fall. Numerous species and varieties are available.

Design Uses

Plant early-blooming *T. cultorum* 'Pritchard's Giant', with large golden-yellow flowers on 30-inch stems, with *T. pumilus,* with yellow flowers on 12-inch stems, Japanese primroses *(Primula japonica),* and forget-me-nots *(Myosotis alpestris)* in borders, or at the edge of a woodland or pond.

Later-blooming *T. ledebourii,* with orange-gold flowers on 24- to 30-inch stems, and *T. ledebourii* 'Golden Queen', with orange-gold flowers almost 4 inches across on stems up to 3 and 4 feet tall (under ideal conditions), are a dramatic feature in a border when mixed with bold plantings of *Iris sibirica* 'Dreaming Spire', with lavender flowers and royal blue falls, and late blooming *I. sibirica* 'White Swirl', with fluted, ruffled, white flowers.

VALERIANA OFFICINALIS—COMMON VALERIAN OR GARDEN HELIOTROPE

Light: full sun or light shade
Soil: moist, rich, well-drained
Zones of Hardiness: 4 or 5 to 9

Size: 3–5 feet tall; 2½–3 feet wide
Habit: tall, hollow stalks arising from basal clumps of feathery, deeply lobed foliage

Bloom Period: late June and July
Flowers: airy clusters of tiny white, pinkish-white, or lavender flowers

Foliage (D): dark green, fernlike

Cultural Notes

Easy to grow in most ordinary soils, *V. officinalis* will also tolerate moist conditions. It is easily propagated by division. About the third or fourth year, plants may need to be dug, divided, and replanted. After blooming, if the flower stalks are cut back, the plant will remain an attractive mass of distinctive foliage right through the summer.

Design Uses

In an informal, cottage-style foundation border, plant *V. officinalis* around pink peonies, *Dictamnus albus* 'Purpurea', lilacs, and old-fashioned continuous-blooming shrub roses such as *Rosa rugosa* hybrid 'Roseraie de l'Hay'. The effect will be lush and overflowing with good foliage contrasts to keep the border interesting right through the growing season.

VERONICA SPECIES AND HYBRIDS— SPEEDWELL

Light: full sun to light shade
Soil: moderately fertile, well-drained, but moisture-retentive
Zones of Hardiness: 3 to 9

Size: 5–30 inches tall, with some up to 4 and 5 feet, according to variety; 2–3 feet wide
Habit: variable, some varieties sprawl, others form dense mats or upright clumps

Bloom Period: May to June and July, some into September, providing they are deadheaded
Flowers: small, saucer-shaped, in white and in shades of blue, purple, pink, and red; arranged densely on numerous upright spikes

Foliage (D): glossy green, ovate to lanceolate; some deeply toothed *V. incana* has silver-gray foliage

Cultural Notes

Depending upon the location and fertility of soil, veronicas will often require division every three or four years to maintain attractive, compact growth and lush flowering. With some varieties, the removal of faded flower spikes will prolong bloom. Some veronicas look quite unattractive once finished blooming, so cut back the plants to encourage new growth. Plants are easily propagated by division in spring or fall.

Design Uses

Plant *V. latifolia* 'Crater Lake', with gentian-blue flowers, along the edges of brick or stone paths so its sprawling habit will soften hard edges. Interplant low-growing, mat-forming varieties such as *V. incana,* with silver-gray leaves and lilac-blue spikes in June, with *V. incana* 'Minuet', with gray-green foliage and soft pink flowers from June to August, and low-growing *V. alpina* 'Alba' as an edging for borders, along the edges of paths, or between stones in paths and terraces.

For the middle of the perennial border, combine taller cultivars such as 'Sunny Border Blue', with dark, violet-blue spikes on 18- to 24-inch stems from June to September, and *V. spicata* 'Blue Peter', with deep blue spikes on multi-branched 18-inch stems from June to August, with late-blooming pink and white astilbes and yellow lilies.

VIOLA CORNUTA—HORNED VIOLET OR TUFTED PANSY

Light: light or partial shade to full sun
Soil: fertile, moist, but well-drained
Zones of Hardiness: 5 to 8

Size: 8–12 inches tall; 10–12 inches wide
Habit: loose mounds or sprawling clumps, depending upon season and age of plant

Bloom Period: April and May to October and November
Flowers: small, pansylike; in bright yellow, white, apricot, deep red, and shades of blue and purple

Foliage (D): medium to dark green, ovate to oval, with rounded teeth

Cultural Notes

Violas prefer partial or light shade and moist soil for a lengthy period of bloom. If plants get leggy in a hot, sunny location, cut back to induce new growth and later flowering. In colder areas of the country, the winter hardiness of *V. cornuta* depends upon the severity of the winter and amount of snow cover. Some winters they come through beautifully in my garden; other years only a few make it. But they are so useful and so welcome early and late in the season, I continue to plant them and encourage them to self-seed.

Design Uses

Plant groups of bright yellow *V. cornuta* 'Lutea Splendens' and *V. cornuta* 'White Perfection' between the stones of paths. As an edging for perennial borders, try massing deep apricot *V. cornuta* 'Chantreyland' and blue *V. cornuta* 'Jersey Gem' between clumps of blue and white *Campanula persicifolia* and shorter-growing shasta daisies, including *Chrysanthemum × superbum (C. maximum)* 'Snow Lady'. The long stems of the violas will mingle with the daisies, and the effect is charming. Combine dark red *V. cornuta* 'Awkward Ruby' with astilbes, European ginger *(Asarum europaeum)*, and *Anemone sylvestris* along partially shady paths, or combine with groups of yellow-flowered perennial foxglove *(Digitalis ambigua)* and *Dicentra eximia* 'Snowdrift' as an edging for shady or woodland gardens.

U.S. DEPARTMENT OF AGRICULTURE PLANT HARDINESS ZONE MAP

	Average Annual Minimum Temperature:	
Zone 1	Below −50°F	
Zone 2	−50° to −40°	
Zone 3	−40° to −30°	
Zone 4	−30° to −20°	
Zone 5	−20° to −10°	
Zone 6	−10° to 0°	
Zone 7	0° to 10°	
Zone 8	10° to 20°	
Zone 9	20° to 30°	
Zone 10	30° to 40°	
Zone 11	Above 40°	

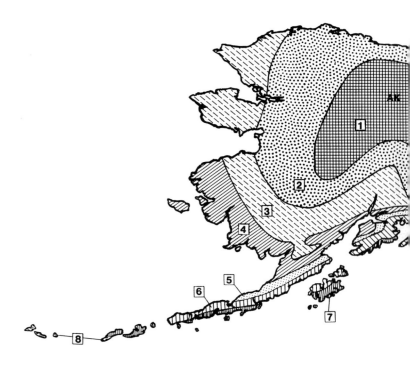

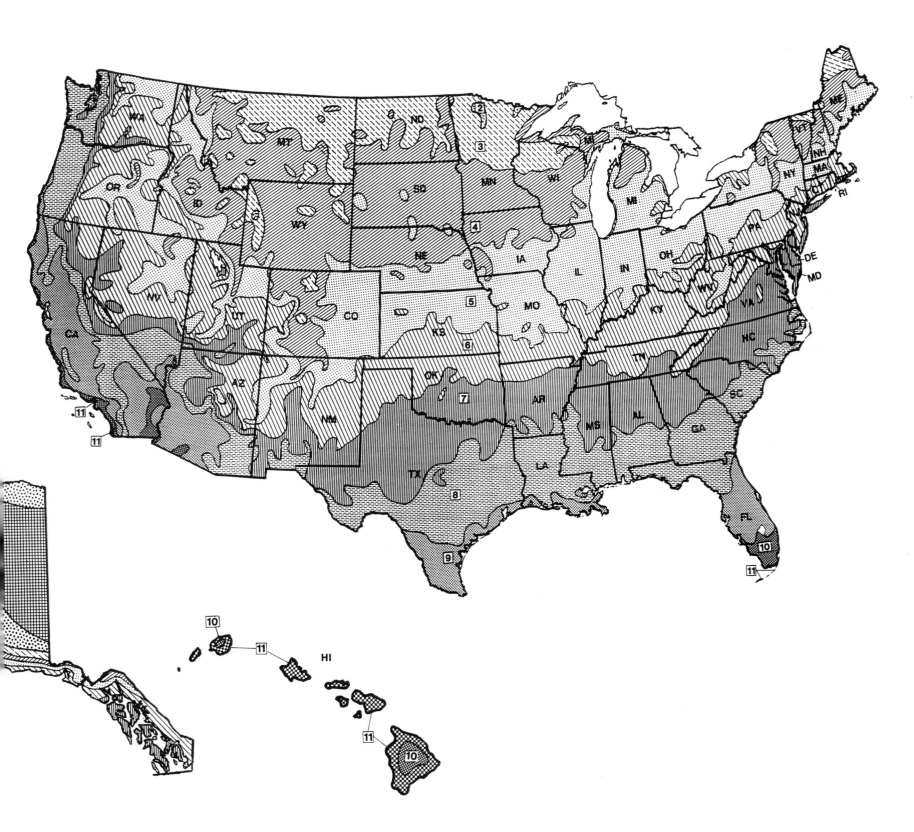

AUTHOR'S NOTE ON CLIMATES

Kinghay, East Knowle, Salisbury
Wiltshire, England

Many North American gardeners labor under the misconception that English gardeners enjoy an ideal climate and therefore "have it easy" and that is why their gardens are so beautiful. Having been in England during some of the worst droughts in generations and seen summers where the sun didn't shine for weeks, I have learned that the reality is quite a different thing. Talking and corresponding with English gardeners during the years of writing this book, I have discovered that their climate and growing conditions (particularly in recent years) are variable and often extremely challenging and that English gardeners, like gardeners here in North America, must contend with the specific challenges of their particular garden site.

To help dispel the myth that gardening in England is easier, and to instill hope in North American gardeners with less than ideal sites and growing conditions, I asked several of the English gardeners featured in this book to write about the weather and climatic conditions of their areas. The following response from Mollie Thorne in southwest England (Chapter 5) shows quite clearly that the grass isn't always greener on the other side of the Atlantic.

Dear Margaret,

It was a pleasant surprise to hear from you, and I'm glad that your book is progressing. I shall be glad to let you have the info you want in regard to temps, wind, rainfall, etc., and have begun recordkeeping today. I shall send you the results when the season has settled down to something in the nature of spring!

For the time being, I am adding here a short item on the general weather pattern in these parts: the most significant thing being that no pattern is now discernible! In the last few years the weather has gone through a change, especially since the Great Drought. There is now little chance of telling when spring has come, or even if winter has—often the early winter months are warm and muggy and the late spring very cold.

This past year has been no exception. Here we are subject to tremendous winds from the S.W., which blast straight across the empty farm lands, and these will continue for most of the year at some level. In the winter we get, as now, strong N. or N.E. winds, bringing bitter frosts. Unfortunately here we do not benefit by a lasting carpet of snow which serves to protect plants to such a great extent. We do have snow (in fact, against all precedent, of late there have been heavy falls, precluding our even emerging from our gate, and the arrival of helicopters to the village to remove persons who have fallen down in the ice and damaged themselves). Such snow, as and when it does fall, will lie for a day or two during penetrating icy winds, which shrivel up all the vegetation, and then we will have a period of warm, muggy weather with winds from the S.W. accompanied very often by deluges of rain. It is not uncommon about here for large floods to occur. Our streams and pond rise to unbelievable heights! Thus, although folk say it is easy to garden in this area, this is far from the case. We are unprotected from all points, although our planting has meant that there are many more amenable micro-climates than when we arrived and I can grow things which would have died earlier. Also, having natural water, we are also naturally low-lying, and receive a good share of frost. Water drains quickly from our land because we are surrounded by ditches, streams, the pond, etc., so that the rain quickly drains. Consequently, we do suffer badly in times of drought, of which in England we have lately had more than enough. Last summer, before the endless drear and rain began, we had a drought here which lasted six weeks, although in other, quite near, areas, rain did fall. It is the *most* appalling weather condition to my mind, and I dread drought more than anything.

This may all sound like a picture of misery, but on the other hand, to get things to grow well here and flourish is, we feel, quite a triumph.

This seems to be a very rambling rigamarole, but I thought I'd put this bit in with the letter—and shall send the exact information later on. I wish you all success with your venture.

All good wishes for the new year.

Yours,
Mollie (Thorne)

SELECTED BIBLIOGRAPHY

Allingham, Helen, and Dick, Steward.
The Cottage Homes of England. London: Bracken Books, 1984.

Austin, David. *The Heritage of the Rose*. Suffolk, England: Antique Collector's Club, 1988.

Batsford, Charles, and Fry, Harry. *The English Country Cottage*. 2d ed. London: B. T. Batsford, 1944.

Beales, Peter. *Classic Roses*. New York: Holt, Rinehart and Winston, 1985.

Bloom, Alan. *Perennials for Trouble-free Gardening:* London: Faber and Faber, 1960.

Brown, R. J. *The English Country Cottage*. London: Arrow Books, 1984.

Clarke, Ethne, and Perry, Clay. *English Country Cottages*. London: Weidenfeld & Nicolson, 1985.

Clausen, Ruth Rogers, and Ekstrom, Nicolas H. *Perennials for American Gardens*. New York: Random House, 1989.

Cook, Olive. *English Cottages and Farmhouses*. London: Thames and Hudson, 1982.

Crockett, James Underwood. *Perennials*. Alexandria, Va.: Time-Life Books, 1972.

Dobson, B. R. *The Combined Rose List*. 1990. Order from Beverly R. Dobson, 215 Harriman Road, Irvington, NY 10533.

Earle, Mrs. C. W. *More Pot-Pourri from a Surrey Garden*. London: Smith, Elder, 1899.

Evans, Tony, and Green, Candida Lycett. *English Cottages*. New York: Penguin Books, 1982.

Ferguson, Nicola. *Right Plant, Right Place*. New York: Summit Books/Simon and Schuster, 1984.

Fish, Margery. *Cottage Garden Flowers*. London: Faber and Faber, 1980.

Genders, Roy. *The Cottage Garden and the Old-fashioned Flowers*. London: Pelham Books, 1969.

Harper, Pamela, and McGourty, Frederick. *Perennials: How To Select, Grow and Enjoy Them*. Tuscon, Ariz.: HPBooks, 1985.

Hebb, Robert S. *Low Maintenance Perennials*. Jamaica Plain, Mass.: Arnold Arboretum, 1975.

Hole, S. Reynolds. *A Book About Roses*. London: Edward Arnold, 1886.

Hortus Third. New York: Macmillan, 1976.

James, Anne Scott. *The Cottage Garden*. Harmondsworth: Penguin Books, 1982.

Jekyll, Gertrude. *Colour Schemes for the Flower Garden*. Country Life, 1908.

————. and Mawley, E. *Roses for English Gardens*. Country Life, 1902.

Krussman, G. *Roses*. English ed. Batsford B.T., 1982.

Reader's Digest Encyclopedia of Garden Plants and Flowers. London: Reader's Digest, 1971.

Robinson, William. *The English Flower Garden*. London: John Murray, 1883.

Taylor's Guide to Perennials. Boston: Houghton Mifflin, 1986.

Taylor's Guide to Roses. Boston: Houghton Mifflin, 1986.

Thomas, Graham Stuart. *Climbing Roses Old and New*. London: J. M. Dent & Sons, 1983.

————. *The Old Shrub Roses*. London: J. M. Dent & Sons, 1980.

————. *Perennial Garden Plants*. London: J. M. Dent & Sons, 1976.

————. *Shrub Roses of Today*. London: J. M. Dent & Sons, 1980.

Wyman, Donald. *Wyman's Gardening Encyclopedia*. New York: Macmillan, 1971.

Yeo, Peter. *Hardy Geraniums*. Portland, Ore.: Timber Press, 1985.

INDEX

Note: Page numbers in *italics* refer to illustrative matter.